AFTERMATH

AFTERMATH

The Cultures of the Economic Crisis

Edited by
MANUEL CASTELLS, JOÃO CARAÇA,
AND GUSTAVO CARDOSO

OXFORD
UNIVERSITY PRESS

Great Clarendon Street, Oxford OX2 6DP,
United Kingdom

Oxford University Press is a department of the University of Oxford.
It furthers the University's objective of excellence in research, scholarship,
and education by publishing worldwide. Oxford is a registered trade mark of
Oxford University Press in the UK and in certain other countries

British Library Cataloguing in Publication Data
Data available

Library of Congress Cataloging in Publication Data
Data available

ISBN 978–0–19–965841–1

Printed in Great Britain by
Clays Ltd, St Ives plc

Contents

Contents

Acknowledgments

We wish to thank the Calouste Gulbenkian Foundation, who provided support to host the Aftermath Network meetings held between 2009 and 2011 in Lisbon, at which the contributors met, discussed the issues, and planned the book. Without their contribution, this book would not have been possible.

Abbreviations

AIG	American International Group
ALBA	Alliance for the Peoples of Our America
BBS	Bulletin Board System
BE	bureaucratic entrepreneur
BPN	Banco Português de Negócios
BPP	Banco Privado Português
BRIC	Brazil, Russia, India, and China
CCP	Chinese Communist Party
CDO	collateralized debt obligation
CDS	credit default swap
CEPAL	Comisión Económica para América Latina y el Caribe
CFDT	Conféderation Française Démocratique du Travail
EB	entrepreneurial bureaucrat
ECB	European Central Bank
ECLAC	Economic Commission for Latin America and the Caribbean
EU	European Union
ICP	Italian Communist Party
IMF	International Monetary Fund
MERCOSUR	Common Southern Market
MNC	multinational corporation
NGO	non-governmental organization
NHS	National Health Service
OECD	Organization for Economic Cooperation and Development
PATO	Plataforma Autonoma de Teatro del Oprimido
PPIC	Public Policy Institute of California
PPP	purchasing power parity
SASAC	State-owned Assets Supervision and Administration Commission
SIV	structured investment vehicle

SOE	state-owned enterprise
TVE	township and village-owned collective enterprise
UDIC	urban development and investment company
UNASUR	Union of South American Nations
UNDP	United Nations Development Programme
WEF	World Economic Forum

List of Contributors

Sarah Banet-Weiser is a Professor in the Annenberg School for Communication and Journalism and the Department of American Studies and Ethnicity at the University of Southern California. She is the author of *The Most Beautiful Girl in the World: Beauty Pageants and National Identity* (1999), *Kids Rule! Nickelodeon and Consumer Citizenship* (2007), and *Authentic^{tm}: The Politics of Ambivalence in a Brand Culture* (2012). She is the co-editor of *Cable Visions: Television beyond Broadcasting* (2007) and *Commodity Activism: Cultural Resistance in Neoliberal Times* (2012), and has published in journals such as *American Quarterly, Critical Studies in Media Communication, Feminist Theory,* and *Cultural Studies.* She is currently the editor of *American Quarterly,* the official journal of the American Studies Association, and the co-editor of the Critical Cultural Communication book series at New York University Press.

João Caraça obtained the D.Phil. in Nuclear Physics at the University of Oxford (1973) and the Agregação in Physics at the Lisbon Faculty of Sciences (1974). He has been Director of the Science Department and is now Director of the Delegation in France of the Calouste Gulbenkian Foundation. João Caraça is also Full Professor of Science and Technology Policy at the Instituto Superior de Economia e Gestão of the Universidade Técnica de Lisboa. He was coordinator of the M.Sc. Course in the Economics and Management of Science and Technology from 1990 to 2003. He is a member of the Governing Board of the European Institute of Innovation and Technology. He also integrates the Steering Group of the European Forum on Philanthropy and Research Funding and is President of the Advisory Board of the Portuguese Business Association for Innovation—COTEC. João Caraça was Science Adviser of the President of the Portuguese Republic (1996–2006) and has published over 150 scientific papers. He also co-authored *Limits to Competition* (1995), co-edited *O Futuro Tecnológico* (1999), and collaborated in *Le Printemps du politique* (2007).

Amalia Cardenas is a Researcher at the Open University of Catalonia. She graduated from the University of California, Berkeley, and from the University of Barcelona. She is conducting research on alternative economic cultures, and on networked social movements in Spain and around the world.

Gustavo Cardoso is Professor of Media and Society at the Lisbon University Institute. His areas of interest are the cultures of the network society, the transformations of the notions of property, distribution, and production of cultural goods, and the role of online social networking. His current research interest focuses on the transformation of digital readership, the future of journalism, and media literacy. Between 1996 and 2006 he was adviser on the information society and telecommunications policies to the Presidency of the Portuguese Republic and in 2008 was chosen by the World Economic Forum as a Young Global Leader. His international cooperation in European research networks led him to work with IN3 (Internet Interdisciplinary Institute) in Barcelona, the World Internet Project at USC Annenberg, COST A20 "The Impact of the Internet in Mass Media," and COST 298 "Broadband Society." Since 2006 he has been the Director of OberCom, the media observatory in Lisbon.

Manuel Castells is University Professor and the Wallis Annenberg Chair of Communication Technology and Society at the University of Southern California. He is also Professor Emeritus of Sociology and Planning, University of California, Berkeley, where he taught for twenty-four years. He is a Fellow of the American Academy of Political and Social Science, the Academia Europaea, the Spanish Royal Academy of Economics, and the British Academy. His main books include the trilogy "The Information Age: Economy, Society and Culture" (1996–2003) and *Communication Power* (2009). He was a founding member of the board of the European Research Council and is a member of the Governing Board of the European Institute of Innovation and Technology.

Joana Conill is a Researcher at the Open University of Catalonia, Barcelona. She graduated in history and cinema from the University of Barcelona. She specializes in the study of agro-ecological cultures and alternative social movements. She also produces documentary films.

List of Contributors

Pekka Himanen is Professor of Philosophy at the Aalto University in Helsinki. He is one of the internationally best-known researchers of the information age, whose works on the subject have been published in twenty languages from Asia to America (English, Chinese, Japanese, Korean, Taiwanese, Indonesian, Russian, Ukrainian, Turkish, Portuguese, Spanish, Catalan, French, Italian, German, Dutch, Croatian, Estonian, Swedish, and Finnish). After obtaining his Ph.D. in Philosophy as the youngest doctor ever in Finland at the age of 20 (University of Helsinki, 1994), Himanen moved to carry out research first in England and then in California (Stanford University and the University of California, Berkeley). The best-known publication of this research is the book *The Hacker Ethic* (2001). Himanen has also co-authored with Manuel Castells the influential book *The Information Society and the Welfare State* (2002), which has been discussed worldwide in the leading academic and political circles. Designated as a Young Global Leader by the World Economic Forum, Himanen is nowadays a popular lecturer around the world.

You-tien Hsing is Professor of Geography and a Senior Fellow at the China Center and at the Institute of East Asian Studies, University of California, Berkeley, after teaching for several years at the University of British Columbia, in Vancouver. She received her Ph.D. from the University of California, Berkeley. Her research focuses on processes of economic development and urban transformation in China. Her published work includes *Making Capitalism in China* (1999), and *The Great Urban Transformation: The Politics of Property Development in China* (2009).

Pedro Jacobetty is a researcher at IN3 (Internet Interdisciplinary Institute) of the Open University of Catalonia, Barcelona, and at the Instituto Universitário de Lisbon (ISCTE-IUL), Centro de Investigacão e Estudos de Sociologia (CIES-IUL), Lisbon. He has worked in the fields of social movements, science and technology studies, education, and communication.

Ernesto Ottone is a Chair Professor of Political Science at the Universidad Diego Portales, Santiago de Chile, and Associate Professor at the Universidad de Chile. He received his Ph.D. in Political Science from the University of Paris III, La Sorbonne. Presently he holds the chair on "Globalization and Democracy" of the Universidad Diego Portales (Chile), the chair on "Globalization and Democracy" of the Universidad General San Martin

(Argentina), and the chair on "Latin America in Globalization" at the Institute of Global Studies/MSHF (France). He has been visiting professor in several universities in Latin America and Europe. He was Deputy Executive Secretary of the United Nations Economic Commission for Latin America and the Caribbean (CEPAL) (2006–8) and the Senior Adviser of President Ricardo Lagos in Chile as Director of Strategic Analysis of the Presidency (2000–6).

Terhi Rantanen is Professor in Global Media and Communications at the London School of Economics and Political Science. Her research interests include globalization theories, global media, global news, post-communist and communist media, media history, and history of media studies. She has published extensively on a range of topics related to global media and especially news. Her publications include *When News Was New* (2009), *The Media and Globalization* (2005), *The Global and the National: Media and Communications in Post-Communist Russia* (2002), and *The Globalization of News* (edited with Oliver Boyd-Barrett) (1998).

Lisa Servon is Professor of Urban Studies and former dean at the Milano School of Management, New School University, New York. She has conducted extensive work on community development, micro-enterprises, uses of information technology in low-income communities, and women and technology. Her books include *Bootstrap Capitalism* (1999), *Bridging the Digital Divide: Technology, Community, and Public Policy* (2002), and *Gender and Planning: A Reader* (2006). Her current research focuses on alternative economic cultures, including a comparative study on the "City Slow" movement.

John B. Thompson is Professor of Sociology at the University of Cambridge and Fellow of Jesus College, Cambridge. He received a BA from Keele in 1975 and a Ph.D. from Cambridge in 1979. He was a Research Fellow at Jesus College from 1979 to 1984. He was appointed Lecturer in Sociology at the University of Cambridge in 1985, Reader in Sociology in 1994, and Professor of Sociology in 2001. He has held visiting professorships at universities in the United States, Canada, Mexico, Brazil, Chile, China, and South Africa. His main areas of research are contemporary social and political theory; sociology of the media and modern culture; the social organization of the media industries; the social and political impact of information and communication technologies; and the changing forms of political communication. Recent publications include *Ideology and Modern Culture* (1990),

List of Contributors

The Media and Modernity (1995), *Political Scandal* (2000), *Books in the Digital Age* (2005), and *Merchants of Culture* (2010). He was awarded the European Amalfi Prize for Sociology and the Social Sciences in 2001 for his work on political scandal. He is currently working on the changing structure of the book publishing industry and the making of bestsellers.

Michel Wieviorka is Professor at the École des Hautes Études en Sciences Sociales (Paris), and the president of the Fondation Maison des Sciences de l'Homme (Paris), where he directs the Collège d'Études Mondiales (Institute for Global Studies). He has been president of the International Sociological Association (2006–10). His main books in English include *The Making of Terrorism* (1993), *The Arena of Racism* (1995), *The Lure of Antisemitism* (2007), *Violence: A New Approach* (2009), and *Evil: A Sociological Perspective* (forthcoming).

Rosalind Williams is the Dibner Professor of the History of Science and Technology at MIT. She attended Wellesley College and received degrees from Harvard University (BA, History and Literature), the University of California at Berkeley (MA, Modern European History), and the University of Massachusetts at Amherst (Ph.D., History). A cultural historian of technology, she explores the emergence of a predominantly built world as the environment of human life, often using imaginative literature as a register of and source of insight into this transition. She has written studies of Lewis Mumford, Jules Romains, Enlightenment thinkers, and technological determinism, amongst other topics. Professor Williams came to MIT in 1980 as a research fellow in the Program in Science, Technology, and Society. In 1982 she joined the Writing Program (now the Program in Writing and Humanistic Studies) as a lecturer. In 1990 she was named Class of 1922 Career Development Professor, and in 1995 became the Robert M. Metcalfe Professor of Writing. From 1991 to 1993 she served as Associate Chair of the MIT Faculty, and from 1995 to 2000 as Dean of Students and Undergraduate Education. From 2001 to 2002 she served a Director of Graduate Studies in the Program in Science, Technology, and Society, and from 2002 to 2006 as head of the Program. In 2006 she was named the Bern Dibner Professor of the History of Science and Technology. From 2004 to 2006 she served as president of the Society for the History of Technology.

The Cultures of the Economic Crisis: An Introduction

Manuel Castells, João Caraça, and Gustavo Cardoso

The crisis of global capitalism that has unfolded since 2008 is not merely economic. It is structural and multidimensional. The events that took place in its immediate aftermath show that we are entering a world with very different social and economic conditions from those that characterized the rise of global, informational capitalism in the preceding three decades. The policies and strategies developed to manage the crisis—with mixed results, depending on the country—may usher in a sharply different economic and institutional system, just as the New Deal, the construction of the European Welfare State, and the Bretton Woods global financial architecture gave rise to a new form of capitalism in the aftermath of the 1930s Depression and the Second World War. This Keynesian capitalism was itself called into question after the crisis of the 1970s and the restructuring that took place under the combined influence of three independent, but interrelated, developments: a new technological paradigm, a new form of globalization, and the new cultures that emerged from the social movements of the 1960s and 1970s (Castells, 1980; [1996] 2010). Cultural change was marked by the irresistible rise of the culture of freedom. The technological innovations that changed the world were nurtured in the campuses of research universities, bringing together the passion of discovery and the insubordination against the corporate establishment (Markoff, 2006). Entrepreneurialism took root in the culture of individuation that bypassed organized social action and state bureaucracies (Giddens, 1991). However, the culture of freedom and entrepreneurialism also paved the way for the wave of deregulation, privatization, and liberalization that shook the world economy, changing the foundations of economic institutions and unleashing free market globalization (Judt, 2010).

The new system, global informational capitalism, and its social structure, the network society, displayed some historically irreversible features (such as the logic of the global network society based on digital networking of all core human activities), together with some elements submitted to eventual change under the impact of crises arising from the contradictions of this model of economic growth (Castells, [1996] 2010; Hutton and Giddens, 2000). Thus, the current crisis stems from the destructive trends induced by the dynamics of a deregulated global capitalism, anchored in an unfettered financial market made up of global computer networks and fed by a relentless production of synthetic securities as the source of capital accumulation and capital lending. Furthermore, the combination of deregulation and individualism as a way of life led to the rise of a new breed of financial, corporate managers focused on their own short-term profits as the guiding principle of their increasingly risky decisions (Zaloom, 2006; Tett, 2009). They rationalized their interests by building mathematical models to sophisticate, and obscure, their decision-making process while disregarding the interests of their shareholders, let alone those of society, or even capitalism at large (McDonald and Robinson, 2009). The "me first" culture is now a key ingredient of business management (Sennett, 2006; Moran, 2009).

However, at the heart of the events that triggered the crises of 2008 and 2011, there was "the complacence of the elites" managing the economy, as Engelen et al. (2011) write in their compelling analysis of the institutional and cultural origins of the crisis. In their words:

the crisis resulted from an accumulation of small, and in themselves relatively harmless, decisions made by individual traders or bankers and banks. It is hard to be so kind about the regulators and the political elite who made and implemented policy in finance. They typically bought into the high modernist macro project of "perfecting the market" and at the sectoral level bought into a "trust the bankers to deliver functioning markets" story. This promised everything and offered very little except the undermining of public regulation, while innovation delivered the exact opposite of the promises, as risk was concentrated not dispersed by a dysfunctional banking system.(Engelen et al., 2011: 9)

We have reached a threshold in the evolution of this particular type of capitalism, which in the autumn of 2008 entered a process of implosion only halted by the intervention of an old acquaintance, the state, which had already been sent to the oblivion of history by the apologists of market fundamentalism. Because one of the key measures to stop the free fall of this form of capitalism was the re-regulation of financial markets and financial institutions, which is tantamount to drastically curtailing lending, easy credit ended. Since easy credit was the fuel of consumption, and consumption had accounted for three-fourths of GDP growth in the USA and two-thirds in Europe (since 2000), economic recession hit both North America and Europe. Demand fell sharply, many firms went bankrupt, and many others downsized. Unemployment and underemployment rose considerably, further reducing demand and straining social spending. The response from governments was at first slow, confused, and uncoordinated. When they realized the severity of the crisis, they focused on emergency stabilization of a financial system on the edge of collapse. Thus, they used tax money and borrowed from global financial markets (including loans from China and the sovereign funds) to bail out the banks and financial institutions, plunging government finance into staggering public debt (Stiglitz, 2010). Secondly, some governments resorted to a sort of neo-Keynesianism, using public investment in infrastructure to stimulate the economy and create jobs quickly. Because of the urgent need to create jobs, most of this public investment went to the least productive infrastructure (transportation and public works) rather than to informational infrastructure (education, research, technology, renewable energy), which would have greater impact on productivity in the long term. Governments extended unemployment insurance and, for a while, kept funding social benefits to maintain social order and to remain in office.

The net result was a deepening of the public debt that fed a budget deficit spiral, as interest owed on unpaid debt became one of the major budgetary items. When new borrowing was needed to finance growing expenses, the financial institutions, resurrected with public money, refused to lend to governments or requested an abusive risk premium on top of market interest rates. As governments were compelled to cut budgets and implement austerity policies, with social benefits bearing the brunt of the cuts, social dissatisfaction mounted, eventually leading to unrest. In short: a financial crisis triggered an industrial crisis that induced an employment crisis that led to a demand crisis that, by prompting massive government intervention to stop the free fall of the economy, ultimately led to a fiscal crisis. When governments started to fail their financial obligations, the political system went into reverse, with parties blaming each other and blocking any salvage plan that would not increase their power over the political competitors. Countries refused to help other countries, unless they were on the edge of bankruptcy, and only under the condition that bailed-out countries would surrender sovereignty (Coriat, Coutrot, and Sterdyniak, 2011). Citizens withdrew their trust and money from political and financial institutions. The economic crisis deepened the crisis of political legitimacy, and ultimately threatened to destabilize society at large (Judt, 2010; Engelen et al., 2011).

Thus, several years since the beginning of the crisis, there is still no ending, since the crisis continues to deepen and spiral, even though a complete collapse has been narrowly avoided for the time being. A leaner and meaner financial system has become profitable again at the cost of refusing to fund recovery or bail out governments. But the deepening fiscal crisis is depriving governments of any leverage on the management of the crisis, while consumers cut their consumption, and the welfare states are reduced to their bare bones. The eurozone is being shaken by the inability of the governments to act together, as Germany uses its economic clout to push toward a tighter fiscal union that would sharply reduce national sovereignty in most European countries. Social protests are mounting, populist movements have erupted in the political scene, and the culture of defensive individualism fuels xenophobia, racism, and widespread hostility, breaking down the social fabric and increasing the distance between governments and their citizens. The culture of fear rises alongside the embryos of alternative cultures of hope.

And yet, as the period of triumphant global informational capitalism was linked to the hegemony of a culture of unrestricted individualism, economic liberalism, and technological optimism, any substantial socio-economic restructuring of global capitalism implies the formation of a new economic culture. Culture and institutions are the foundations of any economic system (Ostrom, 2005). Since culture (a specific set of values and beliefs orienting behavior) is a material practice, we should be able to detect the signs of such culture in the spontaneous adaptation of peoples' lives to the constraints and opportunities arising from the crisis. The observation of these proto-cultural forms and of their interaction with the contours and evolution of the economic crisis constitutes one of the themes of the reflection proposed in this volume.

To illustrate the social landscape that characterizes this crisis and its aftermath, we will now focus on key features of the process in two different contexts: the United States and Portugal. They are, of course, very different countries, and the crisis and its management have specific manifestations in both of them. Furthermore, since the crisis continues to metamorphose as we write, the description that follows will be history by the time you read these pages. However, by proceeding with a brief overview of events in the immediate aftermath of the crisis in two dissimilar contexts, we may ground in observation the issues raised in this introduction that will be analyzed in depth in the chapters of this volume.

The global financial crisis that exploded toward the end of 2008 and sent the global economy in a tailspin **started in the United States**, the seedbed of global informational capitalism, which has been the predominant breed of capitalism since the 1980s. As mentioned above, the crisis was the direct consequence of the specific dynamics of the global informational economy, and it resulted from the combination of six factors.

First, the technological transformation of finance provided the basis for the formation of a global financial market around global computer networks and equipped financial institutions with the computational capacity to operate advanced mathematical models. These models were deemed to be capable of managing the increasing complexity of the financial system, operating globally interdependent financial markets through electronic transactions effected at lightening speed.

Second, the liberalization and deregulation of financial markets and financial institutions allowed the quasi-free flow of capital across companies and across the world, overwhelming the regulatory capacity of national regulators.

Third, the securitization of every economic organization, activity, or asset made financial valuation the paramount standard by which to assess the value of firms, governments, currencies, and even entire economies. Furthermore, new financial technologies made possible the invention of numerous exotic financial products, as derivatives, futures, options, and securitized insurance (for example, credit default swaps (CDSs)) became increasingly complex and intertwined, ultimately virtualizing capital and eliminating any semblance of transparency in the markets, so that accounting procedures became meaningless.

Fourth, the imbalance between capital accumulation in newly industrializing countries (such as China and several oil-producing countries) and capital borrowing in the United States facilitated a credit-led expansion in the USA that resulted in a wave of adventurous lending to a crowd of eager consumers who became accustomed to living on the edge of debt, pushing the lenders far beyond their financial solvency. Indeed, this moral hazard was discounted by the irresponsible lenders, always confident of the federal government's willingness to bail them out, should the need arise, as it inevitably would.

Fifth, because financial markets only partially function according to the logic of supply and demand, and are largely shaped by "information turbulences" and "irrational exuberance," the mortgage crisis that started in 2007 in the United States, after the bursting of the real-estate bubble, reverberated throughout the global financial system and in the international real-estate and mortgage markets (Akerloff and Shiller, 2010).

Sixth, the lack of proper supervision in securities trading and financial practices enabled daring brokers to bolster the economy and their personal bonuses through adventurous lending practices.

The paradox is that the crisis was brewed in the cauldrons of the "new economy," an economy defined by a substantial surge in productivity as the result of technological innovation, networking, and higher education levels in the workforce. Indeed, in the United States, where the crisis began, cumulative productivity growth reached almost 30 percent between 1998 and 2008. However, because of shortsighted and greedy management policies, real wages increased by only 2 percent over the decade, and in fact weekly earnings of college-educated workers fell by 6 percent between 2003 and 2008. And yet, real-estate prices soared during the 2000s and lending institutions fed the frenzy by providing mortgages, ultimately backed by federal institutions, to the same workers whose wages were stagnant or diminishing. The notion was that productivity increases would ultimately catch up with wages as the benefits of growth would trickle down. It never happened, because financial companies and realtors reaped the benefits of the productive economy, inducing an unsustainable bubble. The financial services industry's share of profits increased from 10 percent in the 1980s to 40 percent in 2007, and the value of its shares from 6 percent to 23 percent, while the industry accounts for only 5 percent of private sector employment. In short, the very real benefits of the new economy were appropriated in the securities market, and used to generate a much greater mass of virtual capital that multiplied in value as it was lent to a multitude of avid consumers–borrowers. Thus, in the United States, between 1993 and 2008, bank lending accounted for only 20 percent of total net lending. The rest came from money market funds, exchange-traded funds, hedge funds, and investment banks that had been transformed into lending agencies in a deregulated environment. Furthermore, most banks also relied largely on securitization, instead of their own deposits, to finance their loans.

Moreover, the expansion of the global economy, with the move of China, India, Brazil, and other industrializing economies to the forefront of capitalist growth, increased the risk of financial collapse as the United States and other markets in the world borrowed capital accumulated in these economies in order to sustain their solvency and imports capability while taking advantage of favorable lending rates (Wolf, 2008). The massive military spending of the US government to foot the bill for the invasion of Iraq was also financed through debt, to the point that Asian countries now hold a large share of US Treasury Bonds, intertwining the Asian Pacific and the US budget in a decisive manner. While inflation was kept relatively in check because of significant productivity growth, there was a growing gap between the size of the lending and the ability of both consumers and institutions to repay what they had borrowed. The percentage of household debt to disposable income in the USA grew from 3 percent in 1998 to 130 percent in 2008. As a result, prime mortgage delinquencies as a percentage of loans increased from 2.5 percent in 1998 to 118 percent in 2008.

And so, a financial crisis of unprecedented proportions unfolded in the USA and in Europe, ending the myth of the self-regulated market, with devastating consequences for firms and household economies. The total market capitalization of the financial markets fell by more than half in 2008. Many financial companies collapsed (Lehman Brothers being only the most notorious of them), and others were brought to near bankruptcy. Hundreds of banks disappeared in the USA. The IMF evaluated the global loss for financial institutions at about $4.3 trillion.

However, there is no such thing as a social vacuum. Social systems do not collapse as a result of their internal contradictions. The crisis, its conflicts, and its treatment are always social processes. And these social processes, as all others, are enacted and shaped by the interests, values, beliefs, and strategies of social actors. This is to say that, when a system does not reproduce its logic automatically, there are attempts to restore it to its former state, as well as projects to reorganize a new system on the basis of a new set of interests and values. The ultimate outcome is often the result of conflicts and negotiations between the standard-bearers of these different logics.

Manuel Castells, João Caraça, and Gustavo Cardoso

In the United States, the severity of the crisis was a key factor in the surprising election of Barack Obama on a platform of social and political reform. However, he was sworn into office in the midst of serious threat of financial collapse. He focused first on bailing out the financial institutions. He then tried to build a social and political consensus to proceed with health reform, stimulate the economy, and regulate the financial system. But stern political opposition from the Republican Party and from a right-wing populist movement, known as the Tea Party, against increasing taxes and government regulation, led to a political stalemate and ultimately derailed many of his reform policies. Given the need to finance the two wars he inherited from the Bush administration, and his inability to increase revenue, particularly after the Republicans took control of the House of Representatives, Obama was unable to pursue public investment at a high enough level to engineer a sustained economic recovery.

Unemployment remained close to a double-digit level, while the fiscal crisis spread in local and state governments. Social spending cuts and layoffs in both private and public sectors fueled resentment. With public confidence at a low, it became politically difficult to raise taxes. To finance a growing deficit, Obama had to accept the conditions of the Republican Congress in order to authorize the increase of the debt ceiling. The fiscal crisis became a time bomb, while the social safety net shrank in the midst of greater need. The most potentially reformist administration since the 1960s was put into survival mode, unable to stimulate the economy or to appease society. Only the financial system felt that happy times were here again, comforted by the presence of close allies in the top echelon of Obama's economic team. The Democratic left that had mobilized for Obama felt discouraged. Right-wing populist movements, heavily financed by the most conservative sectors of the corporate world (for example, Koch Industries), went on the offensive to take control of the political system and reshape the economy in line with their interests. In spite of growing technological innovation, entrepreneurialism, and productivity in the United States, dependence on foreign investment and lending increased, and economic imbalances and social differences were intensified. The old global, informational model was being restored in a much reduced version, but at the price of disconnecting large segments of the economy and society from the competitive core of American corporate capitalism, with wealth and power increasingly concentrated in the hands of a small elite, paradoxically supported by a populist movement largely consisting of white working-class citizens of middle America. This revamped model of financial capitalism does not seem to be sustainable.

Portugal offers a vivid example of the evolution of the crisis from the USA to Europe and from its financial to its economic dimensions, with its path toward political crisis and the limits of national European political autonomy vis-à-vis the US-based rating agencies and the Berlin–Paris axis governing the European Union. The 2007 subprime crisis in the United States quickly spread to Europe and, eventually, to Portugal. In Portugal, a small country with an already fragile economy, financial unrest had severe consequences. Portuguese living standards had increased greatly in the twenty-five years after the revolution of April 25, 1974. During the 1990s, productivity increased, private sector investment grew, a National Health Service was consolidated, and generalized access to public education was achieved. In the early 2000s, Portugal had not only one of the lowest newborn death rates in developed countries, but also one of the European Union's lowest unemployment rates. In the areas of entrepreneurial innovation dissemination practices, university enrollment, high-school graduation rates, and high- and low-tech exports, Portugal had achieved better results than its neighboring countries in the eurozone periphery.

But the economic policies shared by all political parties since the early 1990s—namely, infrastructure projects funded by the state (Expo 98 World Fair, stadiums for the 2004 European Football Championship, and new motorways)—had little positive impact on growth. Although expansion was nearly stagnant during the first half of the 2000s, Portugal had, by 2007, once again achieved economic growth and an increase in job creation. It is within this framework that, in September 2007, the first signs of the global financial crisis hit Portugal. By then the effects of mortgage crisis in the eurozone had already become a liquidity crisis for the euro, hampering access to credit in the real economy. This is the moment when the European Central Bank (ECB) started its almost four-year-long policy of injecting more capital into the monetary system.

Also in Europe, the bursting of the subprime bubble deteriorated the assets of the financial sector, bringing liquidity problems for financial institutions and thus leading to a banking crisis. The stock markets plunged, damaging the assets of eurozone countries. In certain cases, this indicated difficulties for government budget control and debt finance, giving birth to a sovereign debt crisis. Furthermore, some of these countries rescued the most affected banks from collapse through the implementation of safety plans or guarantees. In the autumn of 2008, Iceland witnessed the implosion and nationalization of its three major banks. In Portugal, the lack of interbank liquidity led to the downfall of Banco Português de Negócios (BPN). In November 2008, BPN was nationalized by the Portuguese government in order to prevent systemic risk, but the confidence in the banking sector had already been shaken. The structural deficits in Portugal over the years led to a debt burden, which was aggravated by two bailouts of national banks (BPN and Banco Privado Português (BPP)) by the Portuguese government. These banks had been accumulating losses because of bad investment and fraud by their board of managers—very similar to Madoff's actions in the USA.

Beyond bank bailouts, European governments responded during 2008 and 2011 to the global economic crisis essentially by resorting to stabilizers and stimulus packages, partly to offset the sudden contraction in private sector demand. These expansionary fiscal policies did prevent a steep decline in output and employment, but left governments with high debt burdens. In the process, debt-holders started questioning eurozone countries' ability to service their national debt, because those in a monetary union cannot resort to currency devaluation—a condition even more delicate for euro countries such as Portugal with a high debt burden but low export/import ratio and slow economic growth. Being part of the eurozone, the country could manage its problems by borrowing money with low interest rates and injecting it into both the private and the public sector, both for investment and consumption. This, in turn, brought even more debt.

Portugal was the third eurozone country to ask for international assistance, after Greece and Ireland. What the bailout of Portugal demonstrates is that there is not an overarching debt crisis in the eurozone; rather, there is a crisis in several countries with more differences among them than EU membership and the euro currency. The bailout of Portugal also shows that it is not only about sovereign debts. It is about where money can be made within the global casino and what is to be gained by the croupiers (the rating agencies) and of course by the gamblers (financial market investors). It is clear that all three bailed-out eurozone countries had gambled on the belief that a single currency would enable them to borrow heavily at lower interest rates and that such a scenario would continue to be sustainable in the medium to long term. But in Portugal the case is somewhat peculiar, for there was not an underlying systemic risk within the bank system; the political system was already achieving economic growth and reforming the public sector. The Portuguese public debt was below the level of nations like Italy or Belgium that had not been subject to bailout. Its budget deficit was lower than that of several other European countries and was able to be reduced, although irregularly, as a result of the government's actions in the previous decade.

So why the Portuguese bailout? The information turbulence fueled by fears of market contagion in Greece and Ireland, together with the possibility of future rating downgrades, became a self-fulfilling prophecy and at the same time offered interesting prospects for profit in short-term selling. By raising Portugal's interest rates to levels beyond economical sustainability, the rating agencies led the country to the only seemingly short-term option: an EU–IMF bailout. One could argue precisely that in Portugal the path from financial to economic to political crisis has been followed all the way. Portugal felt the need for bailout because of the political frailty of the current political institutions of the eurozone and their inability to deal with crisis and to think differently and experiment with different approaches. In doing so, the governments of the European Union and the ECB have been pushing the crisis into the political domain, where it is experienced in the streets and squares, fueling the undermining of the democratic institutions of modernity. Along that process, governments and the EU allowed new players, such as rating agencies or coalitions of countries (for example, the Berlin–Paris axis), to undermine their power. Could the European Union have supported Portugal as an alternative to bailout? Probably, yes. The ECB could have bought Portuguese bonds, as it did a few months later when both Italy and Spain were being targeted in the very same ways, where central bank-led intervention prevented prospective bailout. The bailout of Portugal shows how future scenario prospects suggested by rating agencies, and acted upon by political and banking institutions of the European Union, undermine economic recovery and political sovereignty.

The Portuguese bailout also shows how the political sphere in the European Union has succumbed to the unregulated financial markets. It shows that the return to the predominance of the political over the financial seems to be increasingly difficult to achieve within the current institutional setting. This explains why people are entrenching themselves in the public squares in search of places where the political might have supremacy—a place where people, in their view, can chose their future.

Thus, **in the immediate aftermath of the crisis, in the USA and in the European Union**, a four-layer economy seems to be emerging:

1. A revamped informational capitalist economy for a much smaller segment of the population—probably the sector dominated by the professional class. There is a new wave of technological and organizational innovation; a kind of new, new economy unfolding, with new products and new processes in fields such as energy, nanotechnology, and bioinformatics. However, because there is a reduced pool of venture capital, this new round of innovation does not have the potential for increasing the consumption of the majority of the population, thus hampering overall economic recovery.
2. A public and semi-public sector in crisis, increasingly unable to generate employment and demand as the fiscal crisis deepens.
3. Survival-oriented, traditional economic activities, with low productivity and high employment potential for low-skill jobs, with an important component of informal economy.
4. An alternative economy sector (not necessarily excluding for-profit production) based on a different set of values about the meaning of life, whose characteristics we will try to explore in this volume on the basis of observation.

Indeed, if people cannot consume as much as they would like, they will have to find fulfillment in something else. But they cannot find fulfillment in something else unless they change their values; that is, unless they generate from within a new economic culture—actually, a variety of economic cultures—unified under the common goal of superseding consumerism. Since new values do not generate in a vacuum, this non-consumerist culture may only grow on the basis of actual social practices that exist in societies around the world, often first enacted by drop-outs of the current economy because of their rejection of what they consider to be a destructive way of life. These are not neo-hippies. They come in all formats, and in some cases under very innovative forms (for example, ethical hackers, to use Himanen's terminology). But the critical remark is that the rise of a new economic culture may result from the historical convergence between a cultural vanguard searching for a different way of life, and the disoriented masses of ex-consumers who no longer have the opportunity to consume anything but themselves—people who have nothing to lose except their canceled credit cards.

However, beyond the shores of North America and Europe, most of the world is *not* in crisis—at least, not in the crisis of global capitalism that shook up the until-now dominant economies. Granted, poverty, exploitation, environmental degradation, epidemics, widespread violence, and uncertain democracy are the daily lot for people living in what are known as emerging economies. Yet, peripheral capitalism, sometimes managed by a Communist party, as in China, is growing to the point of becoming the most dynamic component of the global economy, assuring in fact a new round of capital accumulation on an even grander scale than in the past. Because of the economic and cultural interdependence between old and new areas of capitalist expansion, the understanding of this crisis and its aftermath is impossible without considering developments in Asia, Latin America, and Africa. In short, we must undertake the analysis of the crisis as a "non-global global crisis of capitalism," and account for the interaction between areas in decline and areas in expansion, looking into the causes and consequences of this asymmetrical development of global capitalism. This is why, at the end of this volume, an analysis of these dynamics from the perspectives of Latin America and China will provide material and hypotheses reflecting on the actual contours of the world emerging in the twenty-first century.

The central theme of the interdisciplinary, multicultural analysis presented in this volume is that the economy is—all economies *are*—culture: cultural practices embedded in processes of production, consumption, and exchange of goods and services. As Viviana Zelizer (2011) has forcefully argued, culture shapes the economy. When there is a systemic crisis, there is indication of a cultural crisis, of non-sustainability of certain values as the guiding principle of human behavior (Aitken, 2007; Akerloff and Shiller, 2010). Thus, ultimately, only when and if a fundamental cultural change takes place, will new forms of economic organization and institutions emerge, ensuring the sustainability of the evolution of the economic system (Nolan, 2009). Our hypothesis is that we may well be in such a period of historical transition. Therefore, we are presenting in a plural perspective a series of studies that examine how certain cultural and social forms led to the crisis, as well as assessing the social productivity of different cultures emerging in the aftermath of the crisis. Which cultures will ultimately come to dominate social practice may determine our collective fate: either to enter a process of social disintegration and violent conflicts, or else to witness the rise of new cultures based on the use value of life as a superior form of human organization.

Manuel Castells, João Caraça, and Gustavo Cardoso

References

Aitken, Richard (2007). *Performing Capital: Towards a Cultural Economy of Popular and Global Finance*. New York: Palgrave Macmillan.

Akerloff, George A., and Shiller, Robert J. (2010). *Animal Spirits: How Human Psychology Drives the Economy and why it Matters for Global Capitalism*. Princeton: Princeton University Press.

Castells, Manuel (1980). *The Economic Crisis and American Society*. Princeton: Princeton University Press.

Castells, Manuel ([1996] 2010). *The Rise of the Network Society*. Oxford: Blackwell.

Coriat, Benjamin, Coutrot, Thomas, and Sterdyniak, Henri (2011) (eds). *20 ans d'aveuglement: L'Europe au bord du gouffre*. Paris: Éditions Les Liens qui Libèrent.

Engelen, Ewald, et al. (2011). *After the Great Complacence: Financial Crisis and the Politics of Reform*. Oxford: Oxford University Press.

Giddens, Anthony (1991). *Modernity and Self-Identity: Self and Society in the Late Modern Age*. Cambridge: Polity Press.

Hutton, Will, and Giddens, Anthony (2000) (eds). *On the Edge: Living with Global Capitalism*. London: Jonathan Cape.

Judt, Tony (2010). *Ill Fares the Land*. New York: Penguin.

McDonald, L. S., and Robinson, P. (2009). *Colossal Failure of Common Sense: The Incredible Story of the Collapse of Lehman Brothers*. New York: Crown Business.

Markoff, John (2006). *What the Dormouse Said: How the Sixties Counterculture Shaped the Personal Computer Industry*. New York: Penguin.

Moran, Michael (2009). *Business, Politics, and Society: An Anglo-American Comparison*. Oxford: Oxford University Press.

Nolan, Peter (2009). *Crossroads: The End of Wild Capitalism and the Future of Humanity*. London: Marshall Cavendish.

Ostrom, Elinor (2005). *Understanding Institutional Diversity*. Princeton: Princeton University Press.

Sennett, Richard (2006). *The Culture of the New Capitalism*. New Haven: Yale University Press.

Stiglitz, Joseph (2010). *Freefall: America, Free Markets, and the Sinking of the World Economy*. New York: W. W. Norton.

Tett, Gillian (2009). *Fool's Gold*. London: Little, Brown.

Wolf, Martin (2008). *Fixing Global Finance*. Baltimore: Johns Hopkins University Press.

Zelizer, Viviana A. (2011). *Economic Lives: How Culture Shapes the Economy*. Princeton: Princeton University Press.

Zaloom, Caitlin (2006). *Out of the Pits: Traders and Technology from Chicago to London*. Chicago: University of Chicago Press.

PART ONE

Prelude

Chapter 1

The Rolling Apocalypse of Contemporary History

Rosalind Williams

Introduction: A case study that did not happen

When a group of scholars met in Lisbon in the summer of 2009, our scholarly mission was based on a seemingly self-evident model of contemporary history. An economic crisis had occured in the fall of 2008. We would examine its aftermath, with special attention to its cultural dimensions. Crisis and aftermath, cause and effect: it seemed straightforward.

To be sure, there were pesky adjectives attached to the key nouns. Was the crisis essentially an *economic* one, or was it better described as *financial*, and if so what was the significance of the distinction? Or was it primarily *political*, as, for example, a "quiet coup" of privileged elites (Johnson, 2009; see also Johnson and Kwak, 2010)? As for an aftermath, what makes it *cultural*? As Raymond Williams (1958) showed well over a half-century earlier, the word and concept *culture* has been evolving since the early nineteenth century, along with other key terms such as *society* and *industry*.

Their mutual evolution has both shaped and reflected changes in the world. What does *culture* mean in the early twenty-first century?

I decided to work through such questions in relation to what seemed a promising case study: the effects of the 2008 *economic crisis* on the University of California at Berkeley. In 2004 the state provided just over 40 percent of the financial support for the University of California system, or $3.25 billion. For Berkeley, with a total budget of about $1.1 billion, state funding provided $450 million, or 35 percent of its funding. The crisis of autumn 2008 led to a severe drop in state revenues, which were especially vulnerable because of their dependence on the personal income tax. In 2009 state support for the entire system dropped from $3.25 billion to $2.6 billion; in 2010, to $1.8 billion. This meant a severe and sudden drop in university income. The next largest sources were all much smaller than state funding ($300 million in federal funding, $150 million each for student tuition and private fundraising, and between $100 million and $120 million from endowment income) and none of them could come close to filling the gap for the coming fiscal year (Birgeneau, 2011b; Freedberg, 2011; Hoey, 2011).

Consequently Berkeley leadership, in partnership with the University of California Office of the President, took immediate, painful measures to reduce expenditures. These affected everyone on campus through reduced services, mandatory furloughs (as a way to reduce salaries), reserve fund raids, and sharp increases in tuition and fees: an 8 percent hike in spring 2009, 30 percent in a second round (fall 2009 and spring 2010), and 10 percent more in fall 2010, for a total increase of nearly 50 percent in just two academic years. Because tuition income remained a source of financial aid, this increase was a net gain for low-income students. For other students, there was no cushion for a sharp, unanticipated increase in the cost of higher education.

In undertaking this case study, I had assumed that the *cultural aftermath* most relevant to the Berkeley campus would be that of campus activism, which had emerged so noticeably during the loyalty oath controversies of the 1950s and the Free Speech Movement of the 1960s (Kerr, 2001–3). Unsurprisingly, given this cultural context, these efforts to reduce expenditures aroused organized protests. While it is common to refer to them as "student protests," the individuals involved were a mix of Berkeley students, non-Berkeley students, and non-student activists, especially union members. All of them received encouragement, and more rarely active participation, from some faculty members, who were overwhelmingly concentrated in a few departments. For students, the primary complaint was the abrupt rise in the cost of their education; a secondary complaint was the reduction in student services, such as library hours. From the unions' point of view, the primary complaints were layoffs, since union employees were protected from salary reductions in the form of furloughs. Faculty complaints were more generalized, focusing on accusations of administrative bloat and complicity with business interests.

The methods were familiar from Berkeley's activist heritage: rallies in Sproul Hall Plaza, demonstrations outside California Hall (site of senior administration offices), and building occupations designed to disrupt the normal campus routine (for example, demonstrators often set off fire alarms, requiring building evacuations and emergency response). An occupation of Wheeler Hall in November 2009 led campus police to call in outside, non-university police for assistance, which ended in confrontations that in turn led to charges of police brutality. Sit-in rallies continued in early December, culminating in a nighttime march by one group of demonstrators, some masked and carrying lighted torches, to the Chancellor's on-campus residence: they threw rocks at the windows and nearly succeeded in setting the building on fire. In the spring of 2010 there were further building occupations, demonstrations at Regents' Meetings, a hunger strike, and a "day of action," which included a march on Sacramento.

These tactics and strategies were familiar ones on the Berkeley campus and were repeatedly explained and defended as part of "Berkeley culture." As a response to the economic crisis, however, they were ineffective. In part this is because protestors' demands were fundamentally inconsistent. Calls to maintain services, jobs, and salaries required more income, while demands to lower tuition and fees, or even to eliminate them, would further reduce the income stream, including that directed for financial aid. The protests also ineffectively targeted campus and system administrators as culprits, although they had no responsibility for the dramatic drop in university income and were struggling to deal with its consequences. Protestors responded by asserting that university leaders would have adequate financial resources if they just spent them more wisely, and/or if the state legislature could be convinced to fund the University of California system more generously.

These arguments failed to persuade the overwhelming majority of staff, students, and faculty at Berkeley, who did not rally to the demonstrators, except for supporting complaints about police actions related to the Wheeler Hall occupation. Sometimes re-enactment of familiar protest tactics even aroused pushback if onlookers regarded them as inappropriate for the situation. At the Regents' Meeting of November 18, 2009, student protestors began singing "We Shall Overcome." Some African American staff members present at the meeting were outraged at this co-option of a civil rights anthem to protest fee increases (Birgeneau, 2011c).

Not long after, on December 2, 2009, the forty-fifth anniversary of Mario Savio's "Put your bodies upon the gears" speech, which inspired the Free Speech Movement, a group of Berkeley students and faculty planned to commemorate the event with speeches on the steps of Sproul Hall. They were prevented from doing so by demonstrators who wanted to substitute their causes for "a dead movement." Instead of letting other students and faculty speak, the demonstrators repeated in unison some lines from Savio's speech. The irony was not lost on those who had planned the commemoration, who felt their right to free speech had been overturned, nor on observers such as a newspaper reporter who commented that:

The demonstration . . . showed continued confusion over the issues. Signs held by the protesters addressed everything from fee hikes to minority enrollment, and several aimed anger at the UC regents—but not at the Legislature, governor or voters, all of whom have a more significant say in how much money the university receives. (Krupnick, 2009)

Campus protests continued in 2011 but around causes that were increasingly detached from the economic crisis—for example, demands for amnesty for demonstrators arrested at earlier events, and protests against alleged police brutality in responding to efforts, inspired by the Occupy Movement, to pitch tents on campus. Despite a campus-wide tumult caused by the last of these events in particular, close to two years of protests had no impact in mitigating budget cuts or in arousing broad-based popular support to restore state funding to the UC system.

In the meantime, the institutional budget of Berkeley underwent a revolution. In 2004 state support was the largest source of income for the university, 35 percent of the total. A long-range budget agreement had been reached between the university system and the state. In the particular case of Berkeley, this agreement pledged that by the year 2011 state support to the campus would total $600 million. When 2011 actually arrived, state funding for Berkeley was $235 million—$365 million less than had been promised. Another $15 million will almost certainly be lost because the state's revenue projections have not been met.

At the beginning of 2012 state support was the fourth largest source of university income, contributing only 10½ percent of the operating budget.

External support for research was the largest source of university income (in excess of $700 million), followed by student tuition and fees (approaching $500 million) and private philanthropy (about $315 million). Berkeley still faces an operating budget shortfall of close to $100 million, which it plans to address by again increasing tuition and fees (though on a more modest scale), admitting larger numbers of non-Californian undergraduates (approaching 20 percent of the student body), raiding emergency reserves, and pressing forward with private fundraising and operational savings (Birgeneau, 2011a, b; Freedberg, 2011; Hoey, 2011).

The near-collapse of state support had redefined the character of the University of California at Berkeley. In a few years it has been transformed from a "state-supported" university to a "state-located" one (Freedberg, 2011; Hoey, 2011). Berkeley has not so much been "privatized" as been transformed into a quasi-federal, quasi-private institution, with a residual but hugely diminished mandate to provide excellent higher education to the citizens of California. This is not because system and university administrators have sought privatization. On the contrary, they have protested the decline in state support and warned of its results (Birgeneau, 2011a).[1]

What has been most privatized is the consciousness of the voters of California. While I was following attention-getting actions on campus, the most important cultural aftermath was taking place in public opinion. Longitudinal data assembled by the Public Policy Institute of California (PPIC) indicate that the economic crisis of 2008, if anything, raised public awareness of the value of education, especially of K–12 but also of higher education, and reinforced desire to support a strong educational system. Only support for public safety rates higher than education as a priority for the state.

This support, however, by no means translates into a conviction that the cuts in state support are a serious problem for the university system. Voters are willing to consider higher taxes or higher fees to support higher education, but they have strong reservations about whether they are truly necessary to maintain the system. One strong sentiment is that the California system of higher education must accept its fair share of cuts at a time when they are required of all services. Another extremely strong sentiment is that

---

[1] John Searle's *The Campus War* (1971) shows how closely events at Berkeley during the past several years repeat those of the 1960s, especially with regard to lack of faculty support for the administration once police are called to campus.

the system must get rid of the "waste" that pervades these institutions, especially the number and compensation of senior administrators.

Finally, and most complex of all, there is a sentiment that, in maintaining excellence and accessibility, "where there is a will there is a way." Institutions can remain excellent if they eliminate bureaucracy, overcompensation, and lax supervision. Individuals and families should pay a significant share of the costs of higher education, even when family income is low. (As of early 2012 families earning $80,000 or less pay no tuition.) While campus protestors and the voting public share a conviction that universities could be well run for much less money, the protestors usually want dramatically lower fees, or none at all, while the voters resist anything resembling a "free ride."

These same voters, however, have strong worries about accessibility to the university system. In one poll, three-fourths of the voters agreed that students have to borrow too much to pay for a college education. At the same time, a majority (55 percent) thought that almost anyone who needs financial help could get loans or financial aid (40 percent disagreed). The principle of universal access is strongly approved, and the threats to this access have voters "very worried" (up from 43 percent to 57 percent between October 2007 and November 2010). But, along with this strong fear of being priced out of the market for public higher education, voters apparently also worry that too-low rates will be taken advantage of by others.

These findings are complex and fluid, but overall they indicate a sharp decline in civic consciousness. First, voters have dramatically lost trust in state government, including its ability to plan for the future of California's higher education system. In a neat if troubling symmetry, the percentage of voters who have some or a great deal of confidence in state government's planning for higher education, as opposed to those who have very little or none, has reversed in just under three years. Between October 2007 and November 2010, confidence dropped from 57 percent to 40 percent, while little or no confidence climbed from 42 percent to 57 percent.

Second, voters perceive the system of higher education not so much as a collective good as a consumer commodity. The university system is looked upon first and foremost as a provider of education that enables young individuals to have a better economic future. When voters are reminded of the role of the university system as a research enterprise, by which it plays a critical part in creating economic opportunities, they acknowledge this role—but their primary view of the university is as an educational institution. Furthermore, the strong belief that this education remains accessible to those who appreciate its value assumes that its value is a private benefit, primarily for the ambitious and deserving. Again, the idea that the system of higher education has a collective benefit is weak at best. When this benefit is expressed at all, it is usually defined as an economic one. The idea that public education has non-economic benefits—to create a well-informed and thoughtful citizenry as the fundamental basis for democratic self-governance—is nowhere visible (Baldassare et al., 2010; see also Simon, 2011).

Is this still the *crisis*? Or the *aftermath*? While such a significant shift of consciousness follows the economic crisis, this does not mean it is an *aftermath* that was caused by the *crisis*. Instead, it may be a revelation of cultural processes already underway that have been reinforced. State university systems have been the backbone of American higher education in its period of unprecedented expansion after the Second World War. They have attracted two of every three American college students, including the overwhelming majority of students from poor or modest families. Within three years of the 2008 economic crisis, even the largest and strongest of the state universities were scrambling to reinvent themselves as quasi-federal quasi-private institutions, as well as to attract non-state students who would pay higher tuitions. The poorer and smaller public institutions were just trying to survive.

Little did I realize, as I began to follow events at Berkeley, how representative it would be of the American cultural aftermath of the economic crisis of 2008—an aftermath that does not correct the causes of a crisis but rather intensifies them. In the country at large, a human disaster triggered by multiple, systematic deceptions and structural flaws in financial systems, especially in housing financing, has led to . . . layoffs of schoolteachers and librarians.

This is oversimplifying the cause and effect, to be sure, but not by much. What disasters do, above all, is reveal how things work normally. "One of the most salient features of severe downturns is that they tend to accelerate deep economic shifts that are already under way." In this case, the disaster has revealed "with rare and brutal clarity" the sorting out of Americans into "winners and losers, and the slow hollowing-out of the middle class" (Peck, 2011; see my comments on disasters as revelations in Rosalind Williams, 2002).

This astounding non sequitur is not only a California story, not only a higher education story, and not only an American story. In both the United

Rosalind Williams

States and the European Union, dangerously high national unemployment has led to calls not for government pump-priming but for austerity budgets that are likely further to slow already sluggish economic growth, although such growth is the most plausible source, over time, of higher employment and balanced budgets. This utterly illogical and self-defeating pattern is proclaimed to be the "new normal." What is happening in the USA and EU today feels like a bewildering fall down the rabbit hole, with no bottom in sight.

When I realized this, I also realized that the Berkeley case study, or any case study, would be unproductive without first reviewing the tacit model with which we began: crisis and aftermath, cause and effect, economic and cultural. Accordingly, this paper now turns to these questions:

- What is the meaning, in today's world, of the oft-used, under-analyzed term *crisis*?
- What is the distinction between a *crisis* and its *aftermath*? When is a *crisis* over and when does the *aftermath* begin?
- In this context, what do we mean by *culture* or *cultures*?
- How do individuals and groups perceive, experience, and understand contemporary events as *history*?

As Master Confucius wisely advises, any effort to bring order to the world should begin by "rectifying names."

If language is not correct, then what is said is not what is meant; if what is said is not what is meant, then what must be done remains undone; if this remains undone, morals and art will deteriorate; if justice goes astray, the people will stand about in helpless confusion. Hence there must be no arbitrariness in what is said. This matters above everything. (Confucius, 1980 edn: bk 13, v. 3)

Let us begin with the terms *crisis* and *aftermath*.

Crisis and aftermath as historical concepts

As soon as the financial world began to quake in the fall of 2008, Americans tried to provide a label for the event. In American English, one that gained and still has some traction is "The Great Recession." This was an exercise of historical calibration, being a term somewhere between the Great

Depression of the 1930s and the milder recessions that have regularly occurred since then. But already we begin to confuse *crisis* and *aftermath*, since depressions and recessions alike are aftermaths of some other triggering event. In the case of the Great Depression, that event is the Crash of 1929, referring to the stock market crash that occurred in October of that year. What happened in 2008 was more general, and before long the whole cluster of events of that fall (a word conveniently serving to describe both the time of year and the trend of events) was simply summarized as "the crisis."

Crisis comes from the Greek word *kerein*, meaning to separate or cut, to make fixed, settled, or stated (as, for example, in the expression "a date certain"). It therefore refers to a sharply defined, climactic event; possibly dangerous, but in any case decisive.[2] The earliest uses of the word, dating back to the 1500s, are in relation to medical and also astrological events, which were believed to be closely related. In this context, *crisis* describes "the point in the progress of a disease when an important development or change takes place which is decisive of recovery or death; the turning-point of a disease for better or for worse . . . "

In the seventeenth century, "crisis" began to be used in a more general sense to apply to politics and commerce, as "a vitally important or decisive stage in the progress of anything; a turning point; also, a state of affairs in which a decisive change for better or worse is imminent; now applied *esp.* to times of difficulty, insecurity, and suspense in politics or commerce." It is notable that, in both the medical and more general usages, *crisis* is defined in contrast to ongoing *progress*—initially progress of an illness, and by the seventeenth century, "of anything." In other words, the idea, or more properly the ideology, of progress emerges as the dominant concept of history at the same time the concept of crisis is beginning to be applied to history as a sinister episode disrupting the underlying march of progress. Their dialectic becomes more evident in the nineteenth century, as, for example, in his much-read translation of Plato published in 1875, Benjamin Jowett writes: "The ordinary statesman is also apt to fail in extraordinary crises." *Crisis* also began to be used in phrases such as *crisis-mongers* (1841), *crisis-centre* (1898, referring to the Near East), and (as a compliment) *crisis-avoiding* (1900).

---

[2] All quotations referring to *crisis* are from the *OED* online <http://www.oed.com> (accessed 3 Mar. 2011).

Rosalind Williams

In the twentieth century, crisis began to displace progress as an ongoing state of affairs. In the interwar period, new hyphenated versions were invented and used to define a general state of anxiety: *crisis-minded* and *crisis-conscious* (1938). In 1940 William Empson, in the aptly titled *The Gathering Storm*, wrote that "The point is to join up the crisis-feeling to what can be felt all the time in normal life." The challenge of *crisis-management*—a term first used by Herman Kahn in writing about the danger of military escalation—became routine. Once the ability to *manage* crisis becomes an attribute of political and military leadership, the question arises: is "normal" history *progress* or *crisis*? And if *crisis* begins to pervade ordinary history, what is the distinction between *crisis* and *aftermath*?

We were a year and a half into our project (I am embarrassed to admit) before I happened to read in a novel (Joseph O'Neill's *Netherland*, 2008) that the English word *aftermath* relates to agriculture. I had ignorantly assumed it had to do with mathematics, but, prompted by O'Neill, I looked it up too in the *OED*.[3] Like *crisis*, *aftermath* is first used in English in the sixteenth century, the earliest use dating from 1523. Also like *crisis*, *aftermath* refers to an organic process: "Second or later mowing; the crop of grass which springs up after the mowing in early summer." For example, a 1601 English translation of Pliny's *History of the World* states that "The grasse will be so high growne, that a man may cut it down and haue a plentiful after-math for hay." The sequence is not of cause and effect, but of an organic cycle whereby a first growth is followed by a second harvest, usually less abundant and desirable than the first. (Poet Andrew Marvell in 1673: "The aftermath seldom or neuer equals the first herbage.")

Beginning in the mid-nineteenth century, *aftermath*, like *crisis*, developed additional, more general meanings, as "a state or condition left by a (usu. unpleasant) event, or some further occurrence arising from it." Examples of the "event" range from disappointed love (Coventry Patmore, 1863: "Among the bloomless aftermath...") to rebellion (Hartley Coleridge, 1851: "The aftermath of the great rebellion"). In the twentieth century, the agricultural origins of the word largely disappeared, as aftermath became applied to great historical events, especially war (Churchill in 1946 proclaiming that the "life and strength of Britain... will be tested to the full, not only in the war but in the aftermath of war").

---

[3] All quotations referring to *aftermath* are from the *OED* online <http://www.oed.com> (accessed 3 Mar. 2011).

A similar and dramatic usage comes in John Hersey's account of the bombing of Hiroshima, first published in the *New Yorker* in 1946, as told through the lives of five survivors. In a new book edition, published thirty-five years later, Hersey almost doubles the length of the account by following the lives of these individuals in subsequent decades. The new second part is titled "Aftermath." The possibility of happier outcomes remained (Martin Luther King, 1958: "The aftermath of nonviolence is the creation of the beloved community, while the aftermath of violence is tragic bitterness"). For the most part, however, *aftermath* has more negative connotations, such as depression or a hangover.

I began to appreciate that tracking only these two words would be inadequate to understanding their interactive evolution. Any sensitive and sophisticated approach to language must not make a "fortress out of the dictionary" (to quote Justice Learned Hand on judicial decision-writing) but must consider the larger purpose or object that is the context (Liptak, 2011). This context was made clearer for me when, in the fall of 2010, I was asked to participate in an MIT panel on "communications in slow-moving crises." The title of the event struck me as an intriguing oxymoron: a crisis is supposed to be a sharp and decisive turning point, so how can it be slow-moving? I puzzled that maybe the self-contradictory concept of a "slow-moving crisis" points to what Leo Marx (2010) has called a "semantic void": a situation when existing language proves inadequate for new historical conditions, because historical changes outstrip linguistic resources to express and analyze them. Marx has argued that such a void existed in the later nineteenth century that began to be filled by the relatively recent emergence of the word and concept *technology*.

I began to pay attention to news reports and commentaries on the 2008 crisis that gave particular attention to its slow-moving qualities. My method, so-called, was entirely impressionistic and could not have been narrower: it relied mainly on daily reading of the *New York Times*. Nevertheless, this extremely limited sampling gave me plenty to ponder about slow-moving crises and other variants of *crisis* and *aftermath*. Almost weekly, columnists Bob Herbert and Paul Krugman complained that, while the crisis was "over" by some financial measures, the "real" crisis, which they defined as economic and most particularly as high unemployment, was not at all over.

A year after the crash, a *New York Times* "News of the Week" section was headlined "The Recession's over, but not the Layoffs" (Goodman, 2009). A year and a half after that, in spring 2011 (this time in written and online versions of *Newsweek* magazine) former British Prime Minister Gordon Brown (2011) ominously predicted that, "if the world continues on its current path, the historians of the future will say that the great financial collapse of three years ago was simply the trailer for a succession of avoidable crises that eroded popular consent for globalization itself."

Also in the spring of 2011—now back to the *New York Times*—the ultimately unsuccessful confirmation hearings of MIT economist Peter Diamond to serve on the board of the Federal Reserve hinged on the assumption that the economic crisis still continued. Senator Richard C. Shelby (R-AL) questioned: "Does Dr Diamond have any experience in crisis management? No." Evidently *crisis management* was the new standard of fitness for service on the Federal Reserve Board (Diamond, 2011).

It was not just the economy. Questions asking "will-this-crisis-really-ever-be-over?" were raised over and over again in reference to American-led wars in Iraq and Afghanistan. "After four years of war," wrote the primary war correspondent for the *New York Times* from Afghanistan, "the endgame here has finally begun. But exactly when the endgame itself will end seems anyone's guess" (Filkins, 2010). The same kind of question—is this event over or not?—dominated 2011 commemorations of the tenth anniversary of 9/11. The official *9/11 Commission Report* is subtitled *The Attack from Planning to Aftermath* (National Commission on Terrorist Attacks and Zelikow, 2011) and at least two of the many books about the attack are titled *Aftermath* (Botte, 2006; Meyerowitz, 2006).

Similar language, describing seemingly never-ending crises, was used to analyze environmental disasters that came after the economic crisis: the Pakistani floods of 2009, the Haitian earthquake in early 2010, the Gulf of Mexico oil spill that began soon after, the Japanese earthquake and tsunami in early 2011, and spring 2011 tornadoes and floods in the American South, Midwest and New England. For example, one report on the Haitian earthquake crisis—or was it the aftermath?—was titled "The Special Pain of a Slow Disaster" (Polgreen, 2010).

One consequence of applying the concept of a slow-moving crisis to economic and military crises as well as supposedly natural ones could be to naturalize the human-generated processes and characterize them as unstoppable forces beyond human control—in short, to deny human agency. But it works in both directions, in that natural disasters can be humanized, in acknowledging their partially human origins as well as their sharply differential human effects. The effect of the Mississippi floods of spring 2011 on people of modest means—"thousands of backyards are under water"—was contrasted with the high ground found by "the financial elites who have built walls around their prosperity, while flooding downstream markets with torrents of toxic assets" (Carroll, 2011). The eruption of Eyjafjallajokull in Iceland in spring 2010 was called an "ash shock" in analogy to an "oil shock" (Jolly, 2011). Most notably, almost immediately after the partial meltdown of nuclear reactors in Japan following the 2011 tsunami—a prime example of a hybridized crisis, composed of both "acts of God" and human error—the global economy was more than ever referred to as being in "meltdown" (Norris, 2011).

By this time it was evident that contemporary discussions of *crisis* and *aftermath* were not only redefining these terms but also generating a set of new metaphors to describe contemporary history. The historical pattern that kept being evoked was one not of logical cause and effect, but rather an aesthetic one. In a sort of collective exercise of free association, an image of fluid flow kept being repeated: a "spill" (especially in 2010, when the Gulf spill was on everyone's mind), a "flood," an "ash cloud," or, most persistently, a "meltdown." At the back of these images no doubt is that of the falling towers of the World Trade Center, which seemed to turn into fluid as they collapsed in a cascade.

In all these cases, the locus of vulnerability sets up ever-expanding circles of trouble, which intersect with those from other such points, in a new historical pattern of intersecting and mutually reinforcing calamities. One *New York Times* essayist gave the name *spillonomics* to the "natural" human tendency to underestimate risks such as that of the Gulf oil gusher (Leonhardt, 2011). Another *Times* commentator, writing as the spewing well in the Gulf of Mexico was finally being brought under control, proposed that the oil well was "more than an environmental catastrophe." He argued that the spill

has become a festering reminder of the disarray afflicting so many areas of national life, from the cancerous political culture to the crisis of unemployment to an intractable war in Afghanistan . . . the imagery insinuated itself into our collective consciousness—gnawing evidence that something enormous and confounding was still operative, despite the labors of our brightest engineers and our most expensive machinery. (Goodman, 2010)

This imagery insinuates itself just as much into collective *sub*consciousness, which, arguably more than waking reason, is the level of human mentality where imaginal activity is most active. Across the spectrum of consciousness, *crisis* and *aftermath*, both "natural" and "human," are conflated in the imagistic pattern of relentless waves of damage endlessly re-enacting rounds of destruction.

When these media accounts of contemporary history are read with sensitivity to tone, allusion, and context, the aesthetic pattern they convey takes us to a level of culture that Michel Foucault called the "positive unconscious" of knowledge: an "archaeology" of knowledge, below the level of conscious discussion, yet shaping that discussion at every moment as taken-for-granted. As Foucault describes it in *The Order of Things* [*Les Mots et les choses*], such an inquiry focuses on "how a culture experiences the propinquity of things, how it establishes the tabula of their relationships and the order by which they must be considered . . . in short, with a history of resemblance . . . " (Foucault, 1970).

The contemporary history of crisis and aftermath is a "history of resemblance" in this sense. As lived experience, this 2008 economic event is perceived and experienced as part of a network of events that resemble it as a spreading, damaging spill: this is how contemporary history is experienced, through the "propinquity" of these "things." The intersecting episodes of spill are "normal accidents," to use Charles Perrow's term (1984), that collectively make up the "new normal" of contemporary history. Crisis is no longer a turning point in history but rather an immanent condition of history, part of its "normal" working, indistinguishable from its own aftermath. In that case, the 2008 crisis has had a cultural dimension of intensifying and accelerating nothing less than the emergence of a new historical consciousness.

History is ultimately an exercise in pattern-making, and, since the late eighteenth century, the dominant pattern of Western concepts of history has been that of linear progress. The assumption that humans were dramatically increasing their material command over non-human nature made it possible for the first time to imagine that history would no longer be stuck in cycles of repetition and frustration. Instead, material capabilities would reshape history into a pattern of gradual but steady social progress. In the later nineteenth and twentieth centuries, the material means of progress gradually came to define its goal as well its means—a critical change in the concept, but one that did not alter the belief that the basic pattern of history was shaped by a gradually expanding set of human powers (Rosalind Williams, 2004; see also Rosalind Williams 1993).

In the early twenty-first century, many events of contemporary history are occurring that do not fit well into this mental model. Belief in historical progress remains strong, especially when technological machines and gadgets are presented as evidence. But when larger systems are involved—especially environmental, military, and economic ones—the pattern of contemporary history associated with them is visualized not as a line but as a pattern of crisis centers spreading with no end in sight. Each center incorporates its own aftermath and sets up interference patterns with other spreading centers so that the problems of the whole are far greater than the sum of the parts. Just as technological devices and systems usually accumulate rather than displace each other, so do conceptions of history that are so closely related to these devices and systems. Historical progress and historical crisis, linear pattern and network pattern, coexist as explanations of the contemporary world.

This coexistence of conflicting historical patterns presents a fundamental contradiction in contemporary thinking about history. To return to the *New York Times,* there is no better example of this than columnist Thomas Friedman, who in 2006 published a best-selling "brief history of the twenty-first century" entitled *The World is Flat,* emphasizing great opportunities for humankind on a flat earth. In 2008 Friedman published *The World is Hot, Flat, and Crowded: Why we Need a Green Revolution and how it Can Renew America.* In 2011 he published an op-ed piece titled "The Earth is Full," warning of the intersecting loops of population growth, global warming, food price rises, oil price rises, and political instability. In this latest appraisal, Friedman warns, "We will not change systems... without a crisis. But don't worry, we're getting there." As we head for a "crisis-driven choice" (here Friedman cites the authority of Paul Gilding, a "veteran... environmentalist-entrepreneur"), humans will manage to find their way to a new sustainability rather than global collapse (Friedman, 2006, 2008, 2011).

The earth is flat and it is full. Its saviors are environmentalists and also entrepreneurs. The historical lifeworld is driven by crisis, but a new sustainability is just over the horizon. These confused and conflicted ways of imagining the patterns of contemporary events emerge from new historical conditions where human demands on the planet are far greater than can be sustained, but where the dominant ideology of capitalist accumulation through technological innovation only intensifies the crisis.

History as lifeworld

In Foucault's words, we are trying to understand "the same ground that is once more stirring under our feet" (Foucault, 1970: p. xiv). How is it the same, and how is it stirring? Or, to ask the question of contemporary history that Leo Marx asks of technology, what are the new conditions of the world that give rise to the need for new words and concepts to apprehend and analyze them?

In *The Order of Things* Foucault remarks that he rejects "the phenomenological approach, which gives absolute priority to the observing subject," when this "leads to a transcendental consciousness." Instead of a "theory of the knowing subject," he seeks a "theory of discursive practice" (Foucault, 1970: p. xiv).

Admittedly there is a long way between the highly selective and impressionistic evidence presented above—basically random snippets of the American mainstream press—and the sweeping hypothesis that cultural concepts of contemporary history are conflicted between deep-seated beliefs in progress and a rising tide of crisis events that challenge these beliefs. Placing this inquiry on a more substantial base of evidence presents a wonderful opportunity for collaborations of historians and social scientists, especially in examining "discursive practice." The tools most important to understanding contemporary perceptions and experiences of history are those of the humanities in general and of literary criticism in particular. Word counts and linguistic maps would be helpful, but these exercises are incomplete. Discerning patterns of contemporary history requires contextual and imaginative readings of various sources to reveal the underlying, less-than-conscious epistemic rules and presuppositions of our epoch.

Also exciting are the possibilities for collaborations of historians and social scientists in other research that studies history "from the bottom up." This vivid spatial metaphor has often been used by historians who seek to study common people as opposed to elites, and in particular to bring into the historical account various neglected groups (workers, the colonized, women, as well as non-human actors). Nevertheless, the assumption persists that the card-carrying professional historian is the one who is doing the work of inclusion. In evaluating the hypothesis of conflicting models of history, we need history from the bottom up in the sense of asking non-historians—people living in history—how they perceive and experience it. How do they describe and account for both change and continuity in the world? How do they see themselves in relation to past and future history? In short, how do they experience their lifeworld as a historical one?

The concept of lifeworld was articulated by early twentieth-century phenomenologists in order to define the everyday world of experience that precedes and grounds scientific inquiry. In 1936 Edmund Husserl described the distinction in this way: 'It is so trivial a remark that the truly vivid, truly lived and truly experientiable world, in which all our life takes place practically, remains as it is . . . and remains unchanged by the fact that we invent a special art called physics" (Husserl, [1936] 1976: 50–1).

In distinguishing semi-conscious, common-sense experience from the abstract approaches of scientific reflection, Husserl is also making a value judgment. He believes the lifeworld, in all its richness and complexity and even confusion, should be valued over the derivative, and in his view more desiccated, scientific models derived from it. When so much effort is put into a scientific explanation of the world, the grounding facts of daily and active participation in it are forgotten. Husserl believed that this diversion of attention was nothing short of a crisis—"the crisis of European sciences," which was causing ongoing damage to the lifeworld itself (for commentary on Husserl and phenomenology, see Abram, 1996: 40–1 and Welton, 1996: 303).

The word *history* could be substituted for *physics*, as a "special art" that implicitly assumes a "truly lived and truly experientiable" world, preceding and grounding the work of historians. The practical consequences are twofold. First, the inquirer seeking to apprehend the world as lifeworld must include evidence through all the senses and forms of cognition, both conscious and less-than-conscious. Second, the validity of lifeworld evidence is evaluated through intersubjective experiences of people in it. Not a priori reasoning but repeated, fundamental human activities (such as creating and using language and social institutions) provide ongoing reality checks of shared experience.

Foucault disapproves of "the phenomenological approach" because it gives "absolute priority to the observing subject," but this priority is not necessary. Instead this approach at its best includes, in an integrated and reflexive whole, the study of the perceiver, who, "from an embodied location, approaches the world as a lived, horizon[t]al field," as well as "the act of perceiving; and the content of the perceived" (Lowe, 1982: 1). In the case of the historical lifeworld, it is apprehended by "the observing subject," but only as the subject is immersed in acts of perception involving discourse and representation, and only as the subject is engaged with the "content" of what she perceives. The complexity is that this content is changing as it is perceived. The historical lifeworld itself has a history. The ground shifts under our feet.

One of the most common ways of describing the contemporary historical lifeworld, in contrast to earlier ones, is that the rate of change is speeding up. As concepts of history as linear progress evolved in the nineteenth and early twentieth centuries, more and more attention was given to "technological change" as a descriptor of historical progress, as opposed to more general social change. The rate of social progress might continue to be gradual, but in the technological sphere what Henry Adams called "the law of accelera-tion" seemed to rule. In his autobiographical *The Education of Henry Adams*, this eminent American historian—a founder and the first president of the American Historical Association—sketched out this "law," using back-of-the-envelope calculations to conclude that exploitation of new sources of energy was causing historical change to speed up, a sort of collective step-ping-on-the-gas-pedal effect. Adams (1918) was careful not to claim this as *progress*, but he did emphasize it was a *sequence* with immeasurable signifi-cance for humankind.

If anything, Adams underestimated the acceleration effect by focusing on energy. Other historians since him have shown that many other material processes exhibit a dramatic "hockey stick" upward break, beginning at the same moment Adams was writing in the early years of the twentieth century: dramatic accelerations of population, industrial production, resource consumption, species extinctions, and other many other measures of human activity affecting the entire planet (McNeill, 2000).

It took twentieth-century historians some time to appreciate how much the tempo of natural history was being sucked into the accelerating pace of human history. Historians of the *Annales* School in the interwar period brought into the study of history "from below" events of *la longue durée*—collective, long-term changes in the material conditions of life, taking place largely below the level of human consciousness. Emmanuel Le Roy Ladurie, for example, in 1968, wrote what is often regarded as a crowning achieve-ment of the *Annales* School in the form of a study of the peasants of Languedoc in which the protagonist is an agrarian cycle lasting three cen-turies. The cycle is followed through massive evidence accumulated from land tax registers, grain prices, population registers, changes in literacy, and many other measures. *Annales* historians contrasted slow-acting events (changes in climate, soil productivity, population, and similar factors) with the more rapidly unfolding histories of *conjuncture* (social and political change on a scale of two or three centuries) and *événement* (of *courte durée*, discernible within a human life span, including people with names and events that take place within one lifetime) (Le Roy Ladurie, 1974; see also McCants, 2002; Long, 2005).

At the same time the *Annales* historians were bringing the natural world into human history, the "hockey stick" material changes were creating a historical lifeworld in which previously *longue durée* events might now take place within a human lifetime. Far from being the unnoticed backdrop to human history, such changes are arousing a high degree of both individual and collective attention. In the terminology of the founding *Annales* historians, a *crisis* would by definition be applied to *historie événementelle*: a sharp and sudden turning point in history. Now *environmental crisis* is a common name for events measured in decades rather than centuries.

This was not the lifeworld of fifth-century BCE Greece, when the concepts and practices of history were first articulated. The inventors of *historiē* as research or inquiry assumed a planet providing a stable, durable, and predictable home for the relatively transient, frail, and contingent accounts of human deeds and words. The time constant of human history seemed vastly different from that of natural (in the sense of non-human nature) history. The contemporary historical lifeworld is utterly unlike that of the Greeks, and also utterly unlike that of the scientific and industrial revolutions, which assumed that expanding intellectual and material powers would lead to human mastery over the planet.

Instead, the historical lifeworld emerging in the early twenty-first century appears to be one of lingering hopes for progress mixed with growing anxiety about intersecting crises. In this lifeworld, progress becomes more and more defined as material "change," which relentlessly accelerates, rather than social progress, which seems as slow as ever. At the same time crises keep coming, reinforcing each other and mutating into seemingly endless aftermaths that are hard to distinguish from the originating crisis.

Many of the subtleties and apparent contradictions among California voters, I believe, are best understood in terms of this conflicted, unstable historical lifeworld. The PPIC polling data suggest not so much a split consciousness as a double consciousness of contemporary history. The pattern of history as progress is still present and powerful, but so is the pattern of history as crisis: the two patterns are layered over each other in the consciousness of many citizens, together providing a compelling template with which to interpret current events. When contemporary history is perceived as a pattern of progress, then it makes sense for the individual (and his family) to invest in higher education, which will lead to a better economic future, as it has long done in the United States. When history is perceived as a pattern of intersecting crises, then distrust of institutions in general becomes detached from any particular circumstances and becomes a free-floating standing accusation. Even universities, which have long enjoyed a higher level of civic trust, are pulled into this force field of rolling mistrust, which is stronger than the perception of benefits from institutions of higher education.

The coexistence of these two patterns of perceiving contemporary history also helps to explain the coexistence of two wildly different narrative threads that dominate discussion of higher education today, including many concerning the University of California. One thread expresses the generalized distrust of universities as institutions because all institutions are corrupt, unfair, and bloated. They cater to spoiled faculty with high salaries, undeserved raises, and short hours; they hire too many pricey administrators; they are not run like a business; they are mired in bureaucracy; they are stuck in old models of teaching, failing to innovate with educational tools; and so on and so on. On the other hand—and here the California polling data are compelling—most parents desperately want their children to have access to these institutions, as do most of the children themselves. Americans consider it as a high privilege to be able to attend most American colleges and universities, and, in the case of public ones, very much fear any decline in accessibility and affordability.

This contradiction is too deep to be chalked up only to confusion, misinformation, or magical thinking, though all three are certainly present. The contradiction is deep because it arises from the challenge of recent events to belief in a historical pattern of progress, which has given rise to beloved but now threatened narratives of progress. The collective problems of American society are far too numerous and interlocking to be solved through individual efforts. Yet there is no trust in collective effort, when all institutions are perceived as corrupt, ineffectual, or both. The perceived inability to create institutions that could be trusted was a cause of the economic crisis. The crisis has reinforced this lack of trust, not as an aftermath but as a transformation of an economic crisis into a crisis of democracy.

History cannot continue as social progress without collective efforts. Are we doomed to see history transformed into a network of mutually reinforcing crises? The need to understand the pattern of history is much stronger than an opinion or mood. It forms the basis for a sense of predictability in life. This is a conservative instinct, in the pre-political sense, which is necessary for survival and adaptability in a world of loss and change. When the sense of predictability is fundamentally threatened, when it appears that history is not working the way it used to, individuals react intensely, if inconsistently. What the polling data rarely reveal is this intensity: for this, qualitative research and interpretation are crucial, as well as attention to the aesthetic and narrative dimensions of accounts of contemporary history (Marris, [1974] 1986; on the intensity of economic passions, see Rosalind Williams, 1982; Latour and Lépinay, 2008).

Conclusion: The sense of an ending

The timescale of history began to expand in the nineteenth century with archaeological and anthropological discoveries of what came to be called *prehistory* (a term introduced to common use by John Lubbock's *Prehistoric Times*, published in 1865). About the same time, the deep future of history began to be contemplated, as scientific theories of entropy made it possible to imagine a distant "heat death" of the universe. History might be accelerating for the time being, but it began to appear that in the end—the far end—everything would run down and run out (Smith, 1998; see also Brush, 1967). In both directions, universal history was assuming a timescale that no longer had a reasonable fit with the human history, especially not with the six millennia or so associated with Christian prophecy.

Since then, human history has even further lost its moorings compared to universal time. While the discovery of deep time is one of the most exciting intellectual adventures of humankind, this excitement is not symmetrical in both directions (Rosalind Williams, 1990: 22–50). For the future, at least, deep time becomes increasingly surreal and frightening. Toward the end of the twentieth century, evidence of mysterious dark energy suggested that the expansion of space might continue to the point where galaxies would no longer be able to transmit their light to each other. Both past and future would fall beyond the edge of detection, and any sentient creatures that existed would be trapped in the cosmic equivalent of a silent grave (Greene, 2011).

In his lectures (and subsequent book) on *The Sense of an Ending*, Frank Kermode emphasizes the importance of this expansion of time to modern literature. Any writer is speaking to fellow humans who find themselves— ourselves—in the "middest." We need to "sense" an ending and we also need it to "make sense." This is true both for our individual and for our collective stories, for it is always our ending that is in view when we think of history's end (Kermode, [1966] 2000). Once the scale of time gets beyond a length measurable in human generations, a new burden is put on literature to provide this sense.

The same is true for history. The story of history does not have to be a grand narrative, or even a narrative or story at all in the usual sense of the word. But what history unavoidably has in common with fiction is pattern, sequence, organization. The most quantitative and data-driven historical research still implies pattern, because its basic questions imply shape and order: what changes and what continues over time. A phenomenological study of our historical lifeworld has to address the question of "what comes after," for the "content" of a lifeworld includes not only countless daily material interactions but also such unavoidable speculations about the meaning of it all. A crucial dimension of a lifeworld is its horizon. There is always an edge to it, and a constant, strong human desire is to look beyond the edge. In this sense, the transcendent is always part of a lifeworld.

Kermode reminds us that human storylines have typically included three alternatives: salvation, endless cycles, and destruction. All of these arguably have a place in contemporary concepts of history. The prospect of salvation is evident both in Christian versions of the rapture, or Second Coming, and in similar visions in other faiths. It is also present in the secular vision of progress, which posits a happy if far-off goal to which history moves. The time of everlasting cycles, which Kermode names *aevum*, is that of generation after generation of human beings learning from, imitating, and repeating the preceding one, in a form of duration that is not immortal but is still lasting—the generative cycle in which creatures (not only human ones) perpetuate their kind in their own kind of eternity (Kermode, [1966] 2000: 79; for more on *aevem*, see also pp. 67–89). In a world where progress seems to be generating crisis, the vision of everlasting cycles has been revived in the concept of *sustainability*.

And then there is destruction, in its religious version of apocalypse and secular version of a convergent, culminating crisis. In Kermode's analysis crisis is no longer imminent—on the historical horizon—but immanent. Crisis has invaded and become caught up with ongoing history: "the older, sharply predictive apocalypse, with its precise identification, has been blurred; eschatology is stretched over the whole of history, the End is present at every moment . . . "(Kermode, [1966] 2000: 26).

As crises multiply and converge, crisis-as-episode begins to evolve into crisis-as-final-destruction-of-the-lifeworld. The far horizon of history draws nigh. Each particular crisis begins to forebode the larger end.

Nothing is more routine than a crisis of capitalism. All crises have their unique features, and they are all devastating in human terms—but nothing is more predictable; and in intellectual terms, these crises are even boring, in the sense that each one only reminds us yet again how capitalism works and how it is so prone to breaking down. Why should we pay special attention to this crisis? Why set up a special group to explore its implications?

I propose that our less-than-conscious motivation for doing so was "a sense of the ending": a sense that this crisis is not routine, but one of many whose reinforcing interactions are reshaping the historical lifeworld. We know that human empire, like earlier more limited empires, will not last forever. The balance between current rates of human population growth and resource use, on the one hand, and planetary resources, on the other, is unsustainable. Yet the scenario of sustainability does not seem present and real. The scenarios that are much more plausible are daunting and frightening: climate change, nuclear warfare, pandemics, scrambles for water and food.

That is because such scenarios are already part of our historical lifeworld. Rather than suggesting a future apocalypse, they embody a rolling apocalypse. We already live with images of the end: blown-off mountaintops in West Virginia, dried-up marshes in southern Iraq, knocked-down neighborhoods in Beijing, and the constant disappearance of non-human species of life. It is no longer only untamed savages and untrodden wilderness to which we bid farewell. All these and many other more ordinary things are disappearing in a rising tide of loss (Lévi-Strauss, 1992: 414).

We do not have to wait for the last fish in the ocean to disappear, nor the last tree in the rainforests to be felled, to imagine their disappearance. We do not have to imagine that Berkeley will disappear as a great university to mourn the passing of a Berkeley distinctive for scholarly excellence in combination with a public mission supported by an idealistic Master Plan. These features of the world are disappearing as we watch. The end is here and now and all around us. Human empire is a new historical space and also a new historical time, suspended between change and eternity, a time where the end of time is integrated into the present. Time goes on, but it is constantly re-enacting its end (see Kermode, [1966] 2000: *passim*). Crisis is no longer a sharply defined episode nor a final cataclysm. It is an indwelling condition, containing its own aftermath, which increasingly dominates the historical lifeworld.

In such a world, the language of fiction is not a distraction but an irreplaceable source of insight into cultural manifestations of historical change—not superficial but fundamental change. When the novelist Haruki Murakami (2010) tells us that the fiction he writes "is itself undergoing a perceptible transformation," because it is being assimilated differently by Western readers who no longer find chaos unreal, he is presenting powerful evidence of cultural change. When he challenges us to "coin new words in tune with the breath of that change," he is speaking to everyone, scholars very much included.

Which brings us to the ending—of this essay—by considering one more example of the role of imaginative literature in expressing "the sense of an ending" for human history. This is the novel *One Hundred Years of Solitude* (1967) by Gabriel García Márquez, hailed upon its publication as a work of "magic realism" and now existing in a world where the conjunction of these two words no longer seems illogical. The hundred years of solitude—a compressed history of civilization—take place in the fictitious town of Macondo, modeled after the author's home in Colombia.

Macondo is also the code name of the site of the Deepwater Horizon drilling rig that exploded in April 2010. (Such code names are routinely used by oil and gas companies for offshore prospects early in the exploration effort, both to guard secrecy before sale and later to provide a conveniently memorable name.) As we know, that story ended in loss of human life, still uncalculated loss of non-human life and support systems, and only a temporary interruption of offshore drilling, in an aftermath that simply continues the crisis.

García Márquez's story ends with a gale roaring through the cursed village of Macondo, a "fearful whirlwind" in which the last survivor of the calamity is "deciphering [the instant that he lived] as he lived it, prophesying himself in the act of deciphering . . . as if he were looking into a speaking mirror," which includes his own approaching death, with no "second opportunity" for himself or for that world (Márquez, [1967] 1991: 422) In our work, we decipher our time as we live it, prophesying as we decipher, while all too aware that the end is all around us.

References

Abram, David (1996). *The Spell of the Sensuous*. New York: Vintage Books.

Adams, Henry (1918). *The Education of Henry Adams, an Autobiography*. Boston and New York: Houghton Mifflin Company.

Baldassare, Mark, Bonner, Dean, Petek, Sonja, and Willcoxon, Nicole (2010). "PPIC Statewide Survey: Californians and Higher Education" <http://www.ppic.org/main/publication.asp?i=963> (accessed Aug. 18, 2011).

Birgeneau, Robert J. (2011a). "Chancellor Birgeneau's Fall 2011 Welcome and State of the Campus Message," Aug. 26 <http://cio.chance.berkeley.edu/chancellor/

Birgeneau/ChancellorBirgeneausFall2011WelcomeandStateoftheCampusMessage.htm> (accessed Sept. 9, 2011).

—— (2011b). "Chancellor Responds to Gov. Brown's budget veto," June 16 <http://newscenter.berkeley.edu/2011/06/16/chancellor-responds-to-gov-browns-budget-veto> (accessed June 21, 2011).

—— (2011c). Telephone conversation, June 15.

Botte, John (2006). *Aftermath: Unseen 9/11 Photos by a New York City Cop.* New York: Collins Design.

Brown, Gordon (2011). "Connecting the Dots: Take back the Future," *Newsweek,* May 23 and 30: 7.

Brush, Stephen (1967). "Thermodynamics and History: Science and Culture in the 19th Century," *Graduate Journal,* 7: 467–565.

Carroll, James (2011). "Amid Disaster, Community," *Boston Globe,* May 23: A9.

Clark, Nicola and Jolly, David (2011). "German Air Traffic Resumes," *New York Times,* May 25 <http://www.nytimes.com/2011/05/26/world/europe/26volcano.html?hp> (accessed April 12, 2012).

Confucius (1980 edn.). *The Analects of Confucius,* trans. James R. Ware <http://www.analects-ink.com/mission/Confucius_Rectification.html> (accessed Mar. 3, 2011).

Diamond, Peter A. (2011). "When a Nobel Prize Isn't Enough," *New York Times,* June 6: A19.

Filkins, Dexter (2010). "In Afghanistan, the Exit Plan Starts with 'If'," *New York Times,* Oct. 17: 11.

Foucault, Michel (1970). *The Order of Things: An Archaeology of the Human Sciences.* New York: Random House.

Freedberg, Louis (2011). "Chancellor: UC Berkeley Morphing into Federal University," *California Watch Daily Report,* Feb. 23.

Friedman, Thomas L. (2006). *The World is Flat.* New York: Farrar, Straus & Giroux.

—— (2008). *The World is Hot, Flat, and Crowded: Why we Need a Green Revolution and how it Can Renew America.* New York: Farrar, Straus & Giroux.

——(2011). "The Earth is Full," *New York Times,* June 7: opinion page.

Goodman, Peter S. (2009). "The Recession's over, but not the Layoffs," *New York Times,* Nov. 8: News of the Week in Review, 3.

—— (2010). "A Spill into the Psyche," *New York Times,* July 18: News of the Week in Review, 1.

Greene, Brian (2011). "Darkness on the Edge of the Universe," *New York Times,* Jan. 16: opinion page.

Hoey, Robin (2011). "Staff Assembly Digests Chancellor's Stark Campus Update," *Berkeley NewsCenter,* May 25.

Husserl, Edmund ([1936] 1976). *Die Krisis der europäischen Wissenschaften und die transzendentale Phänomenologie,* in *Gesammelte Werke,* vi. The Hague: Martinus Nijhoff.

Johnson, Simon (2009). "The Quiet Coup," *Atlantic,* May <http://www.theatlantic. com/magazine/archive/2009/05/the-quiet-coup/7364/> (accessed April 12, 2012).

—— and Kwak, James (2010). *Thirteen Bankers: The Wall Street Takeover and the Next Financial Meltdown.* New York: Pantheon.

Kermode, Frank ([1966] 2000). *The Sense of an Ending: Studies in the Theory of Fiction* (with a New Epilogue). Oxford: Oxford University Press.

Kerr, Clark (2001–3). *The Gold and the Blue: A Personal Memoir of the University of California, 1949–1967.* Berkeley and Los Angeles: University of California Press.

Krupnick, Matt (2009). "Protesters Shut down Free Speech Movement Tribute," *Contra Costa Times,* Dec. 3.

Latour, Bruno, and Lépinay, Vincent Antonin (2008). *The Science of Passionate Interests: An Introduction to Gabriel Tarde's Economic Anthropology.* Chicago: Prickly Paradigm Press.

Le Roy Ladurie, Emmanuel (1976). *The Peasants of Languedoc.* trans. John Day. Urbana and Chicago: University of Illinois Press. (Published in French in 1968.)

Leonhardt, David (2011). "Spillonomics: Underestimating Risk," *New York Times,* May 31.

Lévi-Strauss, Claude (1992). *Tristes Tropiques,* trans. John and Doreen Weightman. New York: Penguin.

Liptak, Adam (2011). "Justices Turning More Frequently to Dictionary, and Not Just for Big Words," *New York Times,* June 12.

Long, Pamela O. (2005). "The *Annales* and the History of Technology," *Technology and Culture,* 46/1 (Jan.), 177–86.

Lowe, Donald M. (1982). *History of Bourgeois Perception.* Chicago: University of Chicago Press.

McCants, Anne E. C. (2002). "There and Back Again: The Great Agrarian Cycle Revisited," *EH.Net Economic History Services,* Dec. 12 <http://eh.net/bookreviews/ peasants-languedoc> (accessed April 12, 2012).

McNeill, J. R. (2000). *Something New under the Sun: An Environmental History of the Twentieth-Century World.* New York and London: W. W. Norton & Company.

Márquez, Gabriel García ([1967] 1991). *One Hundred Years of Solitude,* trans. Gregory Rabassa. New York: HarperPerennial.

Marris, Peter ([1974] 1986). *Loss and Change.* London: Routledge and Kegan Paul.

Marx, Leo (2010). "Technology: The Emergence of a Hazardous Concept," *Technology and Culture,* 51/3 (July), 561–77.

Meyerowitz, Joel (2006). *Aftermath: World Trade Center Archive.* London: Phaidon Press.

Murakami, Haruki (2010). "Reality A and Reality B," *New York Times,* Nov. 29: opinion page.

National Commission on Terrorist Attacks and Zelikow, Philip D. (2011). *The 9/11 Commission Report: The Attack from Planning to Aftermath* (Authorized Text, Shorter Edition). New York: W. W. Norton & Company.

Norris, Floyd (2011). "Japan's Meltdown and the Global Economy's," *New York Times*, Mar. 18.

Peck, Don (2011). "Can the Middle Class Be Saved?", *Atlantic*, 308/3 (Sept.), 63.

Perrow, Charles (1984). *Normal Accidents: Living with High Risk Technologies*. New York: Basic Books.

Polgreen, Lydia (2010). "The Special Pain of a Slow Disaster," *New York Times*, Nov. 11: F1.

Searle, John (1971). *The Campus War: A Sympathetic Look at the University in Agony*. New York and Cleveland: World.

Simon, Jason (Director, Marketing and Communications Services, Office of the President, University of California) (2011). Telephone conversation, Aug. 17.

Smith, Crosbie (1998). *The Science of Energy: A Cultural History of Energy Physics in Victorian Britain*. London: Althone.

Welton, Donn (1996). "World," in D. Borcher (ed.), *Encyclopedia of Philosophy Supplement*. Basingstoke: Macmillan Reference.

Williams, Raymond (1958). *Culture and Society, 1780–1950*. London: Chatto & Windus.

Williams, Rosalind (1982). *Dream Worlds: Mass Consumption in Late Nineteenth-Century France*. Berkeley, Los Angeles, and London: University of California Press.

—— (1990). *Notes on the Underground*. Cambridge, MA: MIT Press.

—— (1993). "Cultural Origins and Environmental Implications of Large Technological Systems," *Science in Context*, 6/2: 377–403.

—— (2002). "A Technological World We Can Live in," *Technology and Culture*, 43/1 (Jan.), 222–6.

—— (2004). "An Historian's View," in Manuel Castells (ed.), *The Network Society: A Cross Cultural Perspective*. Cheltenham: Edward Elgar.

Chapter 2

The Separation of Cultures and the Decline of Modernity

João Caraça

(It is) a long way to modernity

A powerful conjunction of radical innovations occurred before the dawn of modernity in Europe. A new lattice of urban settlements emerged in the twelfth and thirteenth centuries. Guilds grew to give their members a socio-political role never before experienced. Bills of exchange were invented as a way of financing trade. Arabic numerals were introduced for better account-ing in notarial operations and cannons first saw the light in European plains, heralding the fall of the feudal order. Further, the use of the maritime compass allowed the adventure of discoveries beyond the perils of the high seas. Artillery developed swiftly to accompany and provide comfort to seafarers, enabling new exchange routes to be opened. The transforma-tion of society through these innovations was accelerated by the prolifera-tion of the printing press, a true revolution in information and communication. The availability of paper much enhanced these phenomena. But the most eventful invention of the dawn of modernity was that of the Florentine masters of the Quattrocento: a new representation of the natural world. Linear perspective brought a new way of looking at reality, the first step toward initiating its transformation. Linear perspective separated clearly the subject, the observer, from the object that was observed. The size of any object relative to those of other objects depicted in a context depends only on its distance from the observer, the subject that is representing reality. Divinities were no longer larger than men: in fact, their apparent magnitude was a function solely of their remoteness from the observer. That these representations came to be accepted as "objective" stems certainly from the fact that they could be assimilated to those obtained through the use of an instrument—the "camera obscura." It was this mental association that allowed conceptually the separation of light (a physical phenomenon) from vision (a physiological capacity).

From a culture of separation . . .

The intellectual strength of modernity springs from the surprising capacity and robustness of "separation" as a method of analysis of natural phenomena. A new culture of critical tendency and experimental basis emerged, progressively validated by the flood of new discoveries pervading Europe—of new lands, new peoples, new skies, and new stars. The old order was discredited and a new worldview took form. This worldview, of a "geometrical" character, consisted of searching for symmetries in nature, which concealed principles of invariance that, in turn, led to the formulation of laws for the natural world. The laws are permanent, eternal, and absolute, describing the behavior of bodies in the universe since times immemorial until infinity. They are formulated in mathematical language, since Galileo declared that the Book of Nature was written in mathematical language, separating it from the other holy book, the Bible, which was written in natural language. The objectivity of the laws of nature was assured by the use of instruments, and their validity was confirmed by the publication of the observations and measurements.

The legitimacy of this separation was granted by the sheer strength of the Reformation in the protestant nations in which the new churches—separated from the secular forces that were building the state—were also in construction. The general climate of growing trade and business related to ocean navigation supported a further separation: that of a private sphere within what until then was the (public) domain of an agrarian society. Cities were the beacons of this spirit of modernity. And new Academies of Sciences were created to enshrine and nurture that spirit. The force of this geometrical worldview was still echoing loudly in the nineteenth century: Cézanne asserted conclusively that all forms of nature could be reverted to the sphere, the cone, and the cylinder.

The triumph of modernity was the victory of this culture of trade, military power, navigation, finance, private appropriation, and new knowledge. It came as no surprise that the first conflict in the disciplines of knowledge was the separation of philosophy from theology, as philosophers started to give priority to the empirical analysis of reality.

This was the first serious challenge to the millenarian affirmation that religious authorities were the sole owners of the way to truth. Philosophers claimed that philosophical intuition was as legitimate as a source of truth as was divine revelation! The separation of mind from matter was then established, as expected.

A subsequent separation was that of natural philosophy (which adopted the designation of "science") from philosophy. Scientists, pursuing a way of theorization based on induction, and supported by empirical, replicable, and verifiable observation, opposed metaphysical deduction as speculation that could not contain elements of truth. This rift was not without consequences: separated from philosophy and the humanities, scientists developed an ahistorical and cumulative conception of scientific knowledge and its progresses, which supported a claim of neutrality in social terms.

Science started as physics, and physics for Galileo was mechanics. The "mechanical" impetus of modernity through advances in engineering, in warfare, and in navigation was so strong that mathematics—which until the sixteenth century had been the way we dealt with nature (through counting and numbers (arithmetic), forms and measurement (geometry), proportions and harmony (music), and positions and motions of heavenly bodies (astronomy))—was abstracted from nature to become simply its language; physics (mechanics) became nature. This helped and enhanced the conception of mathematics as a symbolic language, enabling the separation of natural beings from natural rules—that is, of objects from models, of ontology from epistemology. This scheme was met by an astonishing success—as overwhelming as the victories that modern European nations were experiencing in their expansion throughout the world. Who could doubt what their eyes were seeing?

The new world of modernity—the terrestrial globe, not the territories around the Mediterranean sea—was nurtured by the separation of space from time, and by the new concepts derived from the empire of the laws of nature. Space became appropriable until infinity and time became linear.

It is no wonder that the new social organizations that were able fully to interpret and conjugate these notions—the new companies or enterprises—provided the economic success of modernity. The new wealth they generated warranted their existence and proliferation. They became aware of the importance of technology in the mastering of time through the invention of machines. It is no wonder also that the Industrial Revolution was intrinsically a revolution in mechanical force and artifacts. The mastery of space was warranted by the development of market economies, through the incorporation and development of city economies (first at the national level and subsequently overseas).

Modernity allowed capitalism to flourish. Capitalism is a regime of economic power based on the private appropriation of the means of production and of the wealth generated by their operation. Its principle is the maximization of the accumulation of capital, which is limited solely by the "scarcity" of resources or by the "ignorance" of knowledge that allows its further accumulation. Capitalism also needs an interstate system that guarantees the legal property of accumulated capital—a fact that is sometimes forgotten. Modernity provided the adequate framework for the endeavor of capital: a powerful engine (the modern enterprise); a search for technological inventions to fuel the engine; a progressive de-materialization of money though financial innovations; and, an interstate system that progressively expanded in the world. Capital accumulation became indefinite.

The growth of economic activity and wealth associated with the Industrial Revolution had an enormous impact on society. A new vector of capital accumulation emerged and the control of the economic system by the markets (that is, the meeting places of long-distance exchanges) was established. The transformation of society was also deep and full of consequences. It brought about further separations in daily life. Industrial societies saw an inversion in the relation between the economic and the social: instead of the economy being embedded in social relations, as in the past, social relations became embedded in the economic system. The economy became separated from society and, further, home became separated from work. The concept of employment was born.

But the system was intrinsically prone to crises—namely, crises of structural adjustment that were due to evolving production structures and infrastructures. Infrastructures are difficult to transform: they require voluminous investments and costly adaptations to the new basic conditions of economic activity. Every two generations, at least since the dawn of the Industrial Revolution, we have witnessed a crisis of this type. The technical infrastructure of production was transformed accordingly (through the 1830s) from a water-powered mechanization into a steam-powered mechanization, then through electrification (from the 1880s onwards) to a full motorization (from the 1930s onward) through cheap oil and mass production. The present situation, which can be described as a computerization of the entire economy, emerged in the 1980s. If we think that crises are terrible and destructive, we better prepare ourselves for the next wave of structural change in the 2030s.

A capitalist market economy lives always in an intimate arrangement with an interstate political system. It needs a strong interstate system to enforce the property laws that allow capital accumulation, as stated before. Capital, in turn, feeds its partner, allowing it to survive. This is why no empires are permitted in interstate systems, only hegemons. Capital is allergic to caps. And hegemons do not live as such forever. They are not able to set the rules of the game indefinitely. Every four generations we have witnessed crises (another type of crises), which degenerate into wars where the hegemons are replaced by other hegemonic nations. We observed this in the decades following 1610 (the Thirty Years War), then 1710 (in the wars triggered by the control of colonial possessions), then 1810 (the Napoleonic Wars) and 1910 (the world wars). With the present expansion of the world system to encompass almost the whole of our planet, we cannot rule out the current "oil wars" as signaling the possible demise of the American hegemon. That a major crisis is developing in Western societies in the first decade of the twenty-first century is probably not a random coincidence. History does not repeat itself; rather, human mistakes tend to repeat themselves, over and over again, creating cycles not of economic development but of human behavior.

Modernity was fashioned by means of a culture of separation. The power of this way of dealing with reality brought enormous wealth and prosperity to modern nations. By the end of the nineteenth century, four values summarized the pre-eminence of the modern culture: nature (an infinite resource able to be transformed by the knowledge of its laws); science (the legitimate way to discover truth); universality (the values and perceptions of European peoples were imposed and accepted in all corners of the world); and sovereignty (each state was like an atom, indivisible and acting as a legitimate component in the interstate system).

The twentieth century pushed forward these concepts under the joyous leadership of the new hegemon across the Atlantic. Further separations ensued, mainly stemming from the overspecialization promoted by the education systems, now being reorganized to respond to market economy objectives such as fierce competition and higher technological levels. Science progressed immensely, propelled by the world wars effort.

It was following this path that science met its defining point of separation. The first science-based technologies saw the light during the 1940s, never to leave our world again. Their transformative power was such that neither the military, nor subsequently the markets, let science return intact to its curiosity-driven realm. Techno-science was born with the atom bomb. Progressively pulling away from curiosity-driven science, techno-science grew enormously and impacted on the economy strongly. Not without problems, of course. The neutrality of science (read techno-science) was definitively dead. "We lost our innocence," uttered Oppenheimer at Alamogordo. He understood then that the long-term and well-established value of science was being lost. But he could not yet foresee its consequences.

...to a separation of cultures

The world was transformed further in the 1950s under the cold war regime. The "oil crises" of the 1970s set the stage for the deployment of the first socially selected product of techno-science: the information and communication technologies. A new period of techno-economic structural development was initiated, a period in which we are now living, approaching the maturity of the solutions that those science-based technologies have provided for the time span of one generation. But these solutions were naturally associated with a whole array of new issues. Information and communication exploded—a second revolution that has profoundly changed the perception of life on our planet. Terrestrial space has "shrunk" and knowledge circulates the world at the speed of light. Finance took increased control of the economy and finally captured it, through further de-materialization of the monetary system (another essential effect of the Industrial Revolution); money became a convention. Finance has been a driving force since the initial stages of globalization: using new technologies, finance extended the capacity of coordination at a distance (meaning: beyond political borders). The end of the cold war further accelerated this tendency, and, as a result, a multitude of new opportunities emerged and new networks were created to exploit them, challenging the existing mechanisms. Fierce competition between actors ensued and the expansion of the market economies was fed by increased inputs of new knowledge relevant for commercial operations: organization and methods, marketing, design, software, specialized training. New services and activities surged with high economic impact. And each of them developed their own culture.

Increased growth and separation gave us much more than just two cultures (the transfer into the twentieth century of the fierce debate of Enlightenment). We can now distinguish in our societies, besides the cultures of science and the humanities, a culture of social science (strengthened through the invention of postmodernism) and well-defined cultures in politics, in business, in the media, in the military, in religion, in education, as well as diverse cultures of risk, of violence, and of individual autonomy.

We evolved a full "macedoine" of cultures. But, what is worse, in this new Babel an individual can switch from rationality (say, in politics) to the realms of the obscure, in just a click, enabling the resurgence of ignorance, and mysticism seems a business like any other.

Therefore, the tremendous task put on the shoulders of the coming generation is paradoxically very simple: strive amid the integration of cultures. The reason is also very simple: modernity is exhausted. As it is argued below, modernity was drained by financial capitalism; it was even led to transform the future (a founding value) into a mockery of itself, through short-sighted, sick, and exclusive preoccupations centered on the present.

We live in a world of uncertainty. But we have always lived in an uncertain world! We were able in the past to generate mechanisms to reduce uncertainty by proposing order and classifying reality. But finally, all institutions evolve—that is, adapt or disappear. Let us take three examples. First, the medieval Church. The church controlled ignorance through the invention of sin and repentance. Its method was based on confession. But religion is prone to fundamentalisms and, thus, averse to diversity. The disregard of the past and of ancestors by modernity quenched and sank the power of the Church of Rome. Second, the nation state. The control of ignorance was obtained via the introduction of an education system and the creation of degrees. This system, which stimulated critical thinking and taught how to evaluate the credibility of sources of knowledge, was implemented along with a powerful method of examinations. But the state is also prone to conflicts of interest, and globalization has been actively promoting its weakness, by destroying its timid impulses to resist financial discipline.

Finally, the markets: market economies control ignorance through the emergence of a vigorous industry of consultants. Consultancy firms achieve their objectives through the free use of advertising. But markets are intrinsically prone to crises: there goes confidence down the drain. Nobody is perfect!

We are living though a deep crisis that originates in a conjugation of different processes: geo-political, techno-economic, cognitive. The separation of cultures has led us here, and we have let these crises entangle with one another like schoolchildren. Everything is connected today. We live in a complex world. We are surrounded by complexity. More, we know today that we are the products of complexity. This is what is new.

All grand challenges we face today, from climate change to life sustainability, from innovation to city management, are complex by nature. But what is complexity? Very simply, complexity is the impossibility of separating a system from its context, a living being from its environment, an object from its measuring instrument. Exit separation!

We can say that we live in (and we are thermodynamically) open systems. The intellectual apparatus devised by the end of the nineteenth century, composed of determinism (that is, information conservation), reductionism (that is, the use of mathematical language), and dualism (that is, the independence of the observer), is severely flawed with respect to the representation of reality. We know that the progressive substitution of human labor by machines—at first mechanical, and now communication driven—has dramatically changed the conditions of work and employment and the social structures in which they were in turn embedded. The effectiveness of advanced economies derives from their capacity for operating science-based innovation systems, but what matters most in their performance is the quality of their governance. But how do we understand the whole? Especially in the absence of a culture of integration? Maybe we will have to define a new epistemic objective, different from that of "progress though the transformation of nature," the aim of modernity.

But, first, we have to understand how values have changed, to assess where and how a new culture is in (desperate) need.

We may discern four cognitive crises unfolding before our eyes (each corresponding to a well-established value of modernity): a crisis of nature; a crisis of science; a crisis of the universal; and a crisis of sovereignty. In each of these crises, a new concept has emerged to perturb and displace the characteristic word of the culture of modernity (nature, science, universality, sovereignty): the environment; knowledge (as in the "knowledge-economy"); the global; and governance.

The notion of environment has today the relevance we attributed in the past to nature. But then we understood nature as a scenario—eternal— where phenomena were taking place. We could attempt to control or transform nature, but nature would always remain, unharmed. Now, with the concept of environment, a big change is occurring: the environment is no longer the permanent scenario, but the stage where the actors perform (in fact there is no scenario). And there is no author, nor a plot: the actors create their own narrative as they play, and they are responsible for the outcomes; inclusively, for the deterioration of the stage. An evil power is creeping in: it declares the future to be worse than today, so the motto has become "let us re-center our efforts on the present"—the opposite of modernity. A feeling of anguish with regard to the future is being installed.

The word knowledge is being redefined as to signify the set of fields (law, organization, marketing, design, software, training) that together with techno-science feed the success of the new services and the new economy in the globalized world. It has displaced science in all policy-oriented documents written after 1990. But science was not just a mere instrument of the economy, a straightforward source of new technologies. Science was for three centuries the main element of support of the worldview of modernity and the most important criterion in the search for truth. Its culture signified the constructive role of error and of objection, one of the most important elements for establishing the concept of citizenship. Science aimed at eternity, and offered a vision for the long term.

The new word knowledge is a vassal of the markets and their daily operations. Markets welcome change but obscure the long term. Their frenetic search for (economic) value makes them myopic. Consequently, knowledge is nowadays suffering from short-sightedness. The feeling of short-termism is rampant.

The notion of globalization has displaced that of universality. For two centuries we enjoyed the rule of the universal. We had permanent, sacred, and eternal rights simply as a result of being born. These rights were introduced to protect the citizen from the powers of the state and to allow the free exercise of citizenship. Of course, the process of exercising one's rights has not been easy nor linear. Social progress and welfare were the culmination of a lengthy fight, punctuated by eventful battles. But globalization has introduced a wicked twist in this framework. In the realm of globalization there are no acquired rights, just contracts where rights have to be negotiated and renegotiated continuously. The place of individual citizens has to be conquered in the markets; their performance optimized, their utility demonstrated. A systematic process of negotiation, profitability, and competition is at work. People are dispensable, and their importance resides in their function—as producers or as consumers. They have been transformed, actually, into resources: human resources! They have to be recyclable (through lifelong learning!), or otherwise they have no value in the markets. They have become a nuisance and can be eliminated if they are of no economic utility. The global world is a computerized jungle. There is a kind of hush all over the world. Oppression is back in town.

Governance has swiftly substituted sovereignty. For centuries, the states (and the balance of force) have been the cornerstones of the order that was established by Westphalia, which contributed to the political stabilization of Europe. The notion of nation state was tentatively exported to the different continents of our planet with mitigated success. Governments have been recognized as legitimate representatives of nations: as those morally responsible for internal security and welfare, and as interlocutors in foreign affairs.

But the globalization of the markets, with a rhetoric anchored in liberalization, deregulation, and privatization, provoked national governments to recede progressively from the economic sphere. This recession motivated the surge, in the national political spheres, of new actors (at a distance) with considerable (economic and political) power. Who governs now? Where are important decisions being taken? Who is accountable? Have we voted for them? Governance is now a popular word, pervading all fields of activity in advanced countries. No wonder people and institutions feel insecure.

The decline of strong values such as those of nature, science, universality, and sovereignty has unfolded mixed senses of anguish, short-termism, oppression, and insecurity. Tomorrow will be worse than today. And the markets make sure we know that today is all we have. Immediate consumption is the only certainty that is allowed. Marketing propaganda forces one to make instant decisions. The pre-eminence of financial capital—because of its intangibility and therefore infinite possibility of accumulation—accelerated this trend to a point of no return. The final act has been the (self-)separation of finance from the economy, in a vain attempt to gain full control over the accumulation processes. In trying to fly too high and unattended, finance let its wings melt down. And the result was the downward spiral of assumptions regarding the future knowledge economy into a deep crisis that may unfold a new order. But whose? For the first time in centuries (except during periods of war) we do not see the light at the end of the tunnel. We have become afraid of the future.

A new narrative

This means, finally, that capitalism has killed modernity. For what purpose, we do not know: we may no longer refer to divine powers or to satanic forces to help resolve this issue. And collective shrinks have not yet emerged from the best universities. We can only recognize this as the Oedipal moment of Western cultural evolution. It is very hard to grasp its meaning. We must combine the signs from these four cognitive crises with those of other crises weakening our national cultures—loss of trust in institutions, a major ongoing war for resources, a possible fading-out of the higher-education system, an eventual future flow of radical innovations from a non-Western powerful global player—to comprehend what has happened and to begin anew. This overall crisis of representation suggests that our states, heirs of the medieval tradition of divine power and omnipotence, no longer own the future. They are turning their eyes and actions away from it, instead concentrating on immediate solutions. The future has been privatized too. We seem to be trapped in a decaying present.

The USA is drifting further away from Europe. The Internet has freed the Americans from their European birth complex. Will the USA be able to maintain its hegemonic status in the twenty-first century by forging new networks? Will the global twenty-first century look similar to the eighteenth-century multi-polar Europe? Nobody knows.

The Europe of Christendom was doomed by its local nature, for being unable to adapt to new arrangements. The way forward for Europe is therefore clear. It either creates new alliances with the South and the East, or its nations will submerge into a sea of oblivion once again, as in the period that followed the fall of Rome. We have to invent a new future. We must wish a future!

The aftermath of these crises must therefore initiate the creation of a new culture of integration. We must renew our enchantment with nature, forging a new alliance, as Ilya Prigogine so nicely proposed. We have to create a culture that embraces the ethics of interrogating systematically the universe, society, and ourselves, cherishing interdisciplinarity and the new mathematics that will address the issues of complexity. We have to let new ontologies flourish. And base our societal dialogue not on cognition but on the recognition of the values of diversity and identity. We will have to redirect higher education in this direction, creating a fully autonomous network of institutes of advanced study and reflection, to function as beacons of this new navigation toward the future. The economy has no eternal and perfect rules, and is not regulated by any law of nature. It is based on a concept of property that may change with the times. But we have an obligation toward the coming generations: we have to grant them a home planet to live in.

The increasingly multi-polar world that we observe today probably means that we are at the ebbing of globalization as we have experienced it. New times are approaching. New policies will have to be devised. But we need to know where we want to go in order to achieve their adequate formulation. We have to construct a new narrative. We have to innovate social practices. And we have to organize and strengthen civil society.

And the epistemic objective of modernity—the transformation of nature— will have, in turn, to be transformed too. Instead of truth, solely, we will have to seek beauty and bounty. We will have to keep intergenerational communication channels open and also stimulate the opening of new ones, in order to keep the future open, in order to deal with and benefit from the global commons of Earth. We will need more participation in city management. And we will need to reinvent the emancipatory role of knowledge. We will have to nurture curiosity over and over again. And we will have to borrow from António Vieira his extraordinary vision—as valid and effective today as it was 300 years ago—when he brightly stated that to assess hope we have to measure the future.

References

Caraça, J. (1999). *Science et communication*. Paris: Presses Universitaires de France.

Cippola, C. (1978). *Clocks and Culture*. New York: W. W. Norton & Co.

Freeman, C. (1994). "The Economics of Technical Change," *Cambridge Journal of Economics*, 18: 463–514.

Giddens, A. (1990). *The Consequences of Modernity*. Oxford: Blackwell.

Polanyi, K. (1957). *The Great Transformation*. Boston: Beacon Press.

Prigogine, I. (1996). *La Fin des certitudes*. Paris: Odile Jacob.

Vieira, A. ([1718] 1982). *História do Futuro*. Lisbon: Imprensa Nacional.

Wallerstein, I. (2004). *World-Systems Analysis*. Durham: Duke University Press.

PART TWO

Which Crisis? Whose Crisis?

What do we mean by crisis? In the polysemic context of a saturated discursive space about the crisis, clarification of what is implied by the name is an essential component of its understanding. Yet, since the purpose of this volume is precisely to assign meaning to the term, overcoming the confusion that surrounds the perception of the 2008–12 crisis, we have to start not from a definition but from observation and analysis. Furthermore, in the scholarly community we built to reflect on this specific crisis, there is a plurality of perspectives, complementary rather than contradictory in our view, which must be expressed in the volume by presenting two different approaches to the process of crisis formation. There are, however, two key analytical arguments that are largely shared in the interpretations presented here.

The first: the crisis is multidimensional and can be understood only in a transdisciplinary perspective. Strict economic theory is not able to explain the process of formation of this crisis. Neither can a sociological or a political science perspective without referring to economic and cultural explanations. Thus, the contributors to this volume, and those contributing to this section of the volume, are social scientists in the broadest sense, able to move and trained for moving freely across boundaries of traditional disciplines to make sense of an observed phenomenon. The two chapters of this section weave the analysis of economy, society, culture, and politics, referring to a variety of contexts, with the only purpose of making sense of a critical moment of social evolution, putting theory and data analysis to the service of understanding human action while unveiling the ideological mystifications that obscure the perception of the crisis.

Which Crisis? Whose Crisis?

The second argument refers to the evolutionary character of this crisis, to its transformative dynamics. The origins of the crisis are rooted in a certain economic culture that organized economic institutions since the early 1990s around the principles of market liberalism and personal greed, and put the extraordinary capacity of the information and communication technology revolution at the service of an expansionary, unregulated, global strategy of financial capital accumulation. Once this global networked economy, rooted in the financial market, imposed its structural logic, economic mechanisms accounted for both its rise and its collapse. However, the consequences of the economic crisis deeply affected the culture and institutions of all societies. Indeed, in the process, the crisis was transformed from a financial crisis into an economic crisis and from an economic crisis into an institutional crisis that ultimately led to a cultural crisis, characterized by the end of trust, and to a multidimensional societal crisis manifested in the end of social solidarity. In spite of a variety of theoretical perspectives and empirical emphases in the two chapters of this section, there is a coherent argument: the so-called economic crisis is an evolutionary process of structural crisis and social change of a certain form of capitalism that was as dynamic as it was unsustainable because of the mismatch between its exponential capacity to create fictitious value and its decreasing institutional ability to manage its relentless expansion. Furthermore, the crisis was not an accident, but an instrument for the rich and powerful of the new system to make the system work to their benefit regardless of the consequences for the economy and society that emerged from this process of transformation. The often quoted Chinese saying—"crisis means also opportunity"—tells this story. But we should recast the real meaning of the saying in the real world: it is crisis for most and opportunity for a few.

Chapter 3

The Metamorphosis of a Crisis

John B. Thompson

Consider two scenes

It is September 14, 2007 and long queues are forming outside the branches of Northern Rock in London, Cambridge, Nottingham, Newcastle, and other cities in the UK, as anxious depositors gather to withdraw their savings. News has just emerged that the bank has sought emergency liquidity support from the Bank of England, which has responded by guaranteeing funds up to $31.5 billion. Northern Rock has tried to reassure its 1.4 million savers that it is not in danger of bankruptcy, but thousands have responded by withdrawing their savings, triggering the first bank run in Britain for decades.

It is June 29, 2011 and Syntagma Square in central Athens is crowded with people, young and old, some carrying signs, others milling around; the square is surrounded by riot police in helmets, gas masks, and protective gear, a shield in one hand and a truncheon in the other. Inside the Parliament Building just to the east of the square, the Greek Parliament is debating the latest austerity measures demanded by the European Union (EU) and the International Monetary Fund (IMF) as a condition of extending a further

emergency loan of €120 billion to enable Greece to meet its interest payments and avert a default on its sovereign debt, which is now hovering at
around €330 billion, or 153 percent of GDP. As the news circulates that
Parliament has approved the draconian austerity measures, violence erupts
in the square. Protestors clash with police, who hurl canisters of tear gas and
stun grenades into the crowds. Some flee, whilst others join the pitched
battles that become increasingly intense, and the protest turns into mayhem.

What, if anything, is the connection between these two seemingly unrelated events, separated by nearly four years of tumultuous disruption in the
global financial markets? Does the violence in central Athens have any
connection with the orderly queues of anxious savers gathering outside
the branches of Northern Rock? Are these manifestations of one underlying
crisis in the global financial system, or manifestations of two quite different
crises, stemming from different sources and unrelated in nature? Are the
queues outside Northern Rock the first signs of a crisis that reached its apex
with the collapse of Lehman Brothers in September 2008 and the massive
state bailouts of banks and other financial institutions that continued
through the autumn of 2008, and are the protests in Athens merely one of
many delayed consequences of what one might call "the aftermath"?

The truth is we do not have good answers to any of these questions. Our
uses of the terms "crisis" and "aftermath" are too loose and imprecise to
capture the realities of what is happening in a world where financial institutions and transactions have become more complex, more interconnected,
and more opaque. We have an understandable tendency to want to define
clear boundaries, to package up reality into neat concepts that enable us to
say, with a kind of reassuring confidence, "here is the event, this is the real
thing, and here are its consequences." But, if the events of the last few years
tell us anything at all about our intellectual proclivities, they should send a
loud warning shot across the bows of any pretension we might have to
understand the full dimensions of what is unfolding around us today. Social
scientists are as prone to retrospective revision as lay actors are: we (that is,
social scientists) are constantly revising our earlier views when we realize
that the world is not developing according to our initial hunches. What
might have seemed like a "crisis," with a discrete beginning and an end,
with preconditions that would be described as its "causes" and aftershocks
that could be described as its "consequences," may, with the benefit of
hindsight, appear as a mere episode in a much larger series of interconnected
events whose "beginning" and "end" are no longer clear, whose real "causes"
we may only partly understand, and where it would be premature to speak of

"consequences," since we have no idea whether we are at the beginning, in the middle, or at the end of the series of events. Of course, as social scientists we must try constantly to build theories of the social world and of what is happening in it: this is the only way we can make sense of it and try to turn the cacophony of social life into a form of knowledge. But it behoves us to remember that, however elaborate our theories might be, the world is always going to be a lot messier than our theories of it.

Given the complexity and opacity of what is happening in the arena of global finance today, this chapter can be nothing more than a very modest contribution to the clarification of a question, and the question is this: are we living through a crisis today, and if so what kind of crisis is it? Is it one crisis with many interconnected episodes, or many different crises that are essentially unrelated to one another? If it is the former, what is it that unites these episodes? If it is the latter, why does each crisis seem to follow so rapidly on the heels of the other?

Before we can try to give a meaningful answer to these questions, we need to try to give some precision to our concepts—none more so than the concept of crisis itself. In order to do this, I want to begin by returning for a few minutes to what remains one of the best attempts to analyze the nature of crises in advanced capitalist societies: Jürgen Habermas's now-classic book *Legitimation Crisis*. Of course, Habermas's analysis applied to a very different historical conjuncture—namely, to the early 1970s, when the escalating costs of social welfare had triggered alarm bells about what was then called "the fiscal crisis of the state"—and there are aspects of his account that now look very dated in view of the changes that have occurred in global capitalism since then. But his clarification of the concept of crisis still has value for us, and his innovative idea of what we could call "the logic of crisis displacement" may provide a clue to help us make sense of what is happening today.

The logic of crisis displacement

In *Legitimation Crisis* Habermas (1988: 1–4) distinguishes two types of crisis that arise in the context of socio-economic life: what he calls a "system crisis" and an "identity crisis." The distinction between these two types of crisis is linked to his broader distinction between "system" and "lifeworld," where a system is a self-regulating order of purposive–rational action in which actions are coordinated by certain mechanisms or "media," such as money and power. A lifeworld, by contrast, is a symbolically structured space of taken-for-granted meanings in which cultural traditions, social interaction, and personal identity are sustained and reproduced. Crises can occur in a system and in the lifeworld, but in each case it has distinctive properties. A system crisis has to do with the breakdown of system integration: it occurs when the self-regulating mechanisms of a system break down, the medium for coordinating actions fails to fulfill its role, and the system seizes up. The classic example is the crisis of overproduction in the economy: capitalist firms produce more goods than the market can absorb, leading to a collapse of prices and a sharp downturn in the economy as revenues decline and many firms are forced to the wall. An identity crisis, by contrast, has to do with the breakdown of social integration: it arises when members of a society become aware of a major disruption and feel that their own lives or "collective identity" is in some way threatened. Not every system crisis gives rise to an identity crisis, but some do, and the question that interests Habermas is: when and under what conditions do system crises become identity crises?

A key part of his answer to this question is summed up in what we could call "the logic of crisis displacement." This is not exactly Habermas's term, although he does speak of crises being "displaced" from one system to another. His argument, in essence, is this: the economic system remains the primary source of crisis in capitalist societies, stemming ultimately from the structural asymmetry between capital and wage labour. However, given that the state has become directly involved in regulating the economy and compensating for the negative consequences of economic growth through the creation of welfare services amongst other things, a crisis originating in the economy can be displaced into the political sphere, where it is expressed as a "rationality crisis." A rationality crisis is the inability of the political system to cope with the conflicting demands that are placed on it—for example, the demand to provide an extensive array of welfare services, on the one hand, and the demand to raise enough revenue through the taxation system to cover its financial commitments. As Habermas (1988: 46) puts it, "The rationality crisis is a displaced systemic crisis which, like economic crisis, expresses the contradiction between socialized production for non-generalizable interests and steering imperatives." A rationality crisis can in turn become a "legitimation crisis" when there is a withdrawal of legitimation on the part of the public—now it becomes an identity crisis rather than another manifestation of a system crisis. A legitimation crisis arises when the economic or political system can no longer count on sufficient levels of support from the population to continue to function—that is, to reproduce itself without resorting to force or violence. A loss of trust or pervasive sense of disillusionment would be a good indicator of the kind of identity crisis Habermas has in mind.

I do not wish to go any further into the details of Habermas's argument—there are many aspects of his account that could be (and have been) questioned, and in any case the argument is tied to a set of historical circumstances that are now well behind us. Three decades of neo-liberal ascendancy in the West have altered fundamentally the relationship between states and capitalist economies and created the conditions for a kind of crisis that Habermas did not foresee. But there are three aspects of Habermas's account on which I do want briefly to dwell, as they will help us to think through more clearly the value as well as the limitations of his account.

1. In the first place, while Habermas was right to stress the importance of the economic system as a principal source of crises, his account of the features of the economy that are likely to give rise to systemic crises is overly indebted to a rather traditional Marxist view of capitalism as a system of production based on a fundamental conflict between socialized production and private appropriation. While this is not of course unimportant, it overlooks another feature of capitalism that is equally (if not more) important for understanding economic crises and that was stressed much more by Max Weber and by economists like Schumpeter and Keynes—namely, the fundamental importance of *money, debt, and borrowing*, both for the functioning of the capitalist economy and for the activities of modern states.

2. A second feature of Habermas's account that limits its usefulness for us today is its implicit focus on the individual nation state and its neglect of the deep and pervasive *transnational interlocking of institutions*. This includes the interlocking of industrial and financial institutions that are nominally based in different countries but that are fundamentally transnational in their modes of operation, but it also includes the transnational interlocking of financial and political institutions via the increasingly complex operations of the bond markets and rating agencies and the activities of international organizations like the IMF or the European Central Bank. To be fair, in recent years Habermas himself has become increasingly preoccupied with the character and consequences of what he calls "the postnational constellation." But the argument he developed in *Legitimation Crisis* was

rather firmly locked in the framework of what Beck (2006: 24–33) has called, appropriately enough, "methodological nationalism."

3. A third aspect of Habermas's argument that remains rather opaque and unsatisfactory is the precise relation between so-called system crises, on the one hand, and what he calls identity crises, on the other. This is, without doubt, a crucial question: under what conditions does a malfunctioning of the economic system become something more than a technical problem to be "fixed" by so-called experts? When does it become something that ordinary people experience as threatening—as something that threatens to disrupt their lives in some non-negligible way, throwing them out of work or destroying their life savings or in some other way impinging detrimentally on their social or personal lives? Habermas is undoubtedly right to pose this question, but the way he answers it in *Legitimation Crisis* is anything but clear.

While these are serious shortcomings that limit the usefulness of Habermas's account today, it is nevertheless worthwhile in my view to hold on to his distinction between different kinds of crisis and to keep in mind his suggestive idea of the logic of crisis displacement. However, it is sensible in my view to change the terminology. I will leave to one side the rather elaborate schema of *Legitimation Crisis* and adopt a more straightforward distinction between a *financial crisis*, which involves a seizing-up of the financial system; a *political crisis*, which involves a breakdown of the political system or serious challenge to the government, which finds itself struggling (and possibly failing) to cope with the demands that are placed on it and which, partly as a result of this, may find that its legitimacy is being challenged or called into question in new or more intensified ways; and a *social crisis*, which is a broader social malaise in which people feel that their world is being disrupted in some fundamental way, the conditions of their lives are being threatened or undermined, and their future thrown in doubt. Each of these types of crisis has its own distinctive characteristics, but a crisis can change form over time—that is, it can evolve from a financial crisis into a political or social crisis. This idea of the evolution or metamorphosis of a crisis is certainly indebted to Habermas's idea of crisis displacement, though "metamorphosis" is a more appropriate term than "displacement" in my view. "Metamorphosis" implies a change in form; it does not imply, as displacement does, that the crisis has moved from one sphere of social life to another. A financial crisis that metamorphoses into a political crisis or a social crisis does not necessarily cease to be a financial crisis: it simply becomes something else. It changes form and, in so doing, it becomes something *more* than a financial crisis per se, taking on new characteristics in the process. Shortly we shall turn our attention to our current circumstances and see whether these concepts and distinctions might help shed some light on the course of events, but first we must situate these events in a broader context.

Capitalism, states, and debt

The 2007–8 financial crisis is often portrayed as a banking crisis stemming from the reckless provision of mortgages to low-income households in the USA (so-called subprime mortgages) and the repackaging of these mortgages via an array of financial instruments that both dispersed and disguised the risk associated with them. While this was undoubtedly a key element, it is only part of the story. The events of 2007/8 are best understood as part of a broader crisis of the financial system that is rooted in a fundamental feature of capitalism: debt. Capitalism depends fundamentally on debt, in the sense that it depends on credit—the promise to pay—and the continuous provision of money, in the form of interest-bearing loans, by banks and other financial institutions to finance both production and consumption.[1] Without credit–debt, the production and consumption of goods and services would cease, and capitalism would grind to a halt. But states have also depended on debt since at least the rise of modern states in sixteenth- and seventeenth-century Europe. Early modern states borrowed heavily in order to finance the building of armies and navies, to wage wars, and to maintain their military forces in a state of constant war-readiness (see Mann, 1993: ch. 11). Funding the cost of war was the biggest financial need faced by early modern states—indeed, the Bank of England was established at the end of the seventeenth century in order to finance the war debts of William III (Alessandri and Haldane, 2009: 3). States also borrowed in order to finance infrastructural developments and, later, to fund a growing range of educational and welfare services. A substantial part of this state expenditure was funded by the issuance of bonds. Government bonds, with fixed rates of interest and maturity dates, were offered for

[1] This account of capitalism and its dependence on money, understood as a social relation of credit–debt, is heavily indebted to the important work of Ingham (2004, 2008).

sale to private investors in the money market and secured against future state revenues raised through taxation and import duties. The issuance of bonds enabled governments to finance state expenditure and service their debt while providing private investors with relatively secure financial return.

The historical alliance between states and private investors that emerged in early modern Europe was an arrangement that served both parties well, but it was also a delicate balance that could easily be disrupted. Banks and private investors were at risk of losing their money if the state defaulted on its loans—historically, sovereign default has been the single biggest cause of banking collapse. France defaulted eight times between 1500 and 1800, and Spain defaulted six times during the same three centuries and then seven times in the nineteenth century alone (Reinhart and Rogoff, 2009: 86 ff.). Over time, banks and private investors sought reassurances from states to protect their investments. Two types of reassurance were particularly important (Ingham, 2008: 77 ff.). In the first place, the state's creditors sought reassurance that inflation was under control, since inflation would erode the value of their fixed-interest investments in government bonds. Second, creditors had to be convinced that state revenues generated by taxation, import duties, and so on would be sufficient to meet the interest payments and enable states to repay loans when they were due, thereby avoiding the risk of default. The rate of interest that a government pays to service its long-term debt is determined by the demand for government bonds, and this in turn depends on the perception of the government's creditworthiness—that is, its ability to control inflation and to generate sufficient revenue to meet the interest and other payments due. Governments attempt to establish their creditworthiness by adhering to what are regarded as prudent policies for managing state expenditure—above all, by keeping inflation under control and adhering to norms of deficit financing that keep overall debts and deficits within what are regarded as acceptable parameters at a particular point in time (the idea of a strict balance of expenditure and revenue in the annual budgets of states was largely abandoned in the course of the twentieth century).

In recent years, credit-rating agencies such as Moody's and Standard & Poor's have come to play an increasingly important role in assessing the creditworthiness not only of private corporations but of states and municipalities too. The assessment of creditworthiness is not new—it has been a persistent feature of the history of borrowing, lending, and debt. But what is new is the hiving-off of this activity into a small number of specialized organizations that carry out the rating of creditworthiness as a systematic commercial activity. The history of these organizations dates back to the beginning of the twentieth century. John Moody established a business for assessing creditworthiness in 1909. Standard & Poor's, which was formed through the merger of Standard Statistics Company and Poor's Publishing Company in 1941, can be traced back to the mid-1850s, when Henry Poor began publishing regular accounts of investments in railroads and other infrastructural developments (Sinclair, 2005: 22–6). The much smaller Fitch Ratings Agency was founded by John Fitch in 1913 as a publishing company specializing in financial statistics. The rating activities of the agencies were initially focused on railroads, canals, industrial corporations, and financial institutions in the USA. However, with the end of the Bretton Woods system in 1971 and the liberalization of financial regulation through the 1970s and 1980s, the scope and power of the rating agencies greatly increased, as investors relied more and more on the agencies to guide their investment decisions. By the early 2000s, the two main agencies were maintaining ratings on around $30 trillion worth of debt in American and international markets (Sinclair, 2005: 4). These agencies have enormous power in the financial markets simply because their ratings—which range from AAA ("triple A") to D ("default") with various gradations in between—directly affect the rate of interest that businesses, governments, municipalities, and so on have to pay to service their debt: the higher the rating, the less the risk of default on repayment to the lender, and hence the lower the cost to the borrower. On the other hand, if the agencies judge the risk of default to be high (or higher than it was) and give a lower rating, the cost of borrowing will rise—a point to which we shall return.

Thus, the historical alliance between states and private investors was something of a Faustian pact. States acquired the resources to finance expenditure and service their long-term debt, but they had to pay a price for this in terms of adhering to policies of low inflation and sound finance. If states deviate from accepted norms, the money markets are quick to punish them. Uncertainty triggers the selling of government bonds, and investors can be lured back only by higher interest rates that increase the burden of state debt. On the other hand, thanks in part to the rise of the welfare state and the broad transformation in the nature of the rights associated with citizenship that was analyzed so well by T. H. Marshall (1992), governments in Western countries have faced a steady increase in expectations on the part of citizens for public services, health, education, and a range of other goods and services that increase the demands on state expenditure, and the attempt to hold down or even reverse these demands in the interests of reassuring the state's creditors and maintaining a steady flow of money at manageable interest rates runs the risk of eliciting deep public dissatisfaction, anger, and protest.

The historical alliance between states and private investors has remained pretty much intact since it was formed in early modern Europe, but there is one crucial respect in which it has changed. In the early modern period, banks were the lenders of last resort, and the biggest risk they faced was sovereign default. Over the last two centuries the tables have turned (Alessandri and Haldane, 2009: 1). The state has now become the last-resort financier of the banks, and, in times of need, it is the state that steps in to bail out the banks rather than the other way round.

The metamorphosis of a crisis

The story of what happened in the financial markets in 2007/8 is now well documented, and there is no need to rehearse the details here.[2] However, it is helpful to reflect briefly on the broad structural transformations that preceded these events and made them possible.[3] The period since the 1970s has been characterized by a massive expansion of the financial sector of advanced capitalist economies, resulting in a substantial growth in the overall volume of debt. This expansion was facilitated and actively encouraged by some governments, which deregulated financial markets and attenuated government oversight in order to attract finance capital and reap the benefits of increased tax revenues. These developments went furthest in the USA and the UK, spurred on by the growing ascendancy of neo-liberalism in the Anglo-Saxon world and the traditional dominance of Wall Street and the City of London as global financial centers. Freed from the constraints of government regulation, banks and other financial institutions greatly expanded their range of activities and searched for innovative ways to generate profits by extending new loans and repackaging and trading financial assets. Bank assets mushroomed, as illustrated by Figure 3.1, which shows the assets of the banking sector in the UK as a percentage of

---

[2] Everyone will have their own preferred accounts of these events; the two that I found particularly insightful were Tett (2009) and Lanchester (2010).

[3] The following draws on the excellent account of the financial crisis in Ingham (2011).

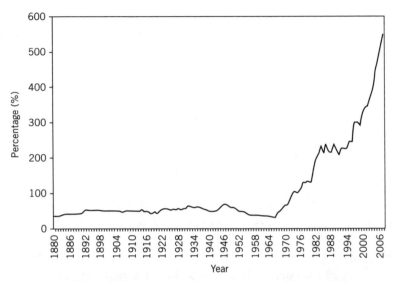

Fig. 3.1 UK banking sector assets as percentage of GDP, 1880–2006

Note: The definition of UK banking sector assets used in the series is broader after 1966, but using a narrower definition throughout gives the same growth profile.
Source: Sheppard (1971) and Bank of England.

GDP. From the late nineteenth century on, the assets of the UK banking system grew roughly in line with overall economic activity, remaining at around 50 percent of GDP. But from the early 1970s on the pattern changed, and by 2001 UK bank assets had grown to more than 500 percent of the annual GDP of the UK (Alessandri and Haldane, 2009: 3). A similar development occurred in the USA, where the assets of the financial industry grew from 1.35 percent of GDP in 1946 to around 110 percent in 2009 (US Federal Reserve, 2010; Ingham, 2011: 234). But banks' assets are loans—that is, debts owed to the banks. A massive increase in outstanding debt on this scale should have been accompanied by an increase in capital and liquidity ratios to offset any losses caused by defaults, but exactly the opposite happened: since the start of the twentieth century, capital ratios fell by over 500 percent in the USA and the UK and liquidity ratios fell by the same amount in half the time (Alessandri and Haldane, 2009: 3). Profits from lending were used to pay high dividends and bonuses and to invest in further speculative activity rather than to strengthen reserves. The net result was a pronounced rise in banking system risk. This was an asset bubble waiting to burst.

The increase in the trading of "derivative" and "securitized" financial assets, using a variety of new financial vehicles that have been analyzed very well by Gillian Tett (2009) among others, has been the focus of a great deal of comment and criticism, but in practice this served merely to exacerbate the underlying fragility of the financial system. The balance sheets of banks had been weakened and rendered vulnerable by the mushrooming of debt and the depletion of reserves. The new "securitized" assets further weakened balance sheets that were already in a parlous state. These new assets were removed from the official balance sheets and held in structured investment vehicles (SIVs) that were created as legally separate entities registered offshore, enabling the banks to evade regulation by USA and UK authorities. The assets were also sliced and diced, packaged and repackaged into different "tranches" of securities (collateralized debt obligations, or CDOs) and sold on so many times that it was no longer clear who was carrying the risk in the event of a default. The illusion was created that the risks associated with default had been all but eliminated by parcelling it up and passing it on to others by means of credit default swaps (CDSs). But the upshot was that banks and other financial institutions did not really know the true value of the assets they were holding on their balance sheets and had no idea what would happen if certain agents in the chain began to default. The securitization of mortgages and other assets was supposed to enable institutions to spread and reduce their risks, but in practice they amplified the risk within the financial system as a whole.

The defaults began in late 2006 and continued through 2007 and 2008, as the fall in USA house prices threw an ever-increasing proportion of US mortgages—especially the so-called subprime mortgages—into arrears.[4] The market price of mortgage securities collapsed, and banks found themselves sitting on trillions of dollars of untradeable CDOs and CDSs. Banks and other institutions that were heavily implicated in the mortgage markets, such as Northern Rock and Lehman Brothers, found themselves highly exposed when the defaults began. On September 15, 2008, Lehman Brothers filed for bankruptcy—the largest corporate bankruptcy in US history. The giant insurance company AIG (American International Group), which used CDSs to insure the obligations of various financial institutions, also found itself in increasingly dire straits; its credit rating was downgraded by the rating agencies and it faced the very real prospect of bankruptcy.

---

[4] For a good account of the dubious and predatory practices that lay behind the collapse of the US mortgage market, see Stiglitz (2009: ch. 4).

Realizing that a second bankruptcy on this scale so quickly after the collapse of Lehman Brothers could be catastrophic, the Federal Reserve Bank stepped in on September 16 and bailed out AIG with an $85 billion credit facility (the total government support to AIG eventually rose to $180 billion). The following day, the US government announced a $700 billion emergency bailout package that allowed the Treasury to purchase so-called toxic assets from banks and other financial institutions. The UK government, which had already taken the lead in this respect when it supported and subsequently nationalized Northern Rock, similarly invested heavily to support the banks in return for substantial shareholdings. The meltdown of the financial system was averted, but it came at a hefty price: by the end of 2009 the US government had spent at least $3 trillion and the UK government had spent £850 billion to support banks and stimulate the economy. The crisis that emerged in the financial sector, stemming from the weak balance sheets of banks that were overexposed to debt, was now firmly displaced into the political sphere. States had averted the collapse of the financial system, at least for the time being, but at what cost?

The expensive rescue packages coupled with the recession triggered by the financial crisis served to shift the spotlight onto states, whose fiscal positions were now significantly weakened by increased debt and sharply declining tax revenues brought on by recession, among other things. Rating agencies and money markets focused their attention on states that appeared to have weak fiscal positions—that is, high debts and declining revenues with which to service the debt. Several countries on the so-called periphery of the eurozone—Ireland, Greece, Spain, and Portugal—became the focal points of concern. The reasons for the fiscal vulnerability of these states varied from state to state. In the case of Ireland, vulnerability was linked to collapse of the banking system and the cost of the rescue, whereas in Greece, Spain, and Portugal the vulnerability had more to do with accumulated debt, the impact of the recession on tourism and debt-financed hotel and housing construction, and the peculiarities of monetary policy in the eurozone.

When member states of the European Union applied to join the euro, they had to promise, in accordance with the Maastricht Treaty, to keep their budget deficits to 3 percent of GDP and to maintain debt-to-GDP ratios of no more than 60 percent. Once they were in the euro, they could borrow money at low interest rates, protected by the creditworthiness of the eurozone's strongest member—Germany. However, the budgetary norms for joining the euro were not strictly enforced, and the cheap money available to member states tended to stimulate further borrowing, as creditors eager to lend more money found willing clients in states eager to borrow more at low interest rates. The true financial position of some states in the eurozone was not entirely clear. It emerged subsequently that investment bankers from Goldman Sachs and other Wall Street banks had secretly collaborated with the Greek and other European governments in the early 2000s to devise financial instruments that enabled them to increase their borrowing while obscuring the true size of their deficits and appearing to remain within Europe's deficit rules. In one deal devised by Goldman Sachs in 2001, shortly after Greece had joined the euro, banks provided Greece with large sums of cash in return for future landing fees at Greek airports—in effect, trading the promise of future revenue for upfront cash (Story, Thomas, and Schwartz, 2010). Since the transaction was classified as a sale rather than a loan, it did not appear as a debt on Greece's balance sheet for that year.

When the new center-left government assumed power in Greece in October 2009, it soon became clear that Greece's fiscal position was much weaker than had been indicated previously. The 2009 budget deficit had been estimated by the previous government to be 6–8 percent of GDP, but it was soon revised upward to 12.7 and then 15.4 percent. Fear of default led the rating agencies to downgrade Greek bonds to junk status. The interest rates on Greek bonds soared—from under 6 percent on 10-year government bonds in early 2009 to over 12 percent later in the year, subsequently climbing to nearly 18 percent in 2011 (see Figure 3.2). The dramatically escalating interest rates on government bonds reflect the growing loss of confidence on the part of the rating agencies and investors in the Greek state (and, to a lesser extent, the Irish and Portuguese states) and its ability to meet its commitments in terms of payments due: the riskier the bonds are perceived to be, the higher the interest they must bear in order to attract investors. The escalating interest rates become punitive and create a vicious cycle. The higher the rate of interest the state has to pay on its bonds, the greater the interest burden becomes, requiring it to raise even more money in the bond market in order to service its debt and thereby increasing the likelihood of a default.

Faced with the very real possibility of sovereign default, states came to the rescue again, only in this case the rescue package came in the form of a €110 billion loan to Greece from the eurozone countries and the IMF. The loan, approved in May 2010, was tied to stringent austerity measures aimed at reducing the size of Greece's debt by cutting expenditure and increasing revenues through higher taxes. A year later it was clear that this was not going to be enough, and a further bailout—a mixture of cash loans, bond

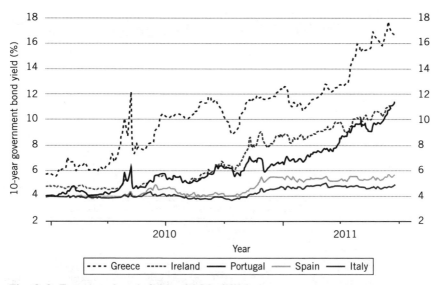

Fig. 3.2 Eurozone bond yields, 2009–2011

Source: Thomson Reuters Datastream

swaps, and debt rollovers amounting to some €120 billion over three years—was approved, again conditional on stringent austerity measures.

Greece has been described as the Lehman Brothers of Europe: Greek default would send shock waves through the financial system and could lead to further defaults in Portugal, Spain, and elsewhere. But, in terms of the structure of credit and debt, Greece is more like the subprime mortgage borrower who finds himself unable to meet the interest payments on his loans, and whose default would expose the fragile position of the balance sheets of the banks that are his creditors. Just as many banks and financial institutions were exposed to defaults in the US mortgage market by virtue of having bought and sold CDOs and CDSs, so too many banks outside of Greece (as well as foreign governments) are heavily exposed to Greek debt—especially in France and Germany, as Figure 3.3 shows. In 2011 Banks in Germany held $22.6 billion of Greek sovereign debt and banks in France held $15 billion; when other forms of Greek debt are added in, such as lending to private banks, these figures rose to $33.9 billion for Germany and $56.7 billion for France. We may have moved on from the specific problems generated by the subprime mortgage market in the USA, but we are still dealing fundamentally with the same crisis—namely, a crisis stemming from banks and other financial institutions with weakened balance sheets that are overexposed to the risk of default. But now the potential

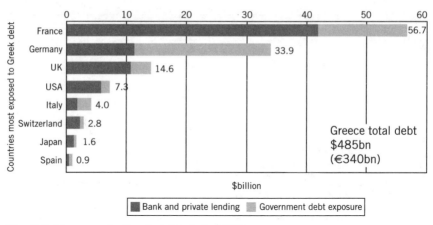

Fig. 3.3 Exposure to Greek debt, July 2011
Source: BIS Quarterly Review

defaulters are states, rather than individuals and households with mortgages they cannot service, and this raises the stakes to an altogether different level. Moreover, given the weakened fiscal positions of many states, it is by no means certain that they would be in a position to rescue their banks a second time if a sovereign default, or series of sovereign defaults, threatened to push them into bankruptcy.

Whilst the crisis we have been living through since 2007/8 is fundamentally a crisis of the financial system, which is rooted in the credit–debt structure of capitalism and the way that the primary institutions of credit–debt—the banks—have evolved since the 1970s, the crisis has shifted into the political sphere and has assumed the form of an actual or potential political crisis. Thanks to this metamorphosis, states and governments are now directly implicated in the crisis and exposed on three fronts. In the first place, they are vulnerable to the charge that their use of public resources to bail out the banks let the bankers off too lightly. Many banks were effectively nationalized, but very little was done to constrain the behavior of bankers, reduce their extravagant salaries, bonuses, and benefits, and re-regulate a sector whose reckless activities had brought the global economy to the edge of collapse. The mixed feelings of bewilderment and anger that many people felt toward bankers and their reckless activities are now redirected toward the governments that were prepared to bail them out in their time of need but appear timid, spineless, and indecisive when it comes to developing and implementing new policies aimed at reforming the financial sector and reducing the likelihood of further bailouts.

The second front on which states and governments are now exposed is more serious: the bailouts and recession have exposed the fragility and vulnerability of the fiscal positions of some states, propelling them—with varying kinds and degrees of external pressure—to clamp down on public expenditure in the hope of reducing their levels of overall debt and the payments required to service it. *The struggle over public spending has become the new frontline of the financial crisis.* The financial crisis has exacerbated the Faustian pact that has always been part of the historical alliance between states and private investors. Since the seventeenth century, states have acquired the resources to fund expenditure and service their debt from the sale of bonds to private investors in the money markets, but to keep the terms manageable they had to strive to adhere to certain norms in terms of inflation and deficit financing that keep overall debts and deficits within acceptable parameters. This produces a constant pressure on states to control or reduce public spending, and this pressure is exacerbated when states find themselves suddenly burdened with substantial additional expenditures (as with the bailouts), or suddenly faced with declining revenues (as happens when tax yields decline in a stagnant or recessionary economy), or both. In these conditions, governments find themselves facing the unpalatable prospect of imposing swingeing cuts in public expenditure and/or raising taxes in an attempt to bring state finances back into line with the norms of deficit financing that are expected by the market, since failure to do so would run the risk of increasing the cost of borrowing and thereby worsening the fiscal position of the state. But the prospect of imposing swingeing cuts and/or raising taxes is unpalatable for governments of any hue, whether left or right, simply because these are two key areas where the actions of the state affect directly the lives of ordinary citizens. Cutting public services, reducing the salaries and benefits of public employees, putting large numbers of people on the public payroll out of work, selling off public assets, restructuring institutions of health and education to shift more of the burden of cost onto private individuals, raising direct and indirect taxation: these and other measures are never going to be easy for any government to introduce and are going to elicit much anger, resentment, and hostility from many sectors of the population, whose quality of life will be directly and materially affected by the changes. Many ordinary people will feel—with some justification—that they are paying the price for a mess created by others.

Let us now consider briefly two snapshots from the frontline of the crisis today. It is Wednesday, June 29, 2011, and Britain is preparing itself for a nationwide strike of public-sector workers called for the following day. It promises to be the biggest strike for many years—more than half a million workers are likely to walk out. Schools, colleges, hospitals, airports, courts, and government offices across the country will be affected; thousands of schools will be closed and travel will be disrupted. Unions have called for the strike to protest against the coalition government's proposed reform of public-sector pensions. The reforms would end final-salary schemes, which link pension payments to salaries at retirement, for all public-sector employees. The amount most employees have to contribute would increase significantly—by 3 percent of earnings, which would double the contribution of many workers—and the pension age would be raised. The strike call was welcomed by many public-sector workers, not just because they are worried about their pensions—though many are—but also because they are angry and resentful about the cuts and the government's strategy of slashing public spending as a way of trying to reduce the budget deficit. They feel they are being forced to make sacrifices and suffer a serious deterioration in their living conditions in order to pay for a crisis that was caused by bankers, who, by all accounts, appear still to be commanding their high salaries and extravagant bonuses and comfortable private pensions. Mary works in the finance department of a benefits processing center in Cannock, just north of Birmingham. She will be joining the strike along with most of her fellow workers. "In all the time I've been working here I've never known finance to strike," said Mary. "Basically, we care about people. The last thing we want to do is to make life more difficult for people" (*Gentleman*, 2011: 6). But this time is different. Mary and her fellow workers are concerned about pensions and changes to their retirement age, but they are also angry about a recent decision to close the whole office within a year and deploy staff to other offices across the Midlands. The changes to pensions were the last straw in a series of decisions that have led to a continuous deterioration in working conditions. "I was shocked at how much it was going to be extra," said Mary, reflecting on the impact of the pension changes on her personal finances. Like others, Mary had used an online pension calculator on the website of the Public and Commercial Services Union to figure out what the changes would mean for her. You fill in three bits of information (age, salary, and length of pension scheme membership) and the calculator tells you instantly how much extra you will have to pay, how much you will lose, and how much longer you will have to work—a simple device that enabled employees to translate the pension reforms into terms they could immediately understand. Mary reckoned that she would have to pay an extra £45 a month in pension contributions out of her £17,000 salary. When changes in the pension contributions of her husband, a teacher, are factored in, they will lose £215 from their monthly household income. "It feels like getting back to being newlyweds and watching every penny. As you get older you expect life to improve, but it's going backwards." She feels that she and her husband are being punished for devoting their lives to public service while those responsible for the crisis get off scot-free. "I feel angry. They bailed out the banks, and we are in this huge financial mess, but it is Joe Public who has to pay the bill."

On the same day, Wednesday, June 29, crowds have gathered in Syntagma Square in central Athens, as members of the Greek Parliament debate the new round of austerity measures that the EU and IMF have demanded as the condition of extending the second emergency loan of €120 billion. The atmosphere is tense. There are pitched battles between protestors and riot police in the streets around Syntagma Square, as youths throw stones and police fire canisters of tear gas and stun grenades into the crowds of protesters. Inside Parliament, the Prime Minister, George Papandreou, pleaded with members of Parliament to pass the legislation endorsing the draconian austerity measures; outside, there was pandemonium in the streets. Just after 4:30 p.m., as news spread that the measures have been passed by the slimmest of margins, the tension in the square rises, the protests turn violent, and the fighting becomes intense. Among the thousands who have gathered in the square day after day are many ordinary Greeks, young and old, who are angry and fed up. Maria Xifara, a bank employee in her 20s, is one of the protesters: "We will not stop, we will not stop," she says forcefully, the anger evident in the tone of her voice. "*They* must stop, the government must stop." "How will you make them stop?" the journalist asks. "With strikes, with demonstrations, with everything—we will come here and protest." Theofrastos Vampourellis, a young unemployed civil engineer, explains why he has joined the protests: "I'm here because youth unemployment is rising up to high levels, we don't have any jobs, we don't have any money, so life is very difficult for us." Sofia Tsadari, a young architect in her early 30s, has her own reasons: "We've seen people losing their homes to the banks," she says, "so this makes people feel that it's a, a . . . social disaster." Georgia Mavriogianni, a 54-year-old mother of three, has been out of work for two years since her small business went bust. "I've never been to a protest in my life but you can see a lot of people are reacting to what's going on. We have reached a dead-end with these politicians and people are waking up and wanting to take part in decision-making." Carlos Margounis, a pensioner, thought the crisis would only deepen because the

Greeks felt cheated and deceived: "In all these years nobody ever talked about the debt problem. Then suddenly we are faced with a stark dilemma: food or interest? Pay off the debt, or continue to live? Well, what would you choose?" (Smith, 2011; Howden, 2011; *Newsnight*, 2011).

Two snapshots from the frontline of the crisis are nothing more than that—two moments captured in time, taken from a myriad of occurrences that happen in different times and places. But they do tell us something important about the crisis unfolding around us. They show very clearly that what we are dealing with today is not *only* a financial crisis (though it is still that) and not *only* a political crisis (though again, it is that too, and now more than ever): we are dealing with what has become a full-blown social crisis as well. The financial crisis has metamorphosed into a political and a social crisis. These snapshots also tell us that, for many ordinary people, the crisis is today more real than ever. Back in the autumn of 2008, the financial crisis had a certain unreality for many ordinary people: these were strange, incomprehensible events taking place in a distant world populated by people you never met engaging in practices you did not understand. If you had savings in banks that were caught up in these events, you might have worried about whether they were safe; you might even have gone to the trouble of withdrawing your savings and putting them somewhere that seemed more secure, as did many who had savings in Northern Rock. But this was still a very small sector of the population, and the government bailout of the banks meant that most people's savings were secure (at least for the time being). The huge sums of money that governments spent on bailing out the banks and stimulating the economy were so gargantuan that they were, to all intents and purposes, meaningless. What is a trillion dollars? What is eight hundred billion pounds? You just had no way of relating to figures of that kind. However, when the government announces that your salary will be frozen or cut, that you will have to pay another £45 a month for your pension and work six years longer than you thought you would have to work, that your taxes will go up and the local library will be closed and your children will have to pay for their own university education, then the crisis is all too real: it impinges directly on your own life and on the lives of those around you. It is now a social crisis that threatens to destroy things you have come to take for granted, to disrupt your life and that of your friends and family, and to have a serious impact on the social and material conditions of your well-being. Now you understand what the crisis means. It no longer seems like an abstract technical problem to be fixed by bankers and technocrats in Washington or London or Brussels who can manipulate numbers and inject vast sums of money into the economy in ways that make little sense to ordinary people. It is now a political and a social problem that impinges directly on your life.

The third front on which states and governments are now exposed is more indeterminate but more worrying and more profound: how could states cope with another round of large-scale defaults? This is precisely the question with which European governments are now faced. If Greece were to default, it would immediately hit the balance sheets of banks in Greece, France, Germany, the UK, and elsewhere, generating further big losses in the financial sector. It is not at all clear what the consequences of this would be, either for the banks themselves or for the euro. If it were to precipitate further defaults in Portugal, Spain, and/or Italy, the crisis could spin out of control and the euro could collapse. That, in essence, is why the governments of France, Germany, and other European states have been so concerned to try to mobilize sufficient support to avert a Greek default, despite the criticism that some European leaders face from their own citizens: they know very well that, since the state is now the last-resort financier of the banks, they will be called upon to prop up the banking system if a sovereign default in Greece—and possibly also elsewhere—were to push European banks over the edge. Their calculation is that the risks involved in rolling over Greece's debt, while considerable, are less than the risks—to banks, to the states that would be called on to support them, and to the global financial system—that would be involved in a sudden and uncontrolled sovereign default on this scale.

Of course, whether rolling over Greece's debt will solve the problem or merely postpone it is a moot point. As the eurozone crisis unfolded it gradually became clear to most observers—and indeed to most political leaders—that the scale of Greece's debt was simply too large to be repayable in the foreseeable future, especially when the deflationary impact of the austerity measures was taken into account. When the second bailout package was finally agreed in February 2012, the total value had risen to €130 billion—the largest bailout in western history—and it included a provision for private banks and investors to accept a 53.5 percent loss (or "haircut") on the nominal value of the Greek debt they hold, amounting to an effective debt write-off of around €100 billion; the hope was that this would bring Greece's debt down to 120 percent of GDP by 2020. But the bailout package also requires the Greek government to impose a new round of stringent austerity measures, including further wage cuts and the layoff of many government workers, and implementing these measures in the face of entrenched, determined, and potentially violent opposition could prove very challenging. Moreover, the additional spending cuts will undoubtedly prolong the recession in Greece, which contracted by almost 12 percent betweeen 2009 and 2011 and where unemployment is hovering around 20 percent. Greece will receive further emergency loans to stave off insolvency, but its future still hangs in the balance. If it fails to achieve the draconian cuts and raise additional revenue through increased taxes and the sale of public assets, future instalments could be withheld, thereby renewing the risk of default. And, even if the situation in Greece can be stabilized, the eye of the financial storm could easily shift to other countries in the eurozone: by mid-November 2011 the yield on ten-year Italian government bonds had risen to over 7 percent, the point at which the smaller economies of Ireland, Portugal, and Greece had to seek aid from eurozone partners and the IMF. Italy is the third largest economy in the eurozone, with a total debt of around €1.9 trillion (2.7 times more than the combined debt of Greece, Ireland, and Portugal) so the challenge of stabilizing Italy—not to mention Spain, Portugal, Ireland, and even Belgium, whose debt has been significantly increased by the need to bail out the leading Franco-Belgium bank Dexia—could dwarf the crisis in Greece. The future of the euro and the eurozone is by no means guaranteed.

This is where we are in 2012: in a very uncertain place, not in the aftermath of a crisis but in the midst of one, where the beginning can be analyzed and documented with some precision but where the end is not yet in sight and the outcome is by no means clear. What began as a financial crisis, apparently stemming from the reckless practices of bankers operating in deregulated financial markets, has changed form, metamorphosing into a much broader crisis that is financial, political, and social in character. Governments and politicians are now in the frontline of the crisis and face enormous challenges, trapped by the Faustian pact that ties their fate to private investors while at the same time facing the wrath of citizens who feel angry and betrayed by them, questioning their legitimacy and actively protesting against the measures they are seeking to impose. And, just as this crisis is now a social crisis as much as it is a financial and political one, so too its future is in the hands of ordinary people, and the way they respond to the sacrifices that are being asked of them, as much as it is in the hands of bankers and politicians. What happens on the streets of Athens, Cannock, Rome, and other cities may be as important, in the months to come, as what happens in the offices of governments and banks in New York, Washington, London, Brussels, Berlin, and elsewhere.

References

Alessandri, Piergiorgio, and Haldane, Andrew G. (2009). *Banking on the State*. London: Bank of England.

Beck, Ulrich (2006). *The Cosmopolitan Vision*, trans. Ciaran Cronin. Cambridge: Polity.

Gentleman, Amelia (2011). "' I Feel Angry. They Bailed Out the Bank But it's Joe Public Who Has to Pay,'" *Guardian*, June 30, 6.

Habermas, Jürgen (1988). *Legitimation Crisis*, trans. Thomas McCarthy. Cambridge: Polity.

Howden, Daniel (2011). "Disaster Averted? Not if you Listen to the Greeks," *Independent*, June 18, 3.

Ingham, Geoffrey (2004). *The Nature of Money*. Cambridge: Polity.

—— (2008). *Capitalism*. Cambridge: Polity.

—— (2011). "Postscript: The Financial Crisis and its Aftermath," in Geoffrey Ingham, *Capitalism*. Cambridge: Polity, 227–64.

Lanchester, John (2010). *Whoops! Why Everyone Owes Everyone and No One Can Pay*. London: Penguin.

Mann, Michael (1993). *The Sources of Social Power*, ii. *The Rise of Classes and Nation-States, 1760–1914*. Cambridge: Cambridge University Press.

Marshall, T. H. (1992). *Citizenship and Social Class*. London: Pluto Press.

Newsnight (28 and 29 June 2011), reporter Paul Mason, June 28 and 29.

Reinhart, Carmen M., and Rogoff, Kenneth S. (2009). *This Time is Different: Eight Centuries of Financial Folly*. Princeton: Princeton University Press.

Sheppard, D. K. (1971).*The Growth and Role of UK Financial Institutions, 1880–1962*. London: Methuen.

Sinclair, Timothy J. (2005). *The New Masters of Capital: American Bond Rating Agencies and the Politics of Creditworthiness*. Ithaca, NY: Cornell University Press.

Smith, Helena (2011). "Papandreou Shuffles Pack But Fails to Quell Protest" *The Guardian*, June 17, 5.

Stiglitz, Joseph (2009). *Freefall: Free Markets and the Sinking of the Global Economy*. London: Penguin.

Story, Louise, Thomas, Landon, Jr. and Schwartz, Nelson D. (2010). "Wall St. Helped to Mask Debt Fueling Europe's Crisis," *New York Times*, Feb. 14.

Tett, Gillian (2009). *Fool's Gold: How Unrestrained Greed Corrupted a Dream, Shattered Global Markets and Unleashed a Catastrophe*. London: Little, Brown.

US Federal Reserve (2010). *Components of US Debt*.

Chapter 4

Financial Crisis or Societal Mutation?

*Michel Wieviorka**

The number of publications devoted to the crisis that started in 2008 is now impressive, and, after three or four years of this crisis, there is a kind of lassitude: do we still need new books and articles dealing with "the crisis"? In fact, yes, at least if we consider a very simple fact— that, at this stage, and so far, the majority of publications have been written by economists or by journalists and, while some do have a sociological slant, none is really a work of the social sciences.

The time required by social scientists to write such publications is obviously not the same as that needed by economists: social scientists must carry out in-depth surveys and work on empirical data that do not necessarily correspond to the ongoing situation. Perhaps, also, as important as it may be, an economic and financial crisis is not something they believe should concern them. It is only with hindsight that we will be able to tell whether the present crisis has, or has not, as such, mobilized social scientists, given

* Translated by Kristin Couper-Lobel.

rise to research programs, and affected the balance between scientific trends and orientations or given rise to new paradigms.

But the experience of the 1929 crisis had already led us to believe that social sciences have considerable difficulties or are rather reticent when it comes to confronting phenomena of this type. As Charles Camic (2007) has demonstrated, the 1929 crisis in the USA—the Great Depression—either produced or accelerated considerable institutional changes in this subject, in particular a reduction in budgets and posts; furthermore, the flow of migrants from Europe, in particular from Germany because of the rise of Nazism, itself consecutive to the crisis, exerted an appreciable influence on their orientations. But let us set aside the institutional aspects and concentrate on the intellectual production directly devoted to the crisis. We observe that social scientists almost entirely neglected this subject and the issues involved, apart perhaps from rural sociology, where a strong research tradition had existed before the Great Depression, whereas, from the outset, economists, political scientists, and lawyers occupied the terrain on a large scale. We also observe that, with the New Deal, the situation did not fundamentally change and, while social scientists did play a role in formulating Roosevelt's policies, this role remained minimal compared to that of their colleagues in political science and law. Can this distance or this avoidance be explained on the basis of the idea that the crisis was perceived as being predominantly economic and thus called for political responses involving a legal formulation? It was, therefore, fitting that the representatives of these disciplines dominated the scene. The question is important, because our analysis of the present crisis will determine whether or not the role of social sciences will be important.

It was not until 1934 or 1935 that American social sciences began to mobilize in relation to the Great Depression. Until then, articles that had appeared in the major academic sociological journals and the addresses of the successive Presidents of the American Sociological Association, for instance, were astonishingly insensitive to the Great Depression—for example, Charles Camic (2007) lists one single research article genuinely concerned with the crisis published by the *American Journal of Sociology* between 1930 and 1934. The idea that social scientists could emerge from their marginalization and be useful and present in action in the face of the crisis began to take shape in mid-1933, when Roosevelt launched the New Deal. Apart from the rural studies that I have previously mentioned, the first important publication was that of F. Stuart Chapin, *Contemporary American Institutions* (1935)—a book "hastily produced and speculative"—which was to be followed by a few empirical studies by other social scientists on the family, unemployment, or, yet again, the effects of the depression in "Middletown," a town studied a few years previously by Robert Lynd (1929), who had "revisited" it. In 1936 a first, and in fact unique, major research program was launched under the impetus of William F. Ogburn and a few well-known names in the subject, published under the generic title of Studies in the Social Aspects of the Depression, which was to give rise to thirteen monographic studies—publications about which all we can really say, along with Camic, is that, on the whole, they did not produce any strong and convincing findings. While they were intended to stimulate empirical research on the Depression, they in fact were indicative of its ending! Ernest Burgess (in Schroeder and Burgess 1938) was to conclude that

social scientists... missed a unique opportunity during the past ten years for increasing our knowledge of the functioning of social institutions as affected by market fluctuations of the business cycle... The greatest depression in the history of the United States has had no adequate recording by students of society. The social sciences individually and collectively failed. (quoted by Camic, 2007: 271)

A consequence, or a dimension, of this failure was to reside in the increasing importance accorded by American sociology to cultural themes and categories, bringing it closer to psychology and social anthropology.

A study of other national experiences would perhaps be required to enable us to relativize this irrevocable observation. The fact remains that the only major study dating from this period to have covered the history of the subject by specifically focusing on the crisis is the now classical study by Marie Jahoda, Paul Lazarsfeld, and Hans Zeisel (1933) on the unemployed workers in Marienthal, a small town in Austria, where a very high level of unemployment rendered the workers and the whole population apathetic and demoralized, despite the trade unions and political left having been powerful there previously.

It must, therefore, be admitted that there is no obvious relationship between the crisis and social sciences, and, to tackle this question, the best way is undoubtedly to begin with the crisis and the analysis that can be made of it.

Two approaches

From the start the majority of commentators told us that the simplest thing to do was to follow the sequence of events. Since then we have been presented with a story that is more or less the same, apart from a few variations in detail. Jacques Attali's book (2008) constitutes a paradigm. We are told that, in the first instance, the crisis was financial: credit for consumer goods and especially the American housing bubble, the sub-primes, securitization, the failures of financial institutions or banks, avoided in the last resort thanks to the intervention of governments, and so on. It spread in the form of a worldwide social and economic crisis: so-called technical unemployment, axing of jobs, closing of firms, poverty, and so forth. It may have dramatic political repercussions, with violence, riots, and populist, nationalist, or extreme left forms of radicalization. Sooner or later after a difficult period it will be resolved. This will be the "way out of the crisis": the economy will pick up again, cleaned up and perhaps strengthened, working more smoothly, thanks to a banking system that has been improved under the leadership of governments that have led the way to a recovery of confidence, and thanks perhaps also to substantial progress having been made in the governance at world level of the economy and finance.

Of course, it appears that this narrative was not entirely false. However, in many respects it is unsubstantiated. Its economism tends to be oversimplistic; economics is the explanation for everything. The Marxist overtones are astonishing on the part of those who have developed them; if we are to believe them, the economic infrastructure controlled the political-ideological superstructure, as if the political actors were in no way responsible for the catastrophe. All that is required is simply to await a reversal of the situation, which is already taking shape and is referred to as the "return of the state."

This narrative also has the overtones of a "saga" with a happy ending along the lines of: "we're going to suffer, we'll have to tighten our belts, but we'll get over it." And those who created it, be they experts, economists, or others, are not lacking in self-confidence. They did not see what was coming, but they present themselves as qualified to explain in a learned fashion what happened, and what the future will be like, even going as far as suggesting the most appropriate public policies to adopt.

Moreover, when they are questioned, they state that some of them had forecast the American scenario, the inevitable bursting of the bubble associated with unbridled credit, in the property market and for consumer goods. At most, they concede that they did not imagine the extension of the crisis to the planet as a whole and with such rapidity; those who have been speaking about globalization for the past twenty years without ever imagining that it could also lead to a "global" crisis are not hesitant to declare that this is the first crisis in globalization. And it is clear now that this narrative did not predict the fact that some countries, and, even further, some regions in the world, would not really suffer from the crisis; it also did not imagine the real economic and political consequences of the crisis, in countries such as Greece or Spain, for instance. And it has been blind to its cultural and social effects, to the forms of resistance and resilience the crisis could cause or reinforce.

Two types of argument

In fact, to be precise, two types of argument characterize the analyses of the present crisis. This can be seen, for example, in France, in the collective thinking of Le Cercle des Économistes (2009).

The first argument, as we have just seen, considers it as a financial phenomenon, at the outset restricted to the USA, which began in August 2007, and which gained momentum in 2008 with the subprime mortgages, the drift of consumer credit, and the existence of liquidities that were disproportionate to borrowers' true capacities, along with the securitization of assets, some of which turned out to be toxic. The financial crisis is described as spreading extremely rapidly worldwide and extending into an economic crisis that itself gave rise to social difficulties and greater political tensions. This narrative lacks imagination; moreover, it did not, for example, foresee the differences between countries or various parts of the world.

This is the approach that predominates among economists, who, in the last resort, date the true beginning of the crisis from the bankruptcy of Lehman Brothers, on September 15, 2008—a date that is said to be as important as October 29, 1929, or "Black Tuesday," when the American stock exchange collapsed. There is a debate within this first approach based mainly on differences of opinion between monetarist economists, and, in particular, between disciples of Milton Friedmann and Keynesian-type economists. The former consider excess liquidity as the main source of the present crisis: in their opinion, the crisis signifies the destruction of excess liquidity, and the dissolution of doubtful debts and other "toxic" assets; it acts as a sort of purge, after which there can be a fresh start and a new cycle of capitalism can take place; it implies intervention on the part of the state, though this should be temporary, and last only until the crisis is over, at which point the state should resume its role, which is, by definition, modest. The Keynesians insist on the process of exhaustion of growth, which should be relaunched by means of various therapies implemented by the state: lowering of interest rates, investment in public works, inputs of liquidity enabling consumption to be stimulated, and so on. We should add that Keynesian economists may be much more open to the perspectives offered by a second type of explanation of the crisis than the monetarists; they see the crisis as a consequence of the disengagement of the state that was inaugurated in the Thatcher and Reagan years, and perhaps even earlier.

Indeed, the second type of argument considers that, in fact, the present crisis is only a point in time—a particularly salient one, to be sure—in a transformation that began to take place in several countries from the mid-1970s. Indeed, a date sometimes serves to mark the beginning of the phenomenon, which at that time was said to have been triggered by the oil crisis linked to the Kippur War: on October 17, 1973, the Arab oil-producing countries suddenly decided spectacularly to increase the price of "crude" oil. According to this point of view, the whole world then entered into a series of transformations marking the end of the thirty post-Second World War years. The developmental model, which at that point was predominant in numerous countries, was characterized in particular by the important role of the state in redistribution—the welfare state—and its large-scale intervention in the organization of economic life, by widespread adhesion to the values of the industrial era: confidence in progress, in science, and in deferred gratification. The management of firms was anxious to maximize efficiency in production and was often characterized by faith in the Taylorian "one best way," in Fordism, and, more generally speaking, in the existence of industrial societies, with a central conflict in which there was a working-class movement that opposed the employers.

This model was also characterized by a high rate of growth: finance was regulated and inequalities were restricted. Apart from its own specific characteristics, which we have no intention of minimizing, the Soviet world was in a way an extreme version of this same model. It was, moreover, at the time of its decline that globalization began to be implemented—a process that gained momentum when the Soviet Union collapsed—challenging national modes of growth. This second type of argument, which is not entirely foreign to the thinking of certain economists, as we have seen, is nevertheless very present in political thinking and among social scientists when they voice their opinions, for example, in the press.

In both cases, on the basis of these somewhat summary images, it is possible to present approaches that are much more detailed. For the first type of argument we would refer to the world market and the spectacular increases in the reserves of foreign currency by countries that export raw materials or by China, Brazil, Russia, and India or other "emerging" countries. We would note the difficulties that have occurred in regulating international trade, in particular with the failure of the Doha trade round, since not only the USA, but also India and China, blocked negotiations in December 2008. We would also stress the incredible inadequacies of the credit-rating agencies, ranging from incompetence to corruption, since they were both judge and jury, in theory objectively ranking securities on behalf of the issuing authorities of these same securities: clients who rewarded them handsomely. If in the analysis we insist on limiting ourselves to the idea of a crisis with relatively limited sources and dates, to one episode among others typical of capitalism; even if it has acquired unusual dimensions and strength, then the answer to this crisis must also be financial and economic. The economy has to be relaunched by consumption and investment until it gains momentum again and the financial industries, duly purged, are able to retrieve their usual mode of functioning. To put it simply, in this first set of arguments, the crisis is at a difficult moment in time: it forces us to appeal to the state and various modes of regulation to get rid of neo-liberal ideologies, though basically there will be no in-depth changes once the economy has been cleaned up and relaunched.

The second set of arguments can also be presented in a more elaborate way. This involves, in particular, demonstrating that, in the processes inaugurated in the mid-1970s, not everything can be classed uniquely under "structural" or "systemic" crisis. Rather, it is a question of a large-scale transformation, a change in which a world is being invented: the internet and digital technologies are helping to create revolutions on the planet, in which new "postmodern" or "post-industrial" values are emerging. While the old world is disintegrating, there is a threat of "stagflation" (a combination of inflation and stagnation); at the same time, the rich are getting richer, inequalities are getting deeper, managers are becoming elements of financial capitalism, and firms are outsourcing an ever larger part of their activities and valorizing flexibility or subcontracting. From this perspective we are forced to introduce two sets of hypotheses concerning the present crisis. Does it denote the end of a long purge, the last step in a long process of emerging from what the French, in the words of the economist Jean Fourastié, have referred to as *"les trente glorieuses"*—the years 1945–1977? Or, instead, is it not an indication that the neo-liberal model, which had been taking shape since the mid-1970s, has failed, since we are now experiencing the end of growth and the need to invent one or several models of development? In the first scenario, after the crisis, we will be able to enter a new world in a more clear-cut way—which seems to be indicated by the expectations linked to sustainable development or "green" growth, or, yet again, by the criticism of consumerism; all of these themes have originated in the challenge to industrial society since the end of the 1960s and have been revived by the present crisis (see, e.g., Stiegler, 2009, which returns to the concerns and the themes of the end of the 1960s). In the second case, we tend to be tempted to return to the mindset of the post-war years, the welfare state, regulation of the economy, managements concerned with organizing work and production and not of simply adhering to the sole interests of shareholders, or, yet again, "Rhenan-type" trade-unionism, to use Michel Albert's terms. But we could also envisage entry into a long period of depression and recession, the failure to invent a new world without the capacity of finding any further inspiration in the developmental models of the post-war years. In other words: if, in this second set of approaches, the lasting return of the state is usually an obvious element in confronting the development of the crisis, the latter may equally well take the form either of an attempt to return to the model of "*les trente glorieuses*" or to the invention of new modes of intervention. In the last-mentioned perspective, it is a question of thinking of the role of the state in terms that depart from the "methodological nationalism" denounced by the German sociologist Ulrich Beck, and that enable us to envisage new, or revised, rules of functioning at supranational, regional (European, for example), or global levels.

Rapprochement

The two major approaches to the crisis that have just been described are not necessarily contradictory, even if extreme and opposite variants of both can be found. Thus, some economists not only consider that the crisis is primarily monetary and financial, but also suggest an elementary solution to get out of it: the return, not only in America but at world level, to the principles of the Glass–Steagall Act, enacted in the United States in 1933, in the weeks that followed the inauguration of the Roosevelt administration. This Act established a strict separation between market activities and deposit banking activities—in other words, a return to making those who lend responsible for ensuring that borrowers are solvent, and to ending securitization, which enabled these same banks to eliminate risk by converting their debts into securities; or, if one prefers, to restoring the separation between the banks and the financial markets, which, in the USA, was abolished in 1999, with the abrogation of the Glass–Steagall Act in the form of the Gramm–Leach–Bliley Act, which made it possible to convert debts that, until then, banks had had to keep, into securities negotiable on the financial markets.

Symmetrically, the second approach can, in the last resort, free itself from any consideration of the short term and the crisis in its financial or even economic dimension and focus on considering the immense changes of which these dimensions are only one specific aspect. The writer Amin Maalouf (2009), for example, speaks of a deregulation of the world, of a zone of turbulence, which is the consequence of a cultural and civilizational impoverishment. Far from offering any idea of "clash of cultures," he is alarmed to see the West ceasing to be true to its own values, central to which he sets the inheritance of the Enlightenment, while, at the same time, according to him, the Arab world is retreating into a cultural and historical impasse. He calls for the refusal of the three temptations: that of the precipice (some people jump into the void with the intention of pulling the whole roped party down with them), that of the wall (withdrawal, retreat, a "backs to the wall" stance while waiting for the storm to pass), and that of the summit (the idea that mankind has come to the twilight of its History). He concludes his thinking by calling for survival to be made mandatory and by hoping for the metamorphosis of mankind.

But somewhere between the analyses restricted to specific sectors and grand meta-social visions, is there no space for a project that analyzes the crisis by articulating opinions devoted to specific aspects, situated in space and time, dominated by mono-disciplinary approaches, and wide-ranging, sociological points of view, possibly open to pluri-disciplinarity with a relatively broad conception of space and time? Until the crisis broke, it was commonplace to insist on the distance separating the financial economy from the real economy; for example, people stressed how absurd it was to see that, the more firms laid off workers and closed plants that were still economically viable, the more their stocks rose on the stock exchange. The crisis demonstrated that powerful links existed between the financial sphere and that of production, since the collapse of the financial system brought in its wake a catastrophe for employment and growth. From that point on, instead of opposing these two worlds, would it not be better to analyze the way in which they are connected? Once again, we can find various proposals here. The most interesting come from economists like Daniel Cohen (2009), explaining that, since the 1970s, finance has been a sphere that is paradigmatic of more general transformations and in the forefront of changes dominated by de-regulation, loss of a sense of responsibility of those involved, and the rise of individualism, even of cynicism, and at the same time of disengagement on the part of states.

Even in its variants, which are furthest from the idea of a structural or systemic crisis, the dominant discourse does include sociological dimensions. For example, we find observations concerning social inequality, which has risen continuously during the years of de-regulation, and questions about the fact that society was able to tolerate such high levels of inequality (see, e.g., the hypercritical and frequently polemic tone of Frédéric Lordon (2009)). We note that, for the young generations, the crisis is a phenomenon into which they were born: they have always known unemployment, blocked horizons, the fear of loss of status, and the perspective of a future with neither landmarks nor hope. We also note some observations about the power of shareholders, which has replaced that of managers, or about the milieu of the traders, including, astonishingly enough, the fact that in France the best students of the Grandes Écoles— the future elites—have, since the 1990s, been choosing to study financial mathematics to gain access to mythical salaries. What distinguishes sociological analysis from economic analysis is not necessarily the opposition between the idea of a classical crisis and a structural crisis. In fact, the distance is greater if we consider the spectrum of categories that are relevant to any consideration of the crisis. From a sociological point of view, apart from the fact that the crisis is not solely financial or even economic in a broader sense of the term, its primary sources possibly lie elsewhere in general cultural, social, and political dynamics. In the last resort, the crisis must be set in the overall context of changes at the global level, which concern demography,[1] our relationship to the environment and to the climate, and our habits in matters of diet, consumption, and production. It punctuates the changes in its domain, which can also be seen in the crises concerning energy or food, and changes that are related to the internet and the considerable space that digital technologies now occupy in our lives. It is

[1] See, e.g., Henri Leridon (2009); he considers that the fall in population growth since 1969 is linked to the emergence of discussions on zero growth and the appearance of the concept of sustainable development.

also explained by political developments, starting with the acceptance, since the mid-1970s, of the withdrawal of the state and a form of deregulation associated with the decline in the classical models and ideologies of the left. Nowadays the left is like an orphan with no parent communism—even social democracy has increasing difficulties in acting as a reference. The crisis is also associated with changes that concern our cognitive models, the way in which we apprehend nature, culture, and their relationship. Finally, it does not affect all social groups in the same way.

There is therefore an immense field for sociological analyses of the present crisis, and not only by merely looking again at the thirteen areas covered by the American series *Studies in the Social Aspects of the Depression* referred to above (family, religion, education, rural life, internal migration, minorities, crime, health, leisure, reading, consumption, social work, and social welfare policies). The main thing to do is to consider which concepts could be useful.

Since no sociological research of any scale seems to have focused on the crisis, there is a temptation to allow a spontaneous form of sociology to occupy the terrain and in that case to insist on the major risks to come: withdrawal of individuals into themselves, in primary groups like the family or into communities; xenophobia, racism, populism, anti-Semitism, search for scapegoats and, finally, fascism or Nazism, the major totalitarian movements. Developments of this sort cannot be excluded, and the media have already given us some occasional examples, in the USA and the UK. But here we have to refuse any oversimplistic determination. After all, in 1933 Roosevelt suggested the New Deal to the Americans and not fascism—nor did the UK become fascist. Today it is true that migrants suffer more than others and that the crisis reveals new migratory geographies. The host countries are making conditions of entry and residence more difficult and expelling undocumented migrants. One direct effect of the crisis is the decline in the financial transfers from migrants to their home countries. But for the time being we cannot speak of waves of racism or xenophobia and even less of fascization of political life. After all, in the USA, it is a black American, Barack Obama, who was elected President, although the crisis had already been declared and his election owes a lot to the fact that he seemed more capable of dealing with it than his Republican opponent.

The very word "crisis" is somewhat foreign to the vocabulary, if not of the social sciences, then at least of sociology. It should be pointed out that it is not always listed in the dictionaries and encyclopedias of sociology (for example, it is not a heading in the recent encyclopedia edited by George

Ritzer and published by Routledge), and, when there is an entry, it is not usually very long. However, though I will not deal with this here, some contemporary sociologists have made it a main focus of study: for example, in France, Edgar Morin (1976) with his "crisology," or Alain Touraine, who edited a collective publication at the same point in time with the eloquent title, *Beyond the crisis* (Touraine et al., 1976).

The two modes of approach, which were described mainly in connection with the proposals of the economists, are an indication of what could be the issues at stake and the theoretical space within which social sciences could deploy research in the face of the crisis. It could be studied while it is still ongoing, focusing on its effects and its implications; it could then be envisaged over time, since the mid-1970s, by seeing therein some of the dimensions of a transformation. The disintegration of one mode of development does not prevent the simultaneous invention of a new mode, which is seeking its way and taking form in all domains, in production, culture, or our modes of knowledge. In this perspective, other crises that are limited geographically, or that belong, at least at the outset, to problems other than finance—for example, in the sphere of energy, new technologies, climate, or food—also have a place in what can be thought of as a general process of change. This, moreover, can have important implications on considerations about the way out of the crisis: whether or not the crisis is long term and not only short term, whether or not it is uniquely financial or even economic, and whether or not it is mingled with dimensions of another type. If it is due to factors that are other than financial and that may even perhaps play a determining role, then answers that are solely financial or even economic will be inadequate and inappropriate.

But under what conditions can the social sciences usefully confront the present crisis, whatever the approach adopted? To answer this question we have to start with these concepts, which can enable them to deal with a transformation as complex as that which engendered the crisis.

Three analytical tools

Social science definitely has analytical tools to offer to those who believe, as we do, that social scientists should make the crisis a priority in their interventions. A comparison enables us make the point forcefully: social scientists cannot continue to go about their business while the boat is sinking.

Michel Wieviorka

The crisis as the problem of a system

The social sciences have developed on the basis of dealing with causes for concern that frequently evoked the idea of crisis. Thus the concept of anomie, popularized by Emile Durkheim, refers directly to the idea of crisis. From this point of view, crisis means that a system (in particular a social, political, or economic one) is not working well, is getting stuck, and changing in a way that cannot be controlled; this engenders reactions in behavior that are themselves linked, for example, to frustrations and fears.

Anomie in Durkheim's definition of the term is the lack or inefficacy of norms in a society. Durkheim introduced the concept of anomie (the word had been used before him by Guyau, 1887) in *The Division of Labour in Society* (1893) and used it primarily in *Suicide* (1897). In particular, he differentiated between anomic suicide and other modalities of the phenomenon: anomic suicide occurs when norms are absent, or else is due to the fact that anomie is long-standing—for example, in industrial work, or in trade, or when an abrupt transition leads to loss of efficacy of norms that no longer succeed in regulating behavior. For example, in times of financial crisis, anomie incites suicide.

In an article that is frequently quoted (Merton, 1938), the concept of anomie was taken up again and transformed by Robert Merton to explain deviance: with Merton, anomie ceases to be in the norms and values that become confused or disappear, as in Durkheim; it resides in the means to succeed in achieving aims or legitimate, clear values that are in no way in crisis: the deviant accepts values that are socially recognized but he uses non-legitimate means to achieve them. The values may, for example, be individual success; the legitimate means to achieve this are, for example, work or education. Now some people are going to use illegitimate means, such as crime or delinquency, to achieve the individual success that others merit as a result of study or professional activities. Now this idea leads to the hypothesis of the conformism of deviants: like everyone else they want money or signs of social success, but they achieve them by means that do not conform.

We should add that the concept of anomie implies that there is a society— an idea that might deserve to be discussed or criticized. The fact remains that, with both Emile Durkheim and the American functionalists of the 1930s, 1940s, or 1950s, the crisis refers in the first instance to the idea of a breakdown in the system, or of a system, and in particular to the idea of a problem of social bond. There is a break or the threat of a break, in solidarity or in the social fabric; there is a lack of confidence.

In some way, spontaneous sociology and also the sociology behind most of the stereotypical discourses on the present crisis accord fairly well with the classical categories and the idea of a close correspondence between society, nation, and the state. In this perspective, measures will be taken by state authorities to restore confidence in economic and financial matters. Furthermore, those in power expect the population to rally behind them in the name of the higher interest of the Nation. The idea that, by combating the crisis efficiently, violence will be avoided, radicalization minimized, and the move to extremes restrained also belongs to this same classical approach. The crisis, here, is a temporary problem in the social system; it is a state of disaster of one or several societies that it is the task of their states to end, with the help of international agreements or negotiations, and by means of appropriate policies—for example, plans for reviving economic growth. Apart from the state, there are not many actors in this type of approach; at the most, there are the actors whose behavior ought to be regulated or governed by public instances—bankers, financiers, and traders who acted improperly in the previous period.

Approaches to the crisis that would originate in Durkheim or in functionalism can lead to the idea that it is time to change the social system, or the type of society, but in most instances they will extend into appeals for an end to the present difficulties and a return to the state ex ante. On this basis, the social scientist can intervene in the discussion—his or her intervention will be aimed at proposing remedies and solutions, rather than helping in the formation of actors and, by clarifying things for these actors, enabling them to improve their mobilization in the face of the crisis. This is why this classical approach is, from my point of view, not so useful.

Crisology

In the mid-1970s, as we have seen, Edgar Morin (1976, 1984) suggested the development of the scientific study of the crisis, or "crisology," and this was a premonitory text because it was written in the historical context where the general transformation that culminated in what we know today as "the crisis" was taking shape. Edgar Morin considered that the crisis can be an event that both reveals and has an effect:

1. *As an event that reveals*: it reveals what usually remains invisible; it forces us to hear things we do not wish to hear. The crisis reveals elements that are inherent to the real and are not merely accidents; it constitutes a moment of truth. Thus we could say that the present crisis reveals unbridled capitalism, in particular financial capitalism, in all its brutality and its extreme injustice. Above all, we see that it constitutes a paroxysm in a process that started long before September 2008.

2. *As an event that has an effect*: Morin considers that the crisis sets in motion not only forces of decomposition, disorganization, and destruction, but also forces of transformation; in these cases it is also a critical point in a process that includes dimensions of construction, innovation, and invention.

This idea of critical point is reinforced by the etymology. The word *krisis* in Greek means decision, and it was first used in medicine: the crisis is the critical point that enables the diagnosis, as Edgar Morin reminds us. From this point of view, the crisis is not only synonymous with congestion, impotence, a situation to be endured, a consequence, and the development of irrational elements. It gives rise to deregulation and hardening of positions, the "paralysis" and "stiffening of what constituted the organizational flexibility of the system," notes Edgar Morin (1984: 144–5). But it also constitutes, on the contrary, a condition that is favorable to the actions and decisions of some actors and becomes an element that enables, or even forces, actors to think and to improve their analysis in order to improve their action. Morin (1984: 140–1) states:

At one and the same time we can grasp the inadequacy and the interest of the concept of crisis: there is something inherent to it which is uncertain since it corresponds to a regression of the determinism specific to the system in question, therefore to a regression in knowledge. But this regression can and must be compensated for by progress in the understanding of the complexity associated with crises.

Continuing in the idea that the crisis both "has an effect" and "reveals," Edgar Morin invites us therefore to admit that the crisis demonstrates that what was a matter of course is in fact a source of difficulties and presents problems: what worked had its limits, its drawbacks, and its inadequacies. The crisis therefore constitutes an incentive to invent something new—but an incentive that is imperative in a very particular context, in which emotions, passions, and fears tend to pervert reason and, in particular, the endeavor to get out of the crisis by rational means. It is a commonplace but one that corresponds to many realities to recall that, in times of crisis, many seek scapegoats, populism is likely to develop, and actors are likely to become more radical; it must be forcefully stated that in times of crisis forms of behavior may also involve sectarianism, and the resort to magic and the irrational, which may assume the garb of messianic movements. The forms of behavior are many and varied and do not conform to any sort of determinism; most of them are all the more alarming, given that actors in a system in crisis develop in ways that are much less foreseeable and much more random than do actors in a system that works. But crisis-type behavior can even take many other forms. In particular, these may also be discouragement and apathy, as Jahoda, Lazarsfeld, and Zeiself (1933) observed in their classical study of unemployed workers in Marienthal, where anomie was the predominant form of behavior at the beginning of the 1930s— before the Nazis transformed it into forms of collective behavior and mobilization.

In a crisis, disorder and rigidity are at work. But, in so far as the crisis is subject to the unknown, in the last resort it does leave room for maneuver, for individual strategies, or for the action of an active minority. The crisis is a disruption of a system in which uncertainties arise, but there are also new opportunities; this disruption is twofold. It operates both in the sphere of social reality and in our knowledge—it opens up new perspectives in action and in learning.

But let us take a step further. Seen from this perspective, is the crisis a characteristic of the system that it affects or does it indicate the way out? If we follow Edgar Morin, it tends to be the first path that we should take. He states that we can only develop a theory of crisis

if we have a theory of society which is also systematic, cybernetic and subject to negative entropy. To understand the crisis, if we want to go beyond the idea of disruption, ordeal and equilibrium, we have to understand society as a system capable of experiencing crises, that is, a complex system which includes antagonisms without which the theory of the society is inadequate and the notion of crisis is unthinkable. (Morin, 1984: 142)

In this case, crisis is a characteristic, in the last resort a property of the complex system constituted by the society, a system that can transform itself or retrieve its own form of regulation. But why not envisage a second path and see the crisis as the convulsion in the transition from one system to another, in any event a deciding phase in a process of change in the system?

Both these hypotheses deserve to be applied to the analysis of actual crises. For example, Lenin in his time adopted the second when he explained that in his opinion the main point was not that the actors be revolutionaries but that the situation be so—that is, defined in terms of crisis. The change in system became possible in Russia in 1917 from the point at which the crisis had become generalized, social, and political but also international and military, and the regime of the Czar was collapsing.

Finally, we also find an interesting question in Morin: does the crisis come from within the system that it affects, or from without? There, too, there is no single answer but separate experiences depending on the crises that are under consideration. The disruption may come from without: for example, in the case of climatic catastrophes. It can also come from within, from a process that at the outset is not a theoretical source of crisis but that produces it, with the result that the system is no longer self-regulating. In Marx, for example, crises in capitalism can originate in a contradiction between the relations of production and the development of the productive forces, which has become too great. The crisis then arises when the system becomes incapable of resolving the difficulties that until then it was capable of resolving. Morin (1984: 143–4) states that the crisis is "the absence of solution (phenomena of deregulation and disorganization) which, as a result, is capable of creating a solution (a new form of regulation, gradual transformation)." Here, he concurs in a way with Michel Dobry (1992), for whom the most interesting aspect of the sociology of crises lies in envisaging not the external disruption but the internal disruption and the processes of deregulation consequent to it—dysfunctioning and deregulation.

Thus, with the "crisology" outlined by Edgar Morin, we have paths or hypotheses that may enable us to tackle the present crises with categories other than those of the stereotypical discourse in which economics and politics predominate. As we shall see, the exercise is worth trying. But the project of creating a new science of "crisology" is not totally satisfying intellectually: crises need researchers that do not isolate them, that do not separate them from their context; they are part of the general collective life; they do not belong to a specific science.

Crisis and conflict

In the social sciences, it is possible to discern ways of thinking that differ from, and are even opposed to, those that focus on society or on the system considered in its totality and in its difficulties to maintain its integration;

these promote an approach based on the idea of an insufficiency, a lack, a loss, or a deficit of conflict. In these cases, the analysis focuses not so much on the system or on the society as on the actors who do not succeed, or no longer succeed, or have not yet succeeded in setting up a conflictual relation, with the crisis representing the complete opposite of this type of relation.

A conflict exists when actors are involved in a relationship, one that they recognize as binding them and opposing them; the actors admit that the relationship involves issues, that these issues are the same for all, and that each of them is endeavoring to control or master them.

These issues can be situated at various levels, and sociological theory may endeavor to rank them. Thus, Alain Touraine (1974) suggested comparing three different levels of conflict, on the one hand, with three different levels of crisis, on the other. He distinguished the highest level in sociological terms, which he called the level of historicity, at which the control of the main orientations of community life are decided:

This distance that society places between itself and its activity, and this action by which it determines the categories of its practice I call historicity. Society is not what it is but what it makes itself be: through knowledge, which creates a state of relations between society and its environment; through accumulation, which subtracts a portion of available product from the cycle leading to consumption; through the cultural model which captures creativity in forms dependent upon the society's practical dominion over its own functioning. (Touraine, 1974: 4)

At the level of historicity, therefore, the conflict, in the vocabulary used by Alain Touraine, refers to the existence of a social movement, which is the action of an actor who is dominated and controlled, engaged in a struggle with the major actors and leaders for the control of historicity. Thus, in an industrial society, the most important issue at stake in the conflict opposing the working-class movement to the employers was the control of the most decisive orientations confronting the organization of labor—namely, the control of investment, and the appropriation and the use of the fruits of labor. As a counterpart, at this level of historicity, the crisis emerges when the social conflict is either not possible or no longer possible, when it is destroyed and overtaken by blocking by the state, its incapacity to act and to represent a social entity not only in its present state but also in its future and in its past; the crisis emerges when there is an absence of state power or when it is reduced to the mere exercise of force and is itself overcome and overwhelmed. A state that is in profound crisis generates reactive forms of behavior, which may ultimately culminate in revolution. For example, in Russia in 1917 there was effectively a social movement of workers, but, if there was a revolution, it was not because the workers and the employers were at loggerheads; it was because the Russian state, as I have said, had collapsed and was losing the war. Moreover, as soon as the Revolution was victorious, the new Soviet power lost no time in crushing the working-class movement and turning the trade unions into "transmission belts" controlled by them. This example nevertheless invites us to recognize that there may be a complex relationship between the social movement and the revolution or the conflict and the crisis, more generally speaking.

Crisis does not necessarily prevent conflict; crisis has an impact on conflict, just as it may also be the origin or the outcome of conflict. Therefore let us be wary of oversimplistic arguments that might evoke an image of a connection between the two, as if the violence of the conflict was inversely related to the extent of the crisis. Reality is more complex. Instead, a more balanced way of putting it would be to say that the sphere of conflict increases when that of the crisis declines and vice versa, but without any notion of this being predetermined or automatic. When this can clarify things, let us be ready to combine in our analyses the hypothesis of conflict and that of crisis, and their interaction when they are mixed. For example, if we take May 1968 in France, we can make an analytical distinction between the dimensions of conflict and of social movement—first the students, then the workers—and elements of crisis, in particular in the university system and the political regime.

Alain Touraine also suggests considering two other levels that are at a lower level, in sociological terms, than that of historicity. At the political or institutional level, there is a crisis if the political system proves to be incapable of dealing with the demands that come from society or from certain sectors of society, if it is blocked, or in the instances when it is incapable of shaping social discussion. For example, Italian terrorism, for which many explanations were advanced in the 1970s and 1980s, was in many respects due to the political crisis. In the context of the rapprochement between the left (the Italian Communist Party, or ICP) and the right (Christian Democrats) moving together toward a "historical compromise," the ICP became incapable of dealing politically with demands that were classically their domain, in particular those that emanated from the youth of the time. Young people, who were often qualified and who, at the time, could find jobs only on production lines, dreamt of another culture and, realizing that the university was becoming a way of parking them, were swept into the violence of terrorist organizations[2]—generally speaking, crisis-type conduct often takes the form of violence.

At the political or institutional level, the conflict, as opposed to the crisis, assumes the garb of pressures from actors to improve their relative position within a political system to gain entry or to increase their influence—this is the main lesson of what is known as the theory of mobilization of resources.

Lastly, and still in the wake of Alain Touraine, at an even lower level, there is an opposition between crisis and conflict within organizations; in these instances the conflict is a relationship within which actors endeavor to obtain a better reward in return for their contribution, and the organizational crisis is a sign of disorganization, an incapacity to deal with internal problems and to face the outside world. It expresses deterioration, a hiatus between values and discourse; here also it may be conveyed by violent forms of conduct.

In all cases, violence may equally well be associated with a conflict and in this case appear as instrumental, like a tool or a resource mobilized by some actors to achieve their aims, or be associated with a crisis, for example, in the form of a riot, of purely expressive—even desperate—forms of conduct.

Now let us consider how these theoretical or general considerations can help in clarifying our understanding of the present crisis.

The crisis as absence, loss, or insufficiency of conflict

Let us begin by considering the specifically social dimensions of the crisis. The effects are all the more devastating as the major principle of conflict that structured societies like those of Western Europe for at least a century and until the mid-1970s—that is, the opposition between the working-class movement and the employers—is no longer fundamental. Until recently it was still possible to contrast the Rhine model of capitalism, in which trade unions and governing boards of firms confronted each other in the context of highly institutionalized conflict, and the neo-American model, which prioritized shareholders and financial, or even speculative, rationales (see, e.g., Albert, 1991).

---

[2] I take this example, since I made an in-depth study of it; see Wieviorka (1988).

Michel Wieviorka

The neo-American model, which seems to have gained the upper hand since then, signified the absolute domination of shareholders over managers, of very short-term economic viability of investment in preference to the long-term stability of the firm. If the economy has suddenly decelerated, is this only due to a lack of liquidity? Is it not also because modes of organization have prioritized flexibility, the implications of which have been so well described by Richard Sennett (2005), at the expense of rationales of production, and encouraging conflict in the structure of social relationships in firms between managers and wage-earners?

Two questions arise here. The first is that of the capacity of trade unionism to make a comeback as a mobilized force in the firm, but also, further, to have an impact as an actor of a political type. Can we imagine a revival of trade union action? Does this not imply new forms of militancy or specifically conditions that encourage wage-earners to join trade unions? There would need to be appreciable changes in the running and management of firms, the end of "neo-American" capitalism, which seems an unrealistic aim and not one that is at the forefront of trade union mobilization at the moment. The second question is: is trade unionism capable of projecting itself into the future by contributing to the invention of new modes of development? Is it not profoundly attached to the previous model, a prisoner of its major orientations, to the point that, when it does succeed in mobilizing, it runs the risk of temporarily reviving the old system rather than contributing to the construction of a new one? At the end of the 1970s and in the 1980s some trade unions, like the Conféderation Française Démocratique du Travail (CFDT) in France, had innovated by presenting themselves—timidly, it is true—as the political operator of new challenges, including, in particular, the ecologists, women, and the anti-nuclear movement. This idea deserves to be re-examined and updated. It does enable the trade union itself to be the traditional defender of wage-earners, jobs, and the standard of living, while at the same time contributing to struggles that are not specific to it but that it recognizes as playing a role in leading us towards a new era.

Now, let us look closely at the conflicts that signpost this entry, in particular, at the alter-globalist struggles.

In the 1990s the realization of the global nature of the major problems in the present-day world was the driving force behind what was best in the alter-globalist movement. At this point, this movement was pleading in favor of another form of alter-globalization: it introduced another principle of conflict into the public sphere.

Since then, it has declined—a collateral victim in particular of the attacks on September 11, 2001, which is not to say that it is, historically speaking, bound to disappear—undermined by extreme politicization, which frequently transforms it into an anti-imperialist, anti-war, and anti-American force. Its decline deprives the discussions about the crisis and the way out of the crisis of a challenge that, in its time, did put an end to the arrogance of Davos. Paradoxically, it is an element in the present difficulties, because it deprives us, in the wake of the decline of trade unionism, of a second principle of conflict. At a broader level, the severity of the present crisis seems to be accentuated by the difficulty that the challenges concerning the planet, the environment, the supranational regulation of economic life, the existence of a world level form of justice, and so on have in constructing a broader sphere for discussion and conflict.

Whether it be a question of trade unionism, of new social movements, or of global movements with their strong cultural and social dimensions, there is one hypothesis that seems to us to merit our attention: for social scientists, consideration of the way out of the crisis should mean analyzing the conditions that would enable the production and stimulation of actors engaged in conflicts.

References

Albert, Michel (1991). *Capitalisme contre capitalisme*. Paris: Seuil.

Attali, Jacques (2008). *La Crise et après?* Paris: Fayard.

Camic, Charles (2007). "Sociology during the Great Depression and the New Deal," in Craig Calhoun (ed.), *Sociology in America: A History*. Chicago: University of Chicago Press, 225–80.

Le Cercle des économistes (2009). *Fin de monde ou sortie de crise?*, ed. Pierre Dockès and Jean-Hervé Lorenzi. Paris: Perrin.

Chapin, F. Stuart (1935). *Contemporary American Institutions: A Sociological Analysis*. New York: Harper.

Cohen, Daniel (2009). *La Prospérité du vice*. Paris: Albin Michel.

Dobry, Michel (1992). "Brève note sur les turpitudes de la crisologie: Que sommes nous en droit de déduire des multiples usages du 'mot' crise?", *Cahiers de la sécurité intérieure (IHESI)*, 7 (Jan.).

Durkheim, Emile (1893). *The Division of Labour in Society*. New York: Free Press.

—— (1897). *Suicide*. New York: Free Press, 1951.

Guyau, Jean-Marie (1887). *Esquisse d'une morale sans obligation*. Paris: F. Alcan.

Michel Wieviorka

Jahoda, Marie, Lazarsfeld, Paul F., and Zeisel, Hans (1933). *Die Arbeitslosen von Marienthal*. Bonn: Allensbach. Eng. trans., New Brunswick, NJ: Transaction Publishers, 2002.

Leridon, Henri (2009). *De la croissance zéro au développement durable*. Paris: Collège de France/Fayard.

Lordon, Frédéric (2009). *La Crise de trop: Reconstruction d'un monde failli*. Paris: Fayard.

Lynd, Robert (1929). *Middletown: A Study in Contemporary Culture*. New York: Harcourt, Brace & Company.

Maalouf, Amin (2009). *Le Dérèglement du monde*. Paris: Grasset.

Merton, Robert (1938). "Social Structure and Anomie," *American Sociological Review*, 3: 672–82.

Morin, Edgar (1976). "Pour une crisologie," *Communications*, 25: 149–63.

—— (1984). "Pour une théorie de la crise," in Edgar Morin, *Sociologie*. Paris: Fayard, 139–53. (First published as Morin, 1976.)

Schroeder, Paul L., and Burgess, Ernest W. (1938). "Introduction," in Ruth Shonle Cavan and Katherine Howland Ranck (eds), *The Family and the Depression: A Study of One Hundred Chicago Families*. Chicago: University of Chicago Press, pp. vii–xii.

Sennett, Richard (2005). *The Culture of the New Capitalism*. New Haven: Yale University Press.

Stiegler, Bernard (2009). *Pour une nouvelle critique de l'économie politique*. Paris: Galilée.

Touraine, Alain (1974). *Production de la société*. Paris: Seuil.

—— et al. (1976). *Au-delà de la crise*. Paris: Seuil.

Wieviorka, Michel (1988). *Sociétés et terrorisme*. Paris: Fayard.

PART THREE

Dealing with the Crisis

The aftermath is a time of change. It is a time when a return to the past is wished for but at the same time we hope to find the rise of the new. As is discussed in this chapter, the search for the return to the old or the rebuilding of the projected new means different things to different people and institutions. What the analysis in this part shows us is the shared need to deal with the crisis and build new narratives and instruments in order to overcome it and adapt to its aftermaths. The approaches to these new narratives on how to deal with the crisis can be built either by new political parties promoting nationalisms, by the state in search of a new identity, by companies and their brands hoping to rebrand the crisis, or by "indignants" in different latitudes and longitudes around the globe trying to make their voices heard.

If economic exchange is organized by cultural meanings, in dealing with the crisis we must also take into consideration insight on the economic practice of advertising. Companies and brands have not turned their backs on the crisis; on the contrary, they have brought to their narratives, through advertisement, the "crisis" as an inevitable obstacle in the road to progress through capitalism. Companies, through their brands, deal with the crisis by asking individuals to overcome and rebuild their lives in the aftermath of a crisis, as both a moral and a national obligation, branding it as a continuous relationship with a special product: capitalism itself.

Products and brands rely on trust-building between people and companies, but trust essentially depends, in a globalized mediated society, on media's ability—be it through mass, self-mass, one-to-many, or interpersonal multimedia—to build it. This part also focuses its analysis on what we do with the consequences of globalization; namely, what is the role of media and how do people react to media's (in)ability to (re)build trust in the aftermath. Media played a fundamental role in the loss of trust in 2007/8, in the search for respondents and the attempts to reconstruct trust through the mediation of new voices. Some of those new voices are focusing on the acceptability of blaming people in other countries for the problems the new global economy has created; other voices are searching for what is common to the problems and what could be common to their solutions. Nationalists and "The Indignants" are some of those voices looking for a space to be heard in the global mediated societies. If the aftermath is a time of big recession, it is also a time for the state to question itself in search of a new identity for dealing with the economic crisis, the welfare state, and cultural identity. The issues raised here lead us to question the ability of actors and institutions to build a project identity based on a more sustainable development model in the network society: does their inability to do so translate the crisis into a more socially and culturally violent environment? The answer lies probably in the need to look beyond the aftermath.

Chapter 5

Branding the Crisis

Sarah Banet-Weiser[*]

As is clear from the varied chapters in this volume, there are complex, multi-layered, and deeply interrelated reasons for, and effects of, the global economic crisis of 2008. During the years 2007/8, around the world, stock markets fell, large financial institutions collapsed or were bought out, and governments in even the wealthiest nations scrambled to develop rescue packages to bail out their financial systems. The collapse of the US subprime mortgage market and the reversal of the housing boom in other industrialized economies had a ripple effect in other nations. The failure of the national economies of Spain and Greece (to name just two) has had resounding effects on the European Union (EU) and global trade. In this chapter, I do not attempt to explain the varied causes of the global economic crisis, or to presume to know what its lasting effects will be. Indeed, it is impossible to predict long-term effects, for the responses by different nation states to the global crisis have been so varied. Many responses are contradictory; it is clear that capitalist exchange does not circulate in the same way

* I would like to thank Kevin Driscoll, Melissa Brough, and Evan Brody for their helpful feedback, suggestions, and research assistantship. I am also grateful to Manuel Castells for the brainstorming sessions that led to this article, as well as the entire Aftermath group for their insightful feedback.

in different spheres of life. The global economic crisis and its aftermaths demonstrate social economist Viviana Zelizer's important point (2011) that economic exchange is organized by cultural meanings.

However, contemporary culture also comes at this dynamic from the opposite direction: cultural meanings are organized by economic exchange. The culture of the economy, and the economy of culture, has generated a variety of impulses and reactions to the Great Recession of the early twenty-first century: there have been financial responses in the form of government bailouts; subversive challenges to capitalism in terms of alternative lifestyles including the global Occupy movements ideological proclamations about what capitalism is and should be; recuperative answers that privilege a new, "leaner," global market; and so on (for more on alternative responses, see Conill et al., Chapter 9, this volume). Here, I am interested in how the cultural meaning of the economic crisis of 2008 is organized by the practice of advertising. In particular, I am interested in how advertising works to brand the crisis as an inevitable obstacle in the progressive march of capitalism, one that individuals are asked as both a moral and a national obligation to "overcome." While I take a somewhat narrow approach, analyzing two specific corporate ad campaigns, the branding strategies employed by these campaigns rely on a broader post-crisis trope, one that uses a recuperative, capital-friendly narrative to mobilize and authorize the American working class to deal with the crisis individually, rather than call a flawed capitalist structure into question. Rhetorics of hope, meritocracy, and new frontiers are used to frame these ads, and thus maintain a narrative of American liberal exceptionalism as well as a neo-liberal mandate for individuals to "take care of themselves" (Foucault, 2010).

More specifically, the ads I analyze position America as "broken" by the global economic crisis. Yet this same malfunction is also framed by these ads as a unique, and perhaps even destined, quality of "Americanness"; through a powerful visual and textual narrative, the ads position US corporate culture as offering the means for individuals to rescue the broken nation. The cases I examine offer particularly clear examples of the relationship between the economics of culture and the culture of economics, and of the ways in which corporate brands may attempt to reconcile their contradictory positions through the reconfiguration of classic American tropes with a contemporary neo-liberal twist.

In Chapter 6 in this volume, Terhi Rantanen points out the role of trust in the twenty-first-century global economic collapse. Along with national budgets and personal savings, trust has been lost in the Great Recession;

trust individuals had in their nations, governments, banks, and media. The downward spiral of trust Rantanen analyzes also partly involves the trust individuals have in brands; the failure of the Big Three automobile manufacturers in the USA (Chrysler, GM and Ford) and the failure of banks such as Lehman Brothers and Goldman Sachs were not simply about the financial failure of companies, but, more diffusely, about the failure of brands in which individuals trusted their lives and their livelihoods. For brands, then, as with banks, the job becomes how to rebuild trust. This means, in part, imagining a powerful narrative to salvage the brand's constitutive story. It also means positioning the individual as a shifted central character in the story of the brand. Rather than call attention to larger infrastructural failures that contributed to the global economic crisis (such as mortgage fraud, corporate greed, and so on), contemporary efforts to brand the crisis frame it as an opportunity for—indeed, a moral obligation of—the individual worker to address. In a time of globalization and global crisis, it is surely the case that the nation is more important than ever; fluid economic boundaries and cultural hybridity do not make the nation obsolete, but rather center its importance ever more firmly, precisely because the nation is under threat (for more on the history of crisis, see Williams, Chapter 1, this volume). Recentering the nation, and the individual citizen's role in the nation, in a brand narrative is one way to reassert cultural control over an otherwise destabilizing crisis narrative. Advertising is a particularly rich and central vehicle through which to do so.

Thus, against press accounts in the USA that breathlessly proclaimed "the death of capitalism" in the wake of the global financial crisis of 2008 (Foster, 2009), I analyze two American advertising campaigns as a method of unpacking the ways in which some US companies did not, in fact, celebrate the death of capitalism in the least, but rather worked to "brand" the crisis in such a way as to obscure some of the lasting ravages of capitalist power on individual and collective subjectivities. The ad campaigns I examine (both well-known American campaigns) work in an affective register, establishing a relationship between consumers and corporations as a media assemblage, a cohering force, in the chaos and uncertainty that accompanies global economic crisis (for more on media assemblage, see Ong, 2006). Historically, advertising has had a crucial role in nation-building, through its reassuring messages to citizens that consumption not only should be a habit, but is more profoundly a national duty (for more on the role of advertising in nation-building, see Sturken and Cartwright, 2009). In the contemporary moment, advertising continues to create narratives that work to validate and confirm the nation and national identity. But, in the aftermath of the 2008 global economic crisis, advertising, as well as other strategies such as corporate public relations and marketing campaigns, go a step further, and brand the crisis for consumers. Indeed, the efforts of contemporary US corporations to brand the crisis as an opportunity for American workers to address renders the global economic crisis culturally consumable.

What is involved in branding the economic crisis? The ad campaigns I examine here narratively account for the Great Recession in abstract terms, placing no specific blame on any one entity. Rather, the ads I examine signify and offer a narrative of how the nation and its citizens need to overcome crisis. The Great Recession has witnessed ongoing shifts in the legitimacies of the liberal welfare state, as well as the coincident turn in attitudes toward social and redistributive programs hitherto managed and administered by the state, which raises troubling questions about the merits and meaning of the nation state, globalization, and the consumer-citizen in the current era (see further Duggan, 2003; Harvey, 2005; Castells, 2009; Brown, 2001; Mukherjee and Banet-Weiser, 2012; and other chapters in this volume). One space that authorizes a specific role of the consumer-citizen as a nation-builder is advertising; as a space of affect, of sentiment, of feeling, advertising provides reassurance in the face of these troubling questions. As Michael Schudson (1986: 232) said about the role of advertising in the USA, advertising is "capitalism's way of saying 'I love you' to itself." But when capitalism has failed, and the world is in economic crisis, how is this love regained, reimagined, rethought?

The normalization of brand culture is not a consequence of the 2008 global economic collapse. To the contrary, branding and brand strategies have influenced liberal and post-Fordist capitalism for decades. However, as I have pointed out, it was certainly the case that part of what occurred in the recent global financial collapse was a failure of brands—brands such as Goldman Sachs, Lehman Brothers, and so on. Brands, and brand culture, are increasingly critical cultural elements in the Western world in the twenty-first century, so, when some of the biggest brands failed, it is not surprising that eventually an effort to rebrand, and thus rebuild, corporate culture would take place.

Here, though, I look at two specific strategies that have worked to rebrand corporate culture, and have in turn worked to brand the crisis itself. Rather than examine the hegemonic behemoths that were so visibly at the center of the crisis, such as the banks, the International Monetary Fund (IMF), and so on, I look at two US spaces that were hit hardest by the financial crisis: the automobile industry and the Rust Belt industrial towns in the north-eastern United States. Using nostalgic, jingoistic representations and rhetoric, the Chrysler automobile company and Levi's clothing brand have launched new campaigns that brand the crisis as a space of possibility—the possibility for an underdog, in the case of Chrysler, and for a new frontier, in the case of Levi's. Before I analyze the specific ad campaigns, however, it is necessary to set the context for their emergence.

Brand culture

Again, because capitalism circulates in culture in varied ways, there are different responses to the current global economic crisis. One cultural response (in the USA and elsewhere) has been to stage the crisis as a kind of "media event" (Dayan and Katz, 1994). As Daniel Dayan and Elihu Katz (1994) have argued, media events are those historic events that are broadcast through the media as they are happening, as a kind of world ritual, what they call "high holidays of mass communication." The ongoing global economic crisis takes shape as a media event in a variety of ways: through staged debates on television, pundits arguing over the causes of the crisis, and hysterical "shock jocks" on talk radio placing blame on liberal politics (Smith, 2011). As Rantanen notes in her chapter in this volume: "The media use primarily a national frame when they try to make sense of global events such as the world economic crisis." While she is discussing the role of the news media in this sense-making, another way the twenty-first century global economic crisis has been constructed as a media event is through the branding of the crisis. As a key component of branding, advertising also has a central role in establishing a narrative, as well as a relationship, between corporate culture and consumers, that assists individuals in interpreting the world economic crisis, again through a national frame. Clearly, advertising is more than discrete media artifacts, and more than simply an economic tool for selling products (see, e.g., Ewen, 2001; Schudson, 1986; Rosalind Williams, 1991; Jackson Lears, 1994; Goldman and Papson, 1996; Sturken and Cartwright, 2009). Advertising is a social and cultural system; it is part of what Raymond Williams (1961) defined as a "structure of feeling," an ethos of intangible qualities that resonate in different ways with distinct communities. As a social and cultural system, advertising and branding help to create this "intangible" ethos that resonates in affective,

111

emotional ways for a variety of citizens. But branding is also part of what Ruth Wilson Gilmore (2007) calls an "infrastructure of feeling," a broader, more diffused environment that undergirds, legitimates, and authorizes capitalist circuits of economic and cultural exchange.

As I have argued elsewhere (Banet-Weiser, 2012), branding became a specifically cultural phenomenon in the USA in the 1980s. During this time, corporations and businesses began to concentrate less on manufacturing and more on the marketing of goods, labor began to be outsourced from the USA in significant numbers, and branding began to take on a heightened economic significance and cultural value, as Naomi Klein (2000) has argued. Within advanced capitalism, brand strategies and management are situated not merely as economic principles or good business, but as the affective stuff of culture. That is, neo-liberal practices do not merely protect existing markets but are also expansive, creating new or transformed markets in areas conventionally seen as outside the market, such as creativity, politics, and religion (Duggan, 2003; Harvey, 2005; see also Banet-Weiser, 2012). Thus, within neo-liberal capitalism, those realms of culture and society once considered "outside" the official economy are harnessed, re-shaped, and made legible in economic—and cultural—terms. One result of neo-liberal practices has been the re-imagining of not just economic transactions and resources, but also practices and institutions such as social relations, individual relations, emotion, social action, and culture itself. Among other things, neo-liberalism, like liberalism, privileges a free market ideology and focuses on the individual at the expense of social and public services. Liberalism, as a political doctrine and ideological practice, centers on the individual: in the political language of traditional liberalism, empowerment is about exercising one's individual rights to speak, to have a voice, to be heard, to "make a difference," and to own and accumulate profit and property (Couldry, 2010). In neo-liberal brand culture, individual empowerment and voice are connected primarily to the market, evidenced in the strategies and practices of branding logic, and in the privileging of the entrepreneurial subject.

Rather than insert brands into existing culture, then, contemporary brand managers seek to build culture around brands through emotive relationships. Marketers talk incessantly of "engagement," new branches of advertising and marketing firms are devoted to using social media as a way to authentically interact with consumers, and marketers in general are accepting a loosening of control over messaging (Banet-Weiser, 2012). Branding strategies focus on cultivating affective, authentic relationships between consumers and producers, and building culture out of these relationships. Within brand culture, consumers produce identity, community, emotional attachments, affective practices, and relationships; brand culture within neo-liberal capitalism provides an infrastructure for this kind of social and political behavior. For marketers in the contemporary USA, building a brand is about building an affective, authentic relationship with a consumer, one based on a set of memories, emotions, personal narratives, and expectations.

To argue that branding attempts to create relationships with consumers is not in turn to insist that advertising, as a component of branding, "works" to persuade individuals to buy particular products. The ad campaigns I examine here, Chrysler and Levi's, are not striking for their success in selling more cars or jeans (although Chrysler does attest to an increase in sales after the Super Bowl ad). Rather, they are conspicuous for the ways in which they establish an affective relationship with consumers, one that brands the economic crisis as a problem, indeed, an inevitable consequence, of entrepreneurial individualism. The affective relationships with brands are slippery, mobile, and often ambiguous, which makes them powerful but also difficult to predict and characterize precisely. Cultural practices are expressed and validated through brands. Not merely an economic strategy of capitalism, brands are the cultural spaces in which individuals feel safe, secure, relevant, and authentic. This is the space in which the Chrysler and Levi's campaigns make sense and shore up ideologies about American exceptionalism and individualism.

As not just economic tools, but also cultural statements within broader brand culture, advertisements cultivate relationships between consumers and brands through the use of resonant tropes and ideologies such as individual empowerment and entrepreneurialism. Advertising has, of course, long relied upon affective rhetoric and a focus on the individual. To take one of the starker examples, in 1984 the Ronald Reagan presidential committee produced a political ad called "Prouder, Stronger, Better." The ad opens to a mélange of images featuring Americans (all white Americans) going to work: a barge in the Hudson river, a man getting out of a taxi, a farmer on a tractor, a young boy riding his bike on his newspaper route. The voiceover, a calm, soothing male voice, begins:

It's morning again in America. Today more men and women will go to work than ever before in our country's history. With interest rates at about half the record highs of 1980, nearly 2,000 families today will buy new homes, more than at any time in the past four years. This afternoon 6,500 young men and women will be married, and with inflation at less than half of what it was just four years ago, they can look forward with confidence to the future. It's morning again in America, and under the leadership of President Reagan, our country is prouder and stronger and better. Why would we ever want to return to where we were less than four short years ago?

"Morning in America" relies upon patriotic tropes and a utopian tone to convey its "product," Ronald Reagan. What is different about advertising within the contemporary moment of branding? While American exceptionalism has long been a trope in advertising, as is evidenced by "Morning in America," in the current moment the role of the individual consumer-citizen is more prominent (see, e.g., the discussion of advertising in Sturken and Cartwright, 2009). In contemporary brand culture, advertising offers a promise, one that can be fulfilled in the relationship between branding and consumer citizens. But in the middle of the Great Recession, what is the promise that is offered? How can advertising and branding infuse an affective relationship into an economic crisis, and rebrand it as an opportunity for affective recuperation? Indeed, economic crisis, financial devastation, and individual loss hardly seem to promise much except for more financial, cultural, and individual ruin. But as Michel Wieviorka argues in this volume, there are a variety of different narratives that are invoked in attempts to explain and justify the global economic crisis. I now turn to two 2011 advertising and branding campaigns by Chrysler and Levi's as a way to demonstrate how, and in what ways, the Great Recession of the twenty-first century is being branded. As the examples I consider here illustrate, advertising and branding narratives offer a promise that seemingly is only available because of the economic crisis; an opportunity to re-build; a rewriting of a historical American mythology of individual enterpreneurship, rugged labor and work ethic, and the open frontier.

Chrysler: Imported from Detroit

During the 2011 Super Bowl in the United States, the Chrysler Group aired an advertisement for its new car, the Chrysler 200. Though Chrysler is run by Fiat chief Sergio Marchionne (Fiat owned the majority share of Chrysler at the time of writing), it is one of the "Big Three" American automobile companies. The two-minute ad (the longest advertisement in Super Bowl history), which cost approximately $9 million, was created by the ad company Wieden + Kennedy. It featured a montage of images and themes around the city of Detroit, MI, and starred native Detroit musician Eminem. At the time of writing, the YouTube version of the ad had almost twelve million viewers (YouTube, 2011).

According to Chrysler's webpage, after the initial Super Bowl ad launched the campaign, the Chrysler Group LLC had its first profitable quarter since it had filed for bankruptcy in 2009. While in 2010 the company suffered a $197 million net loss, their profits improved in 2011, increasing net revenues by 35 percent in the second quarter of 2011 (Chrysler Group LLC, 2011). Chrysler CFO, Richard Palmer, said about the ad: "It clearly had a fairly big impact also on market levels with (the) Eminem Super Bowl ad being extremely well-viewed on YouTube . . . And [introduced] the tag line 'Imported from Detroit'." (This tagline is especially interesting in the context of nation branding, which, in its current form, seems very much a phenomenon of globalization/global markets.)

The Chrysler Super Bowl ad is part of a larger ad campaign launched by Chrysler in 2011, titled *Good Things Come to Those Who Work*. The ad is a homage to the city of Detroit, featuring iconic landmarks, cityscapes, and working people. The ad opens to shots of factories, cutting quickly to interstate road signs that introduce the name "Detroit." The camera pans to landmarks of Detroit: the iron fist of Joe Louis, a Diego Rivera mural, the United Auto Workers gear monument, the Campus Martius ice rink, the opulent Renaissance Center. The camera then cuts to downtown Detroit, dazzling with buildings and architectural detail from an earlier historical moment, when Detroit was one of the richest cities in the USA. The voiceover begins:

I got a question for ya. What does this city know about luxury? Huh? What does a town that's been to hell and back know about the finer things in life?

Well, I'll tell ya. More than most. You see, it's the hottest fires that make the hardest steel. Add hard work and conviction, and the knowhow of generations that runs deep in every last one of us . . . [music begins, Eminem's 'Lose Yourself']

That's who we are. That's our story. Now, it's probably not the one you've been reading in the papers, the one that's being written by folks who've never even been here and who don't know what we're capable of. Because when it comes to luxury it's as much about where it's from as who it's for.

Now, we're from America, but this isn't New York City. Or the Windy City. Or Sin City. And we're certainly no one's Emerald City.

The voiceover culminates with a shot of hip-hop star Eminem driving a black Chrysler 200 down historic Woodward Avenue, and ends when he pulls up to the iconic Fox Theater, built in 1928 and restored in 1988, with the marquis reading "Keep Detroit Beautiful." As the music crescendoes, Eminem walks into the theatre, where an African-American gospel choir is on stage, softly singing. Eminem turns to the camera and points, saying: "This is the Motor City. And this is what we do." The ad fades to black with the Chrysler logo, and the tagline appears: "Imported from Detroit."

The Super Bowl ad resonated with many Detroit citizens as well as others (as can be seen from the number of views of the ad on YouTube); the blogosphere and television talk shows covered the ad as if it were an isolated television event. The cinematography, the nods to history, the mixing of labor and luxury, the reference to the fact that the city has "been to hell and back," all resonated with American mythologies of work ethic, nationalism, the underdog, and Horatio Alger narratives of meritocracy and bootstrap mentality. It also spoke to American paranoia about outsourced labor ("The Chrysler 200 has arrived. Imported from Detroit"), and the impact neo-liberal labor practices have had on the economic vitality of US cities based in industry, such as Detroit. The tagline "Imported from Detroit" also asks viewers to reimagine Detroit as a burgeoning, vibrant urban center, rather than a city of despair (Spence, 2011).

Indeed, Detroit's infrastructure has long been in despair, fraught by economic recession, racial tension, and drastic unemployment. The Chrysler ad centrally features Woodward Avenue, the thoroughfare that divides the east of Detroit from the west. This is the same avenue that is historically the home of African Americans in Detroit, who were forbidden because of racist housing policies to live in white neighborhoods (Sugrue, 1996; Lipsitz, 2006). Detroit has been, and continues to be, one of the most racially segregated urban cities in the USA; historically, de-industrialization, unemployment, poverty, and "white flight" meant for Detroit, among other things, that "increasing joblessness, and the decaying infrastructure of inner-city neighborhoods, reinforced white stereotypes of black people, families, and communities" (Sugrue, 1996: 8).

Obviously, there is much to comment upon regarding the disconnect between the advertisement's aggressive jingoistic and regionalist ideology and the various ways in which the city of Detroit is emblematic of so much that was part of the global economic crisis. Not only had the city of Detroit shaped the current state of the auto industry, and been shaped by it, but Chrysler in particular was one of the first companies to need federal bailout funding after the global economic collapse of 2008. That the Chrysler ad is the most expensive ad in Super Bowl history (at a staggering $9 million for two minutes) obscures the fact that Chrysler has received $15 billion in bailout funds from the US government since 2008, and has subsequently closed down numerous plants in the Detroit area—and thus cost thousands their jobs (Flint, 2009; Freire, 2011). As the city of Detroit has been increasingly devastated by economic recession, with the unemployment rate soaring (in 2011 it remained higher than any other big city in the USA), as the school system has failed (recent news of the Detroit public school system has reported that in some classrooms the student:teacher ratio is 60:1), as racial conflict and violence continue to be a problem in one of the most starkly segregated urban centers in the USA, and as the city's government is widely rumored to be a hotbed of nepotism and handouts for friends of city officials, many Detroit citizens have felt that the Big Three automobile companies housed in Detroit (Chrysler, GM, and Ford) have merely sat by and watched (*Detroit Free Press*, 2008; Flint, 2009; *Corrupt Authority*, 2010; Bureau of Labor Statistics, 2011; Corey Williams, 2011). Indeed, historically, the automobile companies of Detroit have discouraged diversification of the city's economy, so that, when the nation fell into a global economic collapse, there was virtually no other economic infrastructure for the city residents to rely upon. (Sugrue (1996) historicizes Detroit's resistance to diversifying its economy.)

But the hypocritical logic that undergirds this ad does not necessarily present cognitive dissonance on the part of the viewer. Rather, this is precisely how the process of branding works; the ad affectively brands the crisis as an opportunity for individuals—in this case, the individuals who reside in Detroit—to re-establish their citizenship, their patriotism, their loyalty, and their trust. The choice of Eminem as a spokesperson for Chrysler, complete with the licensing of his hit song "Lose Yourself" as the background anthem for the campaign, resonates with the nostalgic visual representation of Detroit in the ad. Eminem was apparently taken with the ad's promise to show Detroit "at its grayest and grimmest" and wanted to be part of showing Detroit in all its rawness and contradiction (Kiley, 2011). The narrative of Detroit, Eminem, and global economic crash resonates with a newly inspired Horatio Alger myth: in 2011 *Advertising Age* magazine referred to Eminem as "the comeback story of the year," which is another association the corporate owners would like to see for Chrysler, as well as for the City of Detroit—and definitely not least, the comeback of capitalism after global economic collapse. As *Advertising Age* (2011) put it in an analysis of the ad campaign: "What starts out as a down-on-our-luck tribute to a broken city morphs into a defiant, we're-back rallying cry."

Chrysler is not the only US company to capitalize on American mythologies of nostalgia and economic anxiety in the aftermath of the 2008 global economic crisis, however. The iconic jean company Levi's also tapped into similar images and ideologies in their 2010 ad campaign *Go Forth*. Both ad campaigns work powerfully at the affective register, both focus on the economic devastation of the US Rust Belt, and both exploit what some have called "ruin" or "poverty" pornography (Stevenson, 2009; Weinstein, 2011).

Levi's: *Go Forth*

The clothing company Levi's created an extensive ad campaign in 2010 that centrally featured the struggling steel mill town of Braddock, Pennsylvania, in the heart of the Rust Belt in north-eastern USA. The campaign, titled *Go Forth*, puts a nostalgic and optimistic spin on the decline of the blue-collar laborer and industry in the USA, and clearly attempts to address American anxiety in a global economic recession. The ads capitalize on a historical rhetoric of American pioneers, and visually resemble the Chrysler Super Bowl ad; not surprisingly, the ad campaign was created by the same firm who created the Chrysler "Imported from Detroit" ad, Wieden + Kennedy. Unlike the Chrysler ad and its depiction of iconic, recognizable images specifically from Detroit, the Levi's ad features more generalized images. While it is implied that the images were shot in Braddock, PA, the visuality of the ads clearly resonate with many small towns in the USA; they conjure a generally recognizable Rust Belt industry town. Unlike the Chrysler ad, the Levi's ads depict images of heartbreak and depression alongside more nostalgic images of a "simpler" time. One ad, for instance, opens with a man and a dog sitting in front of a campfire in a vast field as a freight train rushes by; followed by panning shots of abandoned buildings framed by the rising sun; old, broken cars and toys under fallen trees; and then a small child jumping into bed with his sleeping father. Instrumental music—horns and strings—play as a child's voice begins the voiceover: "We were taught how the pioneers went into the west. They opened their eyes and made up what things could be. A long time ago, things got broken here. People got sad and left."

The ad then depicts the town beginning to move and wake up: people performing everyday routines, moving around, going to work. The music picks up momentum, and the child continues: "Maybe the world breaks on purpose, so we can have work to do. People think there aren't frontiers anymore; they can't see how frontiers are all around us."

The music stops abruptly, and the tagline appears on the screen: "Go Forth. Levi's." The ad is emotionally powerful, the images lush and arresting. The dramatic music juxtaposes with the deliberate and innocent voice of the child to create an affective montage that reinforces struggle, labor, and an American mythology of the frontier. As with other frontiers conquered by the USA (expressed historically ranging from Native American genocide, nineteenth-century colonialism, Manifest Destiny and westward expansion, the space race with the Soviet Union, and the Iraqi War, to name but a few), the rhetoric of this ad emphasizes American destiny and inevitability: "Maybe the world breaks on purpose, so we can have work to do." The stunning abstraction of the ad's rhetoric—"things got broken here"—corresponds with an ahistorical neo-liberal conceit that economic crises present opportunities for individual entrepreneurs to imagine, create, and conquer a seemingly endless field of new frontiers. The voiceover, mapped onto images of an economically depressed Rust Belt industry town, capitalizes on a larger project of rebranding the 2008 global economic crisis. This branding effort, represented in ads such as the ones I discuss in this chapter but also found within corporate public relations, media representations, and nationalist marketing, reimagines the global economic crisis as one that was inevitable—but not because of the downward spiral of corporate greed or misuse of funds, but because this is what Americans do: they "fix things." Orchestrating this resolution, the ad insists, is a uniquely American destiny.

This point is brought to bear even more strongly in another series of ads in the Levi's *Go Forth* campaign. Two ads, "O Pioneers!" and "America," also created by Wieden + Kennedy, are more abstract than the previous *Go Forth* ad in their juxtaposition of images: quick shots of individuals, almost all young adults, in various situations. Both ads use the poetry of Walt Whitman as their voiceover. The "America" ad opens with a black and white shot of a broken neon sign depicting the word "America," sinking in a pool of water. This is followed by a melange of images, shot with indie film aesthetics, including quick shots, hand-held camera work, and no real discernible narrative linking the images together. The striking opening image of a broken America is juxtaposed with shooting fireworks, a subway ride, telephone poles in a stark landscape, and an American flag fluttering in a breeze. The voiceover is a recording of the Whitman poem "America," presumably by Whitman himself, recorded in 1890, scratchy and nostalgic:

America
Centre of equal daughters, equal sons
All alike endear'd, grown, ungrown, young or old
Strong, ample, fair, enduring, capable, rich
Perennial with the earth, with freedom, law, and love
(Whitman, 1892)

The ad ends dramatically, with the neon sign "America" restored, hovering above the water line, gloriously lit up. The Levi's tagline, "Go Forth," sketched on a blanket held by young people, fades to black.

The other ad in the Whitman series, "O Pioneers!," is similarly melancholic and nostalgic. It opens with a young woman holding her hand to the air in imitation of a statue, a man running alone through a field, young people embracing, dressing (in Levi's jeans, of course), standing in abandoned buildings, driving. There is no coherent visual narrative, but the images are held together by the recorded reading of a portion of Walt Whitman's 1865 "Pioneers! O Pioneers!":

Come, my tan-faced children,
Follow well in order, get your weapons ready;
Have you your pistols? Have you your sharp edged axes?
Pioneers! O Pioneers!

For we cannot tarry here,
We must march my darlings, we must bear the brunt of danger,
We, the youthful sinewy races, all the rest on us depend,
Pioneers! O Pioneers!

O you youths, western youths,
So impatient, full of action, full of manly pride and friendship
Plain I see you, western youths, see you tramping with the foremost,
Pioneers! O Pioneers!

We debouch upon a newer, mightier world, varied world,
Fresh and strong the world we seize,
Pioneers! O Pioneers!
(Whitman, 1872)

The positioning of Whitman's odes to Western expansion, the use of a quintessential American poet to sell a quintessential American brand, and the stark images of industrial ravages after the economic collapse of 2008 clearly mark the Levi's campaign as a deliberate attempt to brand the crisis as a nostalgic narrative of hope and capital-friendly opportunity, rather than a crisis that calls into question the very structure of capitalism and corporate legitimacy. As reporter Seth Stevenson (2009) points out, the ad "acts as a galvanizing call to generational action: Times may be tough, but we've been here before, and America's youth will not be broken." Casting the current global economic crisis as part of a cyclical dynamic, Levi's relies on the continuing currency of American liberal exceptionalism—we have been here before, we overcame crisis then, we can do it again—as a way to brand the current crisis as one in a series that Americans have overcome and through which they have proven their strength. Indeed, Levi's positions the contemporary crisis as a sort of "evidence" of American destiny to overcome and flourish; after all, as Whitman reminds us: "We debouch upon a newer, mightier world, varied world, Fresh and strong the world we seize." Seizing this world, however, in the twenty-first century, means branding nationalism and the crisis as a deeply interrelated, inevitable dynamic: Americans are, Whitman tells us, "perennial with the Earth, with freedom, law, and love."

The Whitman Levi's ads make liberal, intended use of historical references and images that are meant to provoke nostalgia. At the same time, the ads are not nostalgic in quite the same way as the Chrysler Super Bowl ad. The Whitman ads also directly aim to resonate with fear through the use of what might be termed apocalyptic aesthetics, heavily relying upon a kind of post-industrial wasteland crisis chic as a visual trope that runs through the ads. There is an element of danger in the visual and poetic narratives of these ads that is juxtaposed with an implicit call for courageous adventure. The ads, rather than reassure, capitalize on unknowns and anxieties. In "America," the broken America sign sets a war zone tone for the rest of the ad: the burned-out buildings, the somber faces, the haunting cinematography. The ads do not celebrate American exceptionalism in quite the same way as the Chrysler ad (or, more generally, in the customary way of most American ads), but rather seek to harness the fear and anxiety generated by global economic crisis in an explicit way in order to rescue viewers from the crisis—or, perhaps more accurately, to encourage viewers, as consumer citizens, to rescue themselves.

In other words, the Whitman ads do not work conventionally to rebuild trust in capitalism. But the fear aesthetics that frame these ads do an important kind of cultural work: they entreat the American audience (and Levi's) to rescue themselves, yet again; this time as optimistic and courageous neo-liberals. In these ads, corporate culture and capitalist exploits become part of the natural, rough, even dangerous landscape that sets the stage for the story of American courage to retell—indeed, rebrand—itself. The ads reinforce a naturalization of the dangers of unregulated neo-liberal corporate capitalism by positioning the individual entrepreneur as the central character in the brand narrative.

Unlike Chrysler, the Levi's ads are part of a larger, broader campaign that involves actual revitalization in the city of Braddock, PA, through grants for arts and culture renewal, urban farming initiatives, and so on. The Levi's project, entitled *We Are All Workers*, had an initial press release that began with:

Amid today's widespread need for revitalization and recovery, a new generation of "real workers" has emerged, those who see challenges around them and are inspired to drive positive, meaningful change. This fall, with the introduction of *Go Forth* 'Ready to Work,' the Levi's brand will empower and inspire workers everywhere through Levi's crafted product and stories of the new American Worker. (Levi Strauss and Co., 2010)

The broader campaign featured eleven short video episodes (posted on YouTube among other social media sites), created in conjunction with the Sundance Film Festival. Unlike the *Go Forth* advertisements, these videos were not shown in theaters or on television, and instead were clearly meant to tap into a genre of indie films/documentaries that featured "authentic" Americans, using "real" people instead of actors. Levi's, with a focus on authenticity and "real" individuals, brands the crisis as a nostalgic opportunity, a context for Americans to build community around the Great Recession. The enterprising subject, or the "modern pioneer" who is featured in the videos, is positioned in this brand culture as having a unique, American bootstrap mentality, and the economic crisis itself is rebranded as a moment of opportunity. The eleven episodes feature individuals who "tell the story of Braddock" through their engagement in practices, funded by Levi's, to revitalize the town: a new community center; the development of a Braddock urban farm; the efforts of the mayor of Braddock, John Fetterman, to enlist the help of what Levi's calls "modern pioneers"—artists, musicians, craftsmen—to rebuild the town. Like the *Go Forth* ads, the videos are moving episodes, with stirring soundtracks, featuring somber and hard-working individuals, dilapidated buildings, hollowed-out schools, boarded-up businesses. As the viewer moves through the eleven episodes, the town is slowly built up through the efforts of these "pioneers," who become central citizens in the Levi's brand community.

Branding the crisis

I do not mean to diminish the possible rewards the collaboration of Levi's with the town of Braddock could bring forth, or the benefits the city of Detroit may reap with the national attention the Chrysler ad demands. However, I do want to point out how these are telling examples of how the use of what Eva Illouz calls "emotional capitalism" works to build brand cultures through multiple spaces (such as conventional advertising in print and television, YouTube, blogs, DIY production, consumer-generated content, and so on) (Illouz, 2007). While I examine specific ads in this chapter, I suggest that the logic undergirding these ads goes beyond merely an attempt to resuscitate failing industries in an economic crisis, but rather are characteristic of broader neo-liberal practices, which seek to expand market logic and strategies beyond simply vaunting a particular product (Illouz, 2003; Littler, 2008). Indeed, the ads naturalize the current economic crisis as a dangerous, if inevitable, moment of unregulated capitalism, one that centers the individual as a responsible savior, even as the role of the state or nation in the crisis is abdicated.

It is clear that Chrysler's ad campaign successfully made emotional and affective connections between branding strategies and the city of Detroit. Similarly, the Levi's ad campaign "Go Forth" tapped into historical ideologies and discourses about American exceptionalism and destiny, and nostalgically branded the 2008 economic crisis as a "new frontier." The way the two ads brand specific cities, companies, and products, however, is only part of the larger branding process; these ad campaigns also work as part of the infrastructure of feeling that brands the crisis more globally as an opportunity for the American working class to buy into an alternative, capital-friendly narrative. This narrative is one that focuses on the individual entrepreneur, not the failing system of capitalism. The maintenance of the narrative of American liberal exceptionalism is positioned side-by-side with a neo-liberal mandate for individuals to take care of themselves.

While the global economic crisis of the twenty-first century is referenced in both ads through vague recognitions that the USA needs "widespread revitalization and recovery," or, more ridiculously, as something that "got broken here," the actual reasons for the crisis—the collapse of neo-liberal practices in banking and trade, the disintegration of the automobile industry in the USA, the global reach and ripple effect of economic devastation—are never interrogated; rather, the individual "authentic," courageous, and optimistic worker is the one who is responsible for making the change:

"We are the Motor City. And this is what we do" (for more on the branding of the "authentic," see Banet-Weiser, 2012).

Indeed, within these ad campaigns, the worker or laborer is collapsed with the brand itself, as well as positioned as the central character in the larger narrative that brands the crisis. Rather than call attention to systemic failure in the global banking industry, or the effects of generations living on credit, or the subprime mortgage crisis, these ads call our attention to the lone, rugged entrepreneur; the individualist laborer who is nostalgically created and positioned as the only way out of what "got broken," the mess that was somehow, and abstractly, "made" so that Americans can come along and "fix things."

The worker is thus positioned in a variety of ways in these campaigns: as hero, as cultural memory, as neo-liberal entrepreneur, as a symbol for a nation under threat. Indeed, Chrysler's ad campaign has the tagline: "Good Things Come to those Who Work." Levi's "Go Forth" campaign even vaguely references the Communist Party (CP) slogan with their "We Are All Workers," but without any of the CP's reference and reliance on communal work. The "We" of "We Are All Workers" is a community of individual workers, each "free" in a "free market," called upon to "go forth and work," with the backdrop of economic crisis that will encourage these workers to be leaner, ever more vigilant, within capitalism. With Levi's help, Braddock, PA, is transformed into a town of "real workers" who are "rolling up their sleeves to make real change happen."

Part of the affective narrative of global neo-liberalism is precisely this focus on the individual as opposed to the state. The ads take a particular position on the nation in the midst of a global crisis. Rather than gesture toward a vague global community that needs to unite in response to global economic collapse, these two corporations position the US nation as under threat—from outside and from within. This is, however, an ambiguous threat, as opposed to placing accountability on concrete identifiable actors and structures.

As is increasingly common in contemporary brand culture, the 2010 Chrysler and Levi's ad campaigns challenge a historical language of advertising, which relied heavily on a product's efficiency and unique qualities in a competitive market. Rather, these ads utilize the language of the brand, what Celia Lury (2004) calls the "logos" of the brand, which is maintained by a personal, individual narrative, one that revolves around lifestyle, identity, and individual empowerment. In this sense, the ads are about much more than a discrete product or thing: the Chrysler automobile, or a pair of Levi's jeans. As Lury (2004: 14) points out: "To assume that the brand is a single thing would be to mistake the multiple and sometimes divergent layers of activity that have gone into producing the brand... [these activities] have multiple histories, are internally divided, in tension with each other, and may even be contradictory or opposed." Thus, while it is important to point out the hypocrisy in the ads—the Chrysler corporation was not only a key player in the current economic crisis, but has also historically abandoned Detroit through de-industrialization and the outsourcing of labor; while Levi's utilizes a nationalist rhetoric to sell American products and shamelessly exploits the disintegrating Rust Belt industrial towns to do so—I am also arguing that it is precisely this kind of disconnect or contradiction that makes the ad campaigns so successful on an emotional or affective register, and what makes them effective as mechanisms to brand the current global economic crisis. These contradictions are part of the brand.

The use of cultural contradictions in advertising certainly did not begin with the 2008 global economic crisis. Advertising has long succeeded in co-opting counter-culture aesthetics, reformulating an aesthetics of resistance into something marketable, thus dissipating any fear or anxiety about what might be the consequences of resistance (see Frank, 1998; Klein, 2000; Heath and Potter, 2004). But the contemporary global economic crisis presents an extreme case for advertisers to mobilize fear and anxiety as a dominant trope—one that is unavoidable for marketers to address.

For instance, the Chrysler ad signals the importance of individual belonging to a particular city, Detroit: "This is what we do." As Adam Weinstein (2011) points out, in such a gesture toward individual citizens of Detroit, the ad effectively positions Chrysler as an "urban core" brand using a tough, gritty image that relies on what some critics have called "poverty porn." As Weinstein scathingly points out, the logic undergirding the ad is profoundly hypocritical:

the fact that a major bailout recipient is dishing beaucoup bucks for a one-off ad to boost its image; the cynical racism (or at least colonialism)of positioning Chrysler as a tough, gritty, 8 Mile-style brand that's perfect for what marketers call the 'urban core' demographic; and using Detroit poverty porn to hawk your product while simultaneously trying to deride the media's recent Detroit poverty porn... But most appalling is the idea that Chrysler is one of the great things about gritty Detroit and America, when in fact it's one of the corporate locusts that choked the city and nation purple with its credit-backed gobbling of skilled labor and its excretion of abandoned worker plants.

But this history is rendered invisible through the nostalgic frame of the Chrysler ad. Rather, the nostalgic view of Detroit referenced in the ad begins in 1908, when Henry Ford opened his first automobile assembly-line plant in Highland Park on the east side of Woodward Avenue. As historian Thomas J. Sugrue (1996: 6) argues in his work *The Origins of the Urban Crisis*, the oft-lauded prosperity of the post-war USA, told in school textbooks, television, and popular media, as well as in scholarship, obscured a profoundly uneven post-war US landscape, where "capitalism left behind huge sections of the United States, mainly older industrial cities in the North and East and rural areas in the South and Midwest."

The multi-leveled problems that have beset Detroit since the post-war period are well known; I reference them to make the point that the Great Recession of 2008 did not devastate Detroit, as the city was already well on its way to economic and cultural devastation. As Charlie LeDuff (2010) points out, in the current moment

"Detroitism" means something completely different. It means uncertainty and abandonment and psychopathology. The city reached a peak population of 1.9 million people in the 1950s, and it was 83 percent white. Now Detroit has fewer than 800,000 people, is 83 percent black, and is the only American city that has surpassed a million people and dipped back below that threshold.

But the history of the city, especially its de-industrialization and poverty, did not garner much national attention (and certainly did not much attract federal or state funding for rebuilding or addressing institutionalized racism and systemic poverty), until 2008, when the Big Three automobile chief executives asked the federal government for bailout money (and, in the process, began the process of declaring bankruptcy). As Weinstein says, it is at this moment, the moment of global economic collapse, the moment of the disintegration of the automobile industry in the USA, that "Detroit was historic, symbolic—hip, even"—and thus, remarkably brandable. As Lester K. Spence (2011) has argued:

After the collapse of the car industry and the implosion of the real estate bubble, there is little else Detroit has to export except its misery. And America is buying. There are no fewer than two TV dramas, two documentaries, and three reality programs being filmed here. Even Time bought a house on the East Side last year for $99,000. The gimmick was to have its reporters live there and chronicle the decline of the Motor City for one year.

Indeed, Detroit provides an exemplary site for the branding of the global economic crisis: one of the hardest-hit cities in the USA, with a history of conflict and triumph, and an urban environment that emphasizes the individual blue-collar laborer in its cultural and regional memory—all narratives intertwine to offer a rich context for a new narrative about branding the economic crisis.

The Levi's ads rely upon a similar strategy of using selective history to brand the current crisis. A title of an article detailing the campaign in the trade magazine *Adweek* frames this strategy sardonically and succinctly: "Walt Whitman is Reborn. To Sell Jeans" (Kiefaber, 2009). As Doug Sweeny, the vice president of Levi's brand marketing, more earnestly notes: "The idea of . . . putting people back to work is clearly top of mind [culturally]" (Kiefaber, 2009). Although the Levi's campaign focuses on economically depressed Rust Belt town Braddock, PA, it is not as pointed in its rhetorical focus on the specificity of the town as the Chrysler ad campaign is with Detroit. Rather, the Levi's ad focuses on a general ideology of American heritage and destiny of the blue-collar working class as a way to symbolize the opportunity presented by the global economic crisis. In so doing, the Levi's campaign, like the Chrysler campaign, obscures material realities—such as ethnic diversity, the ravages of Manifest Destiny, and the fact that many Americans actually do want to "go forth" and work but there are no jobs available. This obfuscation was pointedly referred to on a Levi's billboard in New York featuring an ad in the "Go Forth" series. The billboard depicted a young white girl running through fields with the text "This country was not built by men in suits." Someone unofficially responded to this claim, writing below it: "It was built by slaves." The obvious strategy of the billboard—to appeal to hard-working Americans, blue-collar workers, not corporate "suits" or over-paid executives—backfired at least in this case because of the way the campaign renders certain historical narratives invisible while privileging the ideology of the "frontier."

The shift in focus of the Levi's campaign from Walt Whitman's idealism to the realities of Braddock, PA, was a strategic change in how the company was branding the economic crisis. As reporter Matthew Newton (2010) puts it:

The first time around, Levi's attempted to channel gritty realism by simulating it. Now, by going on-location to Braddock—a Rust Belt town that's lost 90% of its population since the American steel industry dried up—Levi's will attempt to capture gritty realism in action. As the site of Andrew Carnegie's first steel mill, Braddock once embodied the spirit of the American worker, which makes the town a receptive home to the words of a poet like Walt Whitman. But that spirit of an unswerving American work ethic has long since been replaced by vacant storefronts and burned-out homes, contentious small town politics and a sense of abandonment...It's obvious Levi's is hoping this move will lend a sense of sincerity to its beleaguered ad campaign. Which, who knows, it very well may. After all, it's a nice gesture—whether PR-motivated or not—for Levi's to invest a million dollars over two years in Braddock.

Both the Chrysler and the Levi's advertising campaigns of 2010 function, not only to rebuild the brand of individual struggling corporations, but, more generally, to brand the current global economic crisis itself. As I have discussed, the economic crisis of 2008 was about many things, one of which was the failure of brands. The job for struggling corporations in the aftermath of the crisis was not only to attempt to regain trust in cars and jeans for consumers. It became, more importantly, about how to restore trust in brands, the market, and, indeed, in neo-liberal capitalism itself. What better way for the USA to re-establish trust for consumers than to position the crisis as a brand: a brand about America, about consumer-citizens, about the inevitable triumph of capitalism? Within contemporary brand culture, branders and marketers invest in establishing an "authentic," affective relationship between products and consumers. In the current environment of post-2008 global economic crisis, the most important "product" in this relationship is capitalism itself.

References

Advertising Age (2011). "Chrysler to Run Two-Minute SuperBowl Commercial," Feb. 2.

Banet-Weiser, Sarah (2012). *Authentic: The Politics of Ambivalence in a Brand Culture.* New York: New York University Press.

Brown, Wendy (2001). *Politics out of History.* Princeton and Oxford: Princeton University Press.

Bureau of Labor Statistics (2011). *Civilian Labor Force and Unemployment by State and Metropolitan Area.* Washington: US Department of Labor.

Castells, Manuel (2009). *Communication Power.* Oxford: Oxford University Press.

Chrysler Group LLC (2011). "Quarterly Profit Reports" <http://www.chrysler-groupllc.com> (accessed July 7, 2011).

Corrupt Authority (2010). "Businessman Latest to Plead Guilty in Detroit City Hall Corruption Scandal," Dec. 24 <http://www.corruptauthority.com> (accessed July 7, 2011).

Couldry, Nick (2010). *Why Voice Matters: Culture and Politics after Neoliberalism*. London: Sage Publications.

Dayan, Daniel, and Katz, Elihu (1994). *Media Events: The Live Broadcasting of History*. Cambridge, MA: Harvard University Press.

Detroit Free Press (2008). "Detroit is Poorest Big City in US," Aug. 27 <http://www.freep. com/article/20080827/NEWS06/808270343/Detroit-is-poorest-big-city-in-U.S.> (accessed July 1, 2010).

Duggan, Lisa (2003). *The Twilight of Equality? Neoliberalism, Cultural Politics, and the Attack on Democracy*. Boston: Beacon Press.

Ewen, Stuart (2001). *Captains of Consciousness: Advertising and the Social Roots of the Consumer Culture*. New York: Basic Books.

Flint, Jerry (2009). "Bailing out Detroit's Bailout Plans," Forbes, Jan. 2.

Foster, Peter (2009). "No End to Capitalism," *Financial Post*, Sept. 18.

Foucault, Michel (2010). *The Birth of Biopolitics: Lectures at the Collège de France 1978–1979*. New York: Palgrave.

Frank, Thomas (1998). *The Conquest of Cool: Business Culture, Counterculture, and the Rise of Hip Consumerism*. Chicago: University of Chicago Press.

Freire, J. P. (2011). "Chrysler Releases $9M Super Bowl Ad while Requesting More Taxpayer Dollars," *Washington Examiner*, Feb. 7.

Gilmore, Ruth Wilson (2007). *Golden Gulag: Prisons, Surplus, Crisis and Opposition in Globalizing California*. Berkeley and Los Angeles: University of California Press.

Goldman, Robert, and Papson, Stephen (1996). *Sign Wars: The Cluttered Landscape of Advertising*. New York: Guilford Press.

Harvey, David (2005). *A Brief History of Neoliberalism*. Oxford: Oxford University Press.

Heath, Stephen, and Potter, Andrew (2004). *Nation of Rebels: Why Counterculture Became Consumer Culture*. New York: Harper.

Illouz, Eva (2007). *Cold Intimacies: The Making of Emotional Capitalism*. Cambridge: Polity Press.

Illouz, Eva (2003). *Oprah Winfrey and the Glamour of Misery: An Essay on Popular Culture*. New York: Columbia University Press.

Kiefaber, David (2009). "Walt Whitman is Reborn. To Sell Jeans," *Adweek*, July 6 <http://www.adweek.com/adfreak/walt-whitman-reborn-sell-blue-jeans-13954> (accessed July 1, 2011).

Kiley, David (2011). "The Inside Story: Chrysler's Risky Eminem Super Bowl Commercial," Feb. 8 <http://autos.aol.com/article/chrysler-eminem-super-bowl-ad/> (accessed July 15, 2011).

Klein, Naomi (2000). *No Logo: No Space, No Choice, No Jobs*. New York: Picador.

Lears, T. J. Jackson (1981). *No Place of Grace: Antimodernism and the Transformation of American Culture, 1880–1920*. Chicago: University of Chicago Press.

LeDuff, Charlie (2010). "What Killed Aiyana Stanley-Jones?" *Mother Jones* (Oct.–Nov.).

Levi Strauss and Co., (2010). "We are all Workers," June 24 <http://www.levistrauss.com/news/press-releases/levis-proclaims-we-are-all-workers-launch-latest-go-forth-marketing-campaign> (accessed July 1, 2010).

Lipsitz, George (2006). *The Possessive Investment in Whiteness: How White People Profit from Whiteness*. Philadephia: Temple University Press.

Littler, Jo (2008). *Radical Consumption: Shopping for Change in Contemporary Culture*. Maidenhead: Open University Press.

Lury, Celia (2004). *Brands: The Logos of the Global Economy*. London and New York: Routledge.

Mukherjee, Roopali, and Banet-Weiser, Sarah (2012) (eds). *Commodity Activism: Cultural Resistance in Neoliberal Times*. New York: New York University Press.

Newton, Matthew (2010). "Levi's Attempts to Salvage 'Go Forth' Campaign with Sincerity," June 24 <http://www.trueslant.com> (accessed July 1, 2011).

Ong, Aihwa (2006). *Neoliberalism as Exception: Mutations in Citizenship and Sovereignty*. Durham, NC, and London: Duke University Press.

"Prouder, Better, Stronger" (1984). Official US Presidential Campaign Advertisement for the Republican Party of the United States of America.

Schudson, Michael (1986). *Advertising, the Uneasy Persuasion: Its Dubious Impact on American Society*. New York: Basic Books.

Smith, Christopher Holmes (2011). "We Have Armageddon! Media Ritual, Moral Panic, and Market Meltdown." Annenberg Research Seminar, Annenberg School for Communication and Journalism, University of Southern California, Los Angeles, California, Aug. 29.

Spence, Lester (2011). "From the DOGG to Eminem: Chrysler Then and Now" <http://www.lesterspence.com> (accessed Mar. 15, 2011).

Stevenson, Seth (2009). "Levi's Commercials, now starring Walt Whitman," *AdWeek*, Oct. 26.

Sturken, Marita, and Cartwright, Lisa (2009). *Practices of Looking: An Introduction to Visual Culture*. 2nd edn. Oxford: Oxford University Press.

Sugrue, Thomas J. (1996). *The Origins of the Urban Crisis: Race and Inequality in Postwar Detroit*. Princeton: Princeton University Press.

Weinstein, Adam (2011). "Chrysler's Deplorable 'Detroit' SuperBowl Ad," *Mother Jones*, Feb. 7.

Whitman, Walt (1872). "Pioneers! O Pioneers," in *Leaves of Grass, 1871–72*. New York: J. S. Redfield.

—— (1892). "America," in *Leaves of Grass, 1891–92*. Boston: James R. Osgood.

Williams, Corey (2011). "Detroit Schools Struggle to Solve Budget Woes," Mar. 20 <http://www.msnbc.msn.com/id/42179951/ns/us_news-life/t/detroit-schools-struggle-solve-huge-budget-woes/> (accessed July 1, 2010).

Williams, Raymond (1961). *The Long Revolution*. Ontario: Broadview Press.

Williams, Rosalind (1991). *Dream Worlds: Mass Consumption in Late Nineteenth Century France*. Berkeley and Los Angeles: University of California Press.

Zelizer, Viviana (2011). *Economic Lives: How Culture Shapes the Economy*. Princeton: Princeton University Press.

Chapter 6

In Nationalism We Trust?

Terhi Rantanen

> As far as the popular imagination is concerned, one way this is being framed
> is to re-install a "business as usual" narrative as quickly as possible. This is
> one predicated on a "fear and insecurity" scenario—economic insecurity in
> particular—which is forging a new category of the "nervous public at
> risk"... The main task is to re-secure the stability of the financial system,
> stimulate the consumer boom once again ("maintain aggregate demand"),
> re-capitalize the banks so that they can re-establish credit circulation and,
> hopefully, re-stimulate the housing market. (Thompson, 2009: 521)

Despite its "greatness," the Great Recession that started in 2008 has been
only to a certain extent entirely global—it has not been and continues not to
be evenly experienced in different parts of the world. A number of countries
practicing state capitalism (Bremmer, 2010), especially in Asia, were actually less affected. However, the crisis has been and continues to be without a
doubt transnational, affecting many nation states, including the USA and
several European countries. It has hit and continues to hit not only
countries, institutions, and people but also the dominant Western idea of
free markets without governmental interference.

The crisis has consisted and continues to consist of different elements that
coexist and overlap. In the beginning, it included a credit crunch that spread

out from the USA to influence the banking sector in Europe and elsewhere. It further resulted in government bailouts of banks and even the nationalization of several established banks in a number of countries. The UK alone, for example, will end up spending between 8 and 13 percent of its GDP rescuing its banks in future years (Tett, 2009: 288). It also affected the housing market, especially in the USA, but also in the UK, Spain, and Ireland, where the value of property has dropped by as much as 50 percent (Boyes, 2009: 214). The Great Recession has contributed to the failure of key businesses, a decrease in consumption, and a serious increase in unemployment. In the European Union (EU) it has led to a situation where the national economies of Greece, Ireland, and Portugal have needed to be rescued by joint EU and International Monetary Fund (IMF) efforts, and to a questioning of the Euro's viability. It has affected and is still affecting nation states in their attempts to provide basic services to their citizens and is increasingly invoked as a justification for the weakening of welfare states. Finally, both ideologically and politically, the crisis has resulted in a return to nationalism. Nationalism, according to Ernest Gellner, holds that nations and states were destined for each other, that either without the other is incomplete and constitutes a tragedy (Gellner, 1983: 1). In the Great Recession, it soon became clear that no nation state can these days single-handedly control its national economy. However, while people began to distrust institutions, including nation states, their faith in nations seemed to hold steady.

How do we analyze this crisis, which has been described as the first crisis of globalization? Is it possible for existing national and international organizations (including the EU and the IMF) to rescue today's global economy? As Ulrich Beck (2007: 153) reminds us, most institutions still appeal to national legitimacy. When the concept of globalization was first introduced in the early 1990s, it was often defined in optimistic terms as the beginning of a new era that could be identified by an increasing connectivity with the potential to lead to "one world." However, with the emergence of the first global economic crisis, the theories of globalization were put to the test. How much do they help us understand what is happening in a world that people increasingly share, even if we do not necessarily want to?

Immediately after the introduction of the concept of globalization, here defined as a process in which "worldwide economic, political, cultural and social relations have become increasingly mediated across time and space" (Rantanen, 2005: 8), a new discussion started about whether globalization actually existed or whether there was anything new about it. The main participants in the debate were labeled as globalization optimists (those who argued that globalization did exist) and globalization pessimists or skeptics (those who argued that globalization did not exist). According to many pessimists, the nation state remained as powerful as ever, and national or international organizations were still the major players in national and international politics and trade (see, e.g., Hirst et al., 2009). Since then, both optimists and pessimists have somewhat shifted from their original positions and modified them accordingly. As a result, the concept of globalization has become more widely accepted, but at the same time it has also been widely acknowledged that nation states have not entirely lost their power. As Holton (1998: 107) writes, while the nation state is far from finished, there is good reason to doubt that states hold the monopoly of power within the politics of globalization. In addition, some of the early proponents of the concept of globalization have stopped using the term altogether and started using adjectives instead of nouns: "the global," "the cosmopolitan," or "the transnational."

Some early theorists of globalization, such as Appadurai (1990), did pay attention to the potential consequences of globalization, pointing out disjunctures between, for example, global financescape and global ideoscape, which were not necessarily moving hand in hand or producing simultaneous (and perhaps positive) changes. However, following a global financial crisis, the success of right-wing populist movements in many European countries has been a surprising result of changes in the European ideoscape. Many of these movements, although anti-establishment in character, are also anti-immigrant and anti-European, offering the most nationalistic solutions to global economic problems. The right-wing populist "True Finns" party, which became the third biggest party in Finland through a landslide success in parliamentary elections in 2011, considers Brussels to be the "heart of darkness" and rejects all financial assistance for what it calls "wasteful countries," such as Greece, Ireland, and Portugal. The party leader says that "We were too soft on Europe" and that "Finland should not be made to pay for others' mistakes" (*Spiegel*, 2011). The return to nationalism as a possible consequence of globalization has received much less attention and has mainly been discussed in relation to non-Western societies such as Russia (Rantanen, 2002) or China (Zhang, 2009).

The other factor absent from the early globalization debate was the role of media and communications. Although media scholars were late to join the original debate, they were just as divided as earlier participants. Media globalization skeptics argued that media globalization did not exist as a concept, either because it was just another word for media imperialism or because there were no truly global media (see, e.g., Sparks, 2007). Others argued that there was indeed something new that could not be completely reduced to national media systems or national audiences and that there was no globalization without the media, especially new media. Since the early stages of the debate, it has become more and more evident that media and communications—whether global, national, or local—play a significant role in a second modernity where social relationships have become increasingly mediated across national boundaries. At the same time, the "optimists" have had to acknowledge that most media institutions still operate in a national framework, even if their ownership, content, and audiences—and, of course, events—are increasingly transnational.

The question this chapter addresses is not a new one; it is a question that has been asked by Anthony Giddens: "what do we do with the consequences of globalization?" (quoted in Rantanen, 2005: 18). In this case, what do we do with economic globalization? What happens when a global economy fails? How do people learn about it? What is the role of the media? How do people react? I shall present an analysis of the deconstruction of global trust following the global financial crisis in 2007. The moments are labeled as (1) loss of trust; (2) search for respondents; and (3) attempts to reconstruct trust through nationalism. I argue that what is at stake is trust, and that, when trust is extended and becomes abstract, there is a return to the national. The long-term result is a growing distrust in traditional institutions such as banks, governments, and the media, which were the pillars of first modernity. At the same time, populist right-wing movements offer an appealing solution in the form of a trust based on narrowly defined nationalism.

Global risk society

Since the Great Recession we have increasingly seen evidence of globalization, but often again in terms of a global crisis. The world has also seen other unexpected and coinciding crises, such as the tsunami in Japan in 2011. Beck (2009) has made a convincing argument that we now live in a global risk society, where risks have become part of daily life and no nation can master its problems alone (Beck and Grande, 2007: 222). According to him, we now face new kinds of risks, not only of natural disasters, but also of catastrophes, which are a combination of the man-made and the natural (Beck, 2009: 19). Nohrstedt (2011: 24) suggests that, instead of naming the current stage a risk society, we should call it a *threat society*. Bauman (2006: 2) writes about fear, "the name we give to our uncertainty, to our ignorance of the threat and of what is to be done—what can and what can't be—to stop it in its tracks—or to fight it back if stopping is beyond our power." As a result, we can argue that not only the sense of risks has increased but also the perception of threat often followed by fear because the latter has become increasingly mediated: not experienced directly but through the media.

Crises in second modernity are also increasingly global. Not only does a tsunami strike the coast of Japan: it strikes a nuclear power station that then starts releasing radioactive materials that affect areas beyond Japan. Nuclear power stations were supposed to be one of the "great achievements" of second modernity, offering "scientific" and "rational" solutions to large-scale problems such as the provision of cheap electricity for all. Increasingly we see "old risks" transformed into "new risks" that involve an unexpected "human" element intervening alongside the forces of nature.

Beck's notion of the global risk society is an important one because increasingly crises touch people not only "there" or "here," but also here and there at the same time. The tsunami in Japan touched us not only because many citizens of our own countries were actually in Japan at the time, but also because we could all identify with the risk and recognize the institutions that had been damaged, especially the nuclear power generation. We recognize the vulnerability of the institutions that typically represent second modernity, of the "progress of mankind" that we increasingly have learned to doubt, if not actively to oppose. "Just 48 hours to avoid another Chernobyl. Britons advised to leave Tokyo," cried the front page of the UK *Daily Telegraph* on March 17, 2011. Media audiences around the world became acutely aware of the tsunami's unforeseen consequences when it hit nuclear power plants. "Panicked Americans rushing to buy anti-radiation drugs," reported the UK *Daily Mail* on the same day. While the media may "nationalize" natural disasters, they also invite a cosmopolitan moment (Beck, 2009: 56–7) and compassion for the victims, however geographically distant.

Unlike natural disasters, which invite assistance from global rescue organizations and non-governmental organizations (NGOs) such as the Red Cross, the global economic crisis turned out to be an event where rescuers were rather reluctant and few in number. Even more importantly, it was more difficult to convince the public that this financial crisis "just happened," in the way disasters do, and that nobody was responsible. The search for organizational and individual responsibility started almost simultaneously with the media coverage. The reactions to a global economic crisis differ significantly from a natural disaster where the people affected are often seen as victims who need other people's compassion and help (Kyriakidou, 2011). What is it about an economic crisis that turns peoples against each other and leads them to accept responsibility only for their fellow citizens, excluding immigrants? I would argue that the missing concept in global risk society is that of trust, which has become too abstract.

Abstract trust

Once upon a time there may have been such a thing as simple trust. This was mostly exercised between individuals and groups. Fukuyama (1995: 26) defines trust as the expectation that arises within a *community* of regular, honest, and cooperative behavior, based on commonly shared norms (my emphasis). Coleman argues that trust can be produced only in small, informal, closed, and homogenous communities that are able to reinforce normative sanctions (Coleman, 1990: 116, quoted in Misztal, 1996: 80). Simmel (1978: 178–9) writes that, without the general trust that people have in each other, even *society* itself would disintegrate, for very few relationships are based entirely upon what is known with certainty about another person, and very few relationships would endure if trust were not as strong as, or stronger than, rational proof or personal observation. Thus, the words "trust" and "faith" do not seem to be entirely disconnected. Even the Latin root word of *crēdĕre* includes both trusting and believing,[1] although the former seems to be based more on rationality than on unquestioning belief.

Trust has now indeed become a tricky word and is closely connected with risk, especially when extended to institutions. However, Luhmann (1979) argues that social order is no longer based on personal trust, as within small communities, but that modern societies are characterized by the increasing importance of trust in *systems*, which is built on the belief that others also trust these institutions, rather than on a feeling of familiarity that creates

---

[1] *OED* online <http://www.oed.com> (accessed on July, 1, 2011).

solidarity (Mizstal, 1996: 74–5). This institutional, collective trust is based more on a contract, often but not always in writing, between an individual and an institution. O'Neill (2002: 85) calls this *informed consent* between two parties, where the expectations are documented. What is thus becoming as important as this, or even more important, is trust in *abstract* systems rather than personal trust based on interpersonal relationships in communities (Giddens, 1992: 82). According to Luhmann (1979: 26), trust remains a risky undertaking. In other words, whenever we trust, we also assume risk or fear of losing trust.

For Giddens, trust is attributed to abstract systems (or parts of these) through the disembedding ("lifting out") of social relations from local contexts of interaction and their restructuring across indefinite spans of time–space (Mizstal, 1996: 89–90; Giddens, 1990: 21–2). Giddens writes about two types of disembedding mechanisms intrinsically involved in the development of modern social institutions. The first of these is the creation of symbolic tokens (that is, money) and the second is the establishment of expert systems. Giddens (1990: 23–4) defines money as abstract, as a mode of deferral, providing the means of connecting credit and liability in circumstances where immediate exchange of products is impossible. By expert systems, Giddens refers to "technical accomplishment or professional practice" beyond most people's knowledge or reach. Both money and expert systems remove social relations from the immediacies of context and promote time–space distanciation (Giddens, 1990: 27–8).

When trust was extended to institutions it came to be executed between ordinary people and *representatives of these institutions*, as in political life where a party is supposed to represent the collective interests of its members and voters who then trust elected representatives to represent these interests. Similarly, a bank manager represents the interests of the bank but also acts as a mediator between the bank and its clients. If and when a bank manager gives a customer a loan, a contract is made where both parties list their obligations. As a result, there is an informed social contract between the client and the customer. There is always a risk, as in any social contract, that one party may abdicate, but established institutions such as banks do their best to convince their clients that they are trustworthy.

Shapiro (1987: 627) is one of the few sociologists who touch upon the question of the media in relation to trust. On the one hand, she argues, organizations and individuals need their own information collection, but, on the other hand, they increasingly rely on the *representations* of the news media, especially with regard to events taking place outside their own physical reach. In this way, the media act on behalf of others, in the same way as, for example, banks. The problem is that all these representative institutions are connected to each other and rely on each other for their information collection. The media need information about banking, but at the same time banking needs information about politics. Politicians need information about banking and rely primarily on the media for this, but the media also need this information in order to fill their columns and airtime. All are dependent on each other and feed each other. They all need to convince people that they are trustworthy and worth their votes, money, or subscriptions. There is no financial crisis without a crisis in politics or in the media, since they are all interconnected. There is a *spiral of trust* that can be either an upward spiral, creating or maintaining trust, or a downward spiral of loss of trust leading to complete distrust and fear.

Misztal (1996: 143) argues that we can see clear connections between collective memory and trust. According to her, collective memory can resist becoming a national, ethnic, or other type of myth only by standing aside from the unreasonable distrust of others and allowing for a new cooperative future to be established on the basis of "forgiving without forgetting." Misztal (1996: 146) quotes Keane (1988), who suggested that an active democratic memory recognizes that the development of fresh and stimulating perspectives on the present depends upon criticisms that remind us of that which we are in danger of forgetting. I would further argue that democratic memory also needs to forget, but is unable to do so because of the media, which frame every new event in terms of a previous one and make use mostly of national spectacles. For Entman (1993: 52), "to frame is to select some aspects of a perceived reality and make them more salient in a communicating text, in such a way as to promote a particular (1) problem definition, (2) causal interpretation, (3) moral evaluation, and/or (4) treatment recommendation for the item described."

I would argue that, while both money and experts were significant for first modernity, the latest phase of second modernity is witnessing three new phenomena: (1) globalization, (2) credit (including credit cards) increasingly replacing "real" money, and (3) the mediation of societies— that is, the role played by the ever-increasing importance of the media. All these contribute to the disembedding of social relationships and the changing nature of contemporary trust, which has to be extended across national borders to institutions that are more distant than ever before.

Terhi Rantanen

Money, banks, and (dis)trust

In the generational collective memory of ordinary people, modern banking is a relatively new phenomenon and some can still remember the time where their salaries were paid to them as cash in a brown envelope. Even today around thirty million people—or 7 percent of adults—in the twenty-seven EU countries do not have a bank account. The number of adults without bank accounts is particularly high in new EU states such as Bulgaria and Romania, where only about half of citizens have an account. One of the main obstacles to opening a bank account is not having a proof of address, affecting not only the homeless but also trainees or migrant workers who move to a different state for a short time (Europa, 2011). People who do have bank accounts still remember a time when they had "savings books" and "money-boxes" and received from an early age a moral lesson about saving money, not living beyond their means, and not buying things on credit. If and when they received a loan from a bank (or a building society), they entered into an informed consent with their local bank manager and the payments were carefully monitored. The relationship was based on trust, respect, and even fear, at least from the customer's point of view. Banks and currency were national institutions, and the idea that one would open an account in a foreign bank was almost unimaginable. Banks were also a source of national pride, like other "great" institutions of first modernity that could be seen as national symbols for independent nation states.

Ordinary people know that banks are here to make money, but at the same time they trust that they will get their own savings back whenever they need them, possibly with interest, although the rate may vary. When entrusting their money to a bank, most people understand that their money is not actually kept in their bank, but invested in a sensible way that guarantees that they will get it back. Most ordinary people do not understand the concept of investment banks, the "shadow system" (Lowenstein, 2010: 57) where bankers who are "comfortable with risks" (Posner, 2009: 323) "bet with other people's money, not their own" (Authers , 2010: 73) with "absence of fear" (Lowenstein, 2010: 79), or "that banks and the mortgage lenders had a tight symbiotic relationship" (Taibbi, 2010: 84) and that the latter achieved unimaginable wealth. Most people did not know about derivatives or hedge funds before the crisis, and still do not know what these terms mean, although since the early 1990s bankers had been responding to failing interest rates by producing more complex and leveraged derivatives products and developing credit derivatives (Tett, 2009: 100).

But even money has now become de-nationalized and much more abstract. Not only has it lost its earlier connection with any valuable metal, since all industrialized countries have already abandoned the pretense that their currency is tied to gold, silver, or anything else of intrinsic value. As Evans and Schmalensee (2005: 29) write, "the introduction of the euro in 2002 reinforced the point that 'faith' is enough, since one cannot convert the euro to gold or silver and has to trust a still loosely connected group of often bickering countries to maintain its value." Increasingly, trust in money and banks has become not only abstract, but also more extended and mediated. The introduction of "plastic money" and credit cards also resulted in greater distanciation between people and money. People were increasingly encouraged to live on debt. Studies show that they are now using credit cards to finance many of their basic needs. Growing numbers of people use consumer credit to finance health expenses, groceries, and other necessities and pay high interest rates on these items that can sink them deep into debt (Gates, 2010: 426). There is no longer an individual bank manager, but loans are increasingly applied for online, and one's reference point at a bank branch is a cash machine that is perhaps less intimidating, but also lacks human flexibility.

Globalization has opened up new markets for banks. As a result, many people experience their "local" bank as no longer local or even national, but as located in another country. Increasingly they also do not know how the national and local institutions they used to trust have invested their money. For example, in the UK, Oxford University deposited £30 million in Icelandic banks. The Metropolitan Police invested £30 million, Transport for London £40 million, Cambridge University £11 million, the National Cat Protection League £11.2 million, and 116 local governments £858 million in Icelandic banks (Boyes, 2009: 127).

Mortgages also became more easily available, even for people whose income level made it difficult for them to make repayments. What ordinary people did not know was that for years banks had been using mortgage securitization, where a number of all types of mortgages are combined and repackaged into bonds to make a new financial product that investors then sell to corporations and governments. This allowed banks to keep lending at levels they could not have done in the past and to keep inviting people to buy properties they could not afford (Gasparino, 2009:18, 157, 241). In the UK, for example, by the end of 2007 banks had sold off 50 percent of outstanding mortgages in securitization vehicles (Brown, 2010: 3). Northern Rock, the fifth largest British lender, once a highly regarded Newcastle-based building society with a strong commitment to its local community (Cable, 2009: 10), had been the first British lender fully to embrace mortgage securitization (Brown, 2010: 23) and by 2007 less than 25 percent of Northern Rock's funding came from retail deposits and mortgage payments, with the rest raised by securitization (Tett, 2009: 229; Brown, 2010: 24).

Securitization is often said to be a major cause of the credit crunch, followed by a decrease in property prices. As Gates (2010: 83) observes, it also amounts to a form of disembedding of debt, removing it from the balance sheets of specific institutions and bundling it together in a pool with other debt, which in turn can be sold off on a secondary market. Cable (2009: 19) writes that the growth of second-hand mortgages on personal loans and the securitization of mortgages have meant that there has been a weakening in banking based upon personal relationships with bank managers. A default on payments now often automatically triggers a court reference, the first step on the road to repossession (Cable, 2009: 19). In the USA, in 2009, a *Consumer Reports* survey reported that only 54 percent of respondents paid off their credit card bills every month, while the remaining 46 percent carried debit balances from month to month. Those people who carried balances of more than $10,000, who are the most profitable group for credit card issuers, were not by and large irresponsible shopaholics but regular members of the middle class (Gates, 2010: 426).

Mistrusting a bank involves a withholding of confidence in its operations. People, of course, can change their bank, but banking systems operate in a similar way across borders, and are connected to and dependent on each other. In their customers' minds, they are highly abstract systems with laws of their own that people do not fully understand. As a consequence, financial crises seem to come as a complete surprise, like volcanic eruptions or tsunamis, since it is very difficult to recognize the warning signs if they are not made public in advance.

The media

The old media like to present themselves as "experts" informing the public about the operations of institutions they consider important. They can be seen as mediating between these institutions and the public and claim to make sense of the former by critically examining their operations. However, the media, like other traditional institutions, are deeply national. The press and broadcasting were "children of the modern nation state, have always been primarily national, directed towards a national community" (Hjarvard, 2002: 71–2).

In relation to the Great Recession, the first question that needs to be asked is whether the media actually reported warnings of the developing crisis. Journalist John Authers (2010: 1) of the *Financial Times* writes in his book that "it was in March 2007 (after the 'Shanghai Surprise' when a 9 percent fall on the Shanghai stock exchange led to a day of turmoil across the world) that he realised that the world's markets had each other in a tight and deadly embrace." Another journalist, Gillian Tett (who also worked for the *Financial Times*), describes in her acclaimed book how in 2005, almost by chance, she spotted increasing activity in the credit sector that was being under-reported by the mainstream media and tried to cover it. However, she concludes that neither politicians nor journalists were discussing derivatives at all before 2008 (Tett, 2009: pp. x–xi). Another journalist who made a film about debt crisis in 2006 was ridiculed as an "alarmist" or a "doom and gloomer" (Schechter, 2009: 20).

Thus the media seem by and large to have failed to cover the evolving crisis, which made the news only when it became a governmental issue. On June 20, 2007, the media in the UK dutifully reported British Prime Minister and former Chancellor of the Exchequer Gordon Brown's speech at the Mansion House, where he congratulated the City of London on its leadership skills and entrepreneurship and claimed that its success had been a direct consequence of the "light touch" policies adopted by the Labour government (Sim, 2010: 95). According to Brown, "this is an era that history will record as a new golden age for the City of London . . . We think globally . . . and nurture the skills of the future, advance with light-touch regulation, a competitive tax-environment and flexibility" (Boyes, 2009: 188).

Less than three months later, on the evening of September 13, 2007, the BBC reported, although this information was not meant to become public until the following morning, that Northern Rock had asked the Bank of England for emergency support. Within minutes the bank's clients began logging on to its website and withdrawing their money, since the bank had relatively few branches and emphasized online accounts. The website crashed, causing more panic and fear. The next day Northern Rock savers formed long queues in front of the bank's branch offices, and television stations started broadcasting pictures of worried savers queuing to take out their money, causing others to join them. These pictures were spread all over the world by old and new media. In one day, Northern Rock depositors withdrew £1 billion (Cable, 2009: 9; Tett, 2009: 228–9; Authers, 2010: 130–1; Brown, 2010: 21; Sim, 2010: 95). Only then did the event become publicly known as an economic crisis, because the media had shown the queues that other institutions did not want the public to see. As Mervyn King, the Governor of the Bank of England, said in an interview in November 2007:

After the run on Northern Rock, and the impact of the television pictures, it became evident that many of the funders of British banks around the world were no longer willing to fund British banks... What was so difficult to predict was the impact which the television pictures sent around the world of people queuing in the street would have on sentiment and opinion... And this was a potential systemic risk that would have caused immense damage to the structure of the banking system, because a range of institutions, a large number, might have found themselves victims of people who felt nervous about whether their deposits were safe because they had seen a bank in which the retail depositors got trapped.... I wish I had communicated earlier than I did during the month of August. (King, 2007; emphasis added)

Vince Cable (2009: 9), British Liberal Democrat MP, who later became a prominent minister in the Conservative–Liberal Democrat coalition government, wrote this about the UK:

A country that prided itself on being in the forefront of financial innovation and sophistication had been *shamed* by the kind of *disaster* normally experienced in the most *primitive* banking systems. The only visual images most British people had of banking panics were television pictures of bewildered and angry Russian *babushkas* impoverished by pyramid-selling schemes disguised as banks in the chaotic aftermath of communism, or ancient black and white photographs of Mittel-Europeans desperately trying to force the doors of imposing but barricaded buildings in the 1920s. But this was Britain in the twenty-first century! (emphasis added)

According to Gordon Brown (2010: 21–2), "to everybody's considerable annoyance, it became clear that somebody had again been leaking information to Robert Peston, business editor of the BBC." Brown (2010: 56) further observed that:

Most people watched it in complete disbelief as our TV screens showed hitherto unbelievable pictures of a bank run in a modern economy. I was at Downing Street watching long queues outside branches of a British high street bank. It was like a scene in a film or a picture in a history textbook, but not something I had ever expected to see in my lifetime or under my watch. . . . For me it was frightening to see such a physical manifestation of the frailty of modern economies. Because of the manner in which the information was leaked, people were terrified they might lose everything, and our main job was to make sure that the British public felt safe and was kept safe. (emphasis added)

The public panic appeared to cease when the Chancellor of the Exchequer fully guaranteed all Northern Rock's deposits, but Northern Rock was soon to experience the first bank run in the UK for over 150 years. Howard Davies and David Green (2010: 76–7) describe the failure of Northern Rock as "an unpleasant shock to the international reputation of the new London model of regulation" and the nationalization of the bank as "embarrassing enough for the Labour government that had come to office on the basis that nationalization was no longer part of its policy." But this was only the beginning of a banking crisis where it turned out that many other banks both in the UK and other countries had ended up with substantially more money out on loan than they had assets to cover at any one time (£500 billion more in the UK by 2007) (Sim, 2010: 99).

In September 2008, the US investment bank Lehman Brothers filed for protection, and several other banks, in countries including the UK, the USA, France, Germany, Ireland, and Iceland, went bust and asked for help. A study by the Bank of England concluded that the cost of the rescue packages around the world came to a sum of £4,473 billion, around 12 percent of total global GDP (Lynn, 2011: 97). Now the crisis received not only media attention but also attention from politicians, governments, and international organizations. There was no longer any way the economic crisis could be hidden or forgotten. Kaletsky (2010: 18) notes that it was "respected commentators, celebrity financiers, and Nobel laureate economists who were appearing during the nadir of the crisis in the world's most serious media—the *Financial Times*, the *Wall Street Journal*, business television and the BBC, who were asked to explain what it was all about, but who had also played a part in the crisis being professionally blind (Posner, 2009: 328) and were hardly without bias." Kaletsky (2010: 136) further asserts that it was a "complete collapse of confidence among the depositors and creditors of every major financial institution—in effect every bank in the world. It was not just a bank or a financial system, but about an entire political philosophy and economic system, a way of thinking about and living in the world". And Boyes (2009: 66) notes that the failure of the financial system was also a failure of journalism.

Why did it take such a long time for all institutions involved to acknowledge that there was a global crisis? Why did the media not cover it earlier? And when they finally did cover it, did they make things worse, as politicians and bankers claim? I have already argued that all of the old institutions of modernity (including the old media) are caught up together in a *spiral of trust* and that this can be transformed into distrust and fear. Most of the time it does not matter if there is increasing distrust in one of the key institutions, but it does matter when all are caught up in mutual distrust. The spiral of trust starts to escalate, either upwards or downwards, when the different institutions become more interconnected, as happened with the banking crisis. Schechter (2009: 24) writes:

You could say that business journalism was in bed with, or embedded in, the institutions the way that war correspondents were embedded in the units in Iraq, but you know, that can go both ways. General journalists, as well as business journalists, are really guilty in this. They have indulged madness in the last five years—we should have been better at whistle blowing than we were. Journalists for the most part missed the build-up to the crisis and did not warn the public. We all kind of believed that we had fallen upon some kind of alchemy that capitalism had changed, and I think everyone got carried away. Even sceptics in the end found it was pretty difficult to maintain scepticism in the face of the tsunami of apparent easy money.

It is sometimes easy to forget that the media cannot make news without making money (see, e.g., Rantanen, 2009). Apart from public broadcasting financed by license fees, the media have a double market: they create audiences that are in turn sold to advertisers (Owen, 1974: 4). The media themselves were in crisis, especially newspapers, which are heavily dependent on advertising, including property advertising (Schechter, 2009: 21). In many countries, newly rich investors had also invested in the media. As Boyes writes about Iceland, pro-business investors bought media outlets, while pleading for de-regulation and open markets. Financially struggling local newspapers became dependent on real-estate agencies buying up advertising space. National newspapers focused their business coverage toward the business community, rather than explain developments to ordinary readers (Boyes, 2009: 64–5).

With ever-increasing entertainization of the media, in which they compete against each other with the latest news for the biggest audience and advertising share, it is also increasingly difficult to sell these audiences news, and especially informed analysis of an evolving crisis, without making it into a dramatic event. This eventually happens when events are framed as catastrophes. Unlike natural disasters, where one cannot blame the volcano or the tsunami, in a financial crisis the media immediately began to look for those who caused the crisis. The usual initial suspects were "greedy bankers, incompetent regulators, gullible homeowners, or foolish Chinese bureaucrats" (Kaletsky, 2010: 2). But a larger and a more collective culprit was needed: other nation states.

Nationalism, politicians, and the media

The media use primarily a national frame when they try to make sense of global events such as the world economic crisis. They are not alone in this, since they are also in the spiral of trust with governments and politicians, and dutifully report what the latter have said in their speeches and at press confidences. Most of the news originates from official sources (see, e.g., Perry, 2007), and even international organizations are framed in national colors by media choosing to interview representatives of their "own country." There are very few truly global old institutions, mainly only international institutions based on national representation. Likewise, there is not one single medium that does not use a national framework, referring in headlines to "Americans," "Brits," "Greeks," "the US," "the UK", or Greece as a homogenous entity.

Increasingly, when EU money was needed to rescue banks in other countries, economists, politicians, and the media started using nationalist rhetoric. For example, the *Observer* announced on October 5, 2008 that "the party is over for Iceland, the island that tried to buy the world" (Sim, 2010: 26). As Chartier (2010: 28) observes, foreign journalists writing about the financial crisis in Iceland were not reluctant to use disaster vocabulary such as "abyss," "paralysis,"' "catastrophe," "sinking," "crash," "chaos," "lost values," "lost generation," "risk of depopulation," "depression," and even "civil war." He also notes how ordinary Icelanders were victimized. *Le Monde* wrote in October 2008:

Credit was almost a religion in Iceland, all the way down to bankruptcy. A loan for the 4 x 4, a loan for the kitchen, television. When the children wanted to buy a house, they mortgaged their parents. All credit cards were deferred debit and everything was paid for using them: cigarettes and even bread. (quoted in Chartier, 2010: 71)

German Chancellor Angela Merkel, in a speech made in December 2008 after Lehman Brothers had just collapsed and governments around the world were trying to rescue banks in trouble by bailouts, talked about Swabian housewives who would advise not living beyond one's needs (Lynn, 2011: 75). In April 2010, *Bild*, the largest newspaper in Europe, reported that a finance policy expert for the Free Democrats in Merkel's government had made a statement that the German government could not promise Greece any help. "Sell your islands, you bankrupt Greeks! And sell the Acropolis too!" screamed a headline. "Supposedly we have no money for tax cuts, no money for fixing our streets, but suddenly our politicians have billions of euros for the Greeks who have deceived Europe" or "Lazy Greeks living well on German taxes." "They took away the gold that was in the Bank of Greece, they took away Greek money, and they never gave it back," proclaimed the Greek deputy prime minister, referring to the Nazi occupation of Greece in the Second World War (Lynn, 2011: 137–46). "Not a euro to the humbug countries that bite the hand that feeds them," proclaimed a newly elected MP of the True Finn party, resisting EU financial aid to the Portuguese government (*Ilta-Sanomat*, 2011).

The return of nationalism is largely possible because of collective memories of trust, distrust, and fear. Most people's collective international memory is of a breaking of trust, supported by their governments, political parties, and the media, such as in wars and international conflicts. Memories of wars extend across generations, transferred to younger generations within families or by the media (Rantanen, 2007). Nation states are based on collectivized memories, and their citizens are constantly reminded in their daily lives of their "belongingness." When all other major Western ideologies are in a vacuum (Sim, 2010: 100), nationalism is still alive and well. It is constantly used to frame events, and is being used to name, blame, and shame, either individually or collectively, those being held responsible for the crisis. In the Great Recession the enemy was another nation state, as in the "Great War" (as the First World War was once called) and almost every war since.

Conclusion

This chapter has explored the relationship between globalization, risk, trust, fear, and the media. It has specifically concentrated on one large-scale global crisis, the financial recession that started in 2008. I argue that economic globalization has progressed with tremendous speed, but politics and the media have remained primarily national. Or, using Appadurai's concepts, we might say that the financescape has moved much faster than the ideoscape. As a result, we see a disjuncture between the two scapes and a sharp rise of nationalism in many countries.

Trust is never unconditional, even in interpersonal relationships. Increasingly, people do not trust blindly without reservation in any institution, not even in religious organizations. According to a 2011 survey, only about half of the respondents in twenty-three countries trusted business, governments, or the media to do what was right. Trust in banks to do the right thing has dropped since 2008 from 46 percent to 25 percent in the USA and from 30 percent to 16 percent in the UK. Trust in media is lower than ever and has dropped to 27 percent in the USA and to 22 percent in the UK. Increasingly, people put their trust, if at all, in non-governmental institutions (Edelman Trust Barometer, 2011). Of course, this survey, like most, was done on a by-country basis, and as a result we are talking about people's trust in national institutions. Trust in the EU seems to be somewhat higher: the European Commission Eurobarometer survey of public opinion in 2010 showed that around 49 percent thought that the EU was a good thing. Even if these numbers are now lower than in the past, according to this study people surprisingly tend to trust the EU more than their own parliament or government (Eurobarometer, 2010).

On the basis of these studies, it looks as if most people live their lives without trusting any of the old institutions that were once considered the pillars of nation states. One of the key features of the global risk society is that trust and risk have become inseparable, like two sides of the same coin. The spiral of trust responds to risks, and if these become bigger than trust then distrust appears followed by fear. One could also argue that people have learned to live without particularly trusting any of the old institutions and would not even use the concept of trust in describing their relationship to these, but that they still need to hold on to something and cannot lose their trust, however abstract, in all institutions at once.

Financial institutions have rapidly become more global than other old institutions. They have stretched the concept of abstract trust to its limits through their operations and representations. Banks have become machines of the modern age: computer systems that cannot be reached or touched because they have become representational and have eliminated almost any human element. People simply do not understand how global banking works with ever-increasing debts. The connection between money and politics is more vague than ever: the EU and the euro are not the same thing (Lynn, 2011: 228) and trust in the euro is even more abstract than trust in the EU. As Posner (2009: 11) writes, often a bubble is generated by a *belief* that turns out to be mistaken that economic fundamentals are changing—that a market, or maybe the entire economy, is entering a new era of growth.

However, people do understand how national politics works. When they are asked to pay for the debts of banks or of other nation states, they turn back to the nationalism they have grown up with through generations and collective memories. Political parties, old and new, with the help of the media, offer national solutions to global problems. Suddenly, it is again acceptable to proclaim that there are, for example, "True Finns" who are different from the "false Finns" who are either migrants or non-believers in a Finnish nationalism based on the holy communion of one language, one ethnicity, and one culture. Likewise, it is acceptable to say publicly that Finns are morally superior to Greeks or Portuguese because they have been "good" while those other people have been "bad." In sum, it has now become acceptable to blame people in other countries for the problems the new global economy has created.

References

Appadurai, A. (1990). "Disjuncture and Difference in the Global Culture Economy," *Theory, Culture, and Society*, 7/2: 295–310.

Authers, J. (2010). *The Fearful Rise of Markets: A Short View of Global Bubbles and Synchronised Meltdowns*. Harlow: Pearson Education Limited.

Beck, U. (2009). *World at Risk*. Cambridge: Polity Press.

—— *A God of One's Own*. Cambridge: Polity Press.

—— and Grande, E. (2007). *Cosmopolitan Europe*. Cambridge: Polity Press.

Boyes, R. (2009). *Meltdown Iceland: Lessons on the World Financial Crisis from a Small Bankrupt Island*. London: Bloomsbury.

Bremmer, I. (2010). *The End of the Free Market: Who Wins the War between States and Corporations?* New York: Portfolio.

Brown, G. (2010). *Beyond the Crash: Overcoming the First Crisis of Globalization*. London: Simon & Schuster.

Cable, V. (2009). *The Storm: The World Economic Crisis & What It Means?* London: Atlantic Books.

Chartier, D. (2010). *The End of Iceland's Innocence: The Image of Iceland in the Foreign Media during the Financial Crisis.* Ottawa: University of Ottawa Press; Quebec: Presses de l'Université du Québec.

Coleman, J. S. (1990). *Foundations of Social Theory.* Cambridge: Belknap.

Davies, H., and Green, D. (2010). *Banking on the Future: The Fall and Rise of Central Banking.* Princeton and Oxford: Princeton University Press.

Edelman Trust Barometer (2011). 2011 Edelman Trust Barometer <http://edelman. com/trust/2011/uploads/Edelman%20Trust%20Barometer%20Global%20Deck. pdf> (accessed Apr. 21, 2011).

Entman, R. M. (1993). "Framing: Toward Clarification of a Fractured Paradigm," *Journal of Communication,* 43/4: 51–8.

Eurobarometer (2010). Eurobaromter 73. European Commission <http://ec.europa. eu/public_opinion/archives/eb/eb73/eb73_first_en.pdf> (accessed Apr. 21, 2011).

Europa (2011). "Commission Recommends Access to Basic and Affordable Bank Accounts for all Citizens," press release. European Commission, July 18 <http:// europa.eu/rapid/pressReleasesAction.do?reference=IP/11/897> (accessed on July 18, 2011).

Evans, D. S., and Schmalensee, R. (2005). *Paying with Plastic: The Digital Revolution in Buying and Borrowing.* 2nd edn. Cambridge, MA: MIT Press.

Fukuyama, F. (1995). *Trust: The Social Virtues and the Creation of Prosperity.* London: Hamish Hamilton.

Gasparino, C. (2009). *The Sellout: How Three Decades of Wall Street Greed and Government Mismanagement Destroyed the Global Financial System.* New York: HarperCollins Publishers.

Gates, K. (2010). "The Securitization of Financial Identity and the Expansion of the Consumer Credit Industry," *Journal of Communication Inquiry,* 34/4: 417–31.

Gellner, E. (1983). *Nations and Nationalism.* Oxford: Blackwell.

Giddens, A. (1990). *The Consequences of Modernity.* Stanford, CA: Stanford University Press.

Hjarvard, S. (2002). "Mediated Encounters: An Essay on the Role of Communication Media in the Creation of Trust in the 'Global Metropolis'," in G. Stald and T. Tufte (eds), *Global Encounters: Media and Cultural Transformation.* Luton: University of Luton Press, 69–84.

Holton, R. J. (1998). *Globalization and the Nation-State.* Basingstoke and London: Macmillan Press.

Ilta-Sanomat (2011). "Persukansanedustaja paljastaa: Kotona ei tv:ta, radiota," interview with Teuvo Hakkarainen, Apr. 21 <http://www.iltasanomat.fi/vaalit2011/ Persukansanedustaja%20paljastaa%20Kotona%20ei%20tvtä%20ei%20radiota/ art-1288384383390.html> (accessed Apr. 21, 2011).

Kaletsky, A. (2010). *Capitalism 4.0. The Birth of a New Economy.* London: Bloomsbury.

Keane, J. (1988) (ed.). *Civil Society and the State.* London: Verso.

Terhi Rantanen

King, M. (2007). Interview with Robert Peston <http://news.bbc.co.uk/1/shared/bsp/hi/pdfs/06_11_07_fo4_king.pdf> (accessed July 18, 2011).

Kyriakidou, M. (2011). "Media Coverage of Distant Suffering and the Mediation of Cosmopolitanism: Audience Discourses of Distant Disasters in Greece." Submitted Ph.D. thesis. Department of Media and Communications, London School of Economics and Political Science.

Lowenstein, R. (2010). *The End of Wall Street.* New York: Penguin Press.

Luhmann, N. (1979). *Trust and Power.* Chichester: Wiley.

Lynn, M. (2011). *Bust, Greece, the Euro, and the Sovereign Debt Crisis.* Hoboken: Bloomberg Press.

Misztal, B. A. (1996). *Trust in Modern Societies.* Cambridge: Polity Press.

—— (2003). *Theories of Social Remembering.* Maidenhead: Open University Press.

Nohrstedt, S. A. (2011). "Threat Society and the Media," in S. A. Nohrstedt (ed.), *Communicating Risks: Towards the Threat-Society?* Göteborg: Nordicom, 17–52.

O'Neill, N. (2002). *A Question of Trust.* The BBC Reith Lectures. Cambridge: Cambridge University Press.

Owens, B. M., Beebe, J. H., and Manning, W. G., Jr. (1974). *Television Economics.* Lexington: Lexington Books.

Perry, J. (2007). "Whose News: Who is the Political Gatekeeper in the early 21st Century." Unpublished Ph.D. thesis. Department of Media and Communications, London School of Economics and Political Science.

Posner, R. A. (2009). *A Failure of Capitalism. The Crisis of '08 and the Descent into Depression.* Cambridge, MA, and London: Harvard University Press.

Rantanen, T. (2002). *The Global and the National: Media and Communications in Post-Communist Russia.* Lanham: Rowman & Littlefield.

—— (2005). *Media and Globalization.* London: Sage.

—— (2009). *When News was New.* Oxford: Wiley-Blackwell.

Schechter, D. (2009). "Credit Crisis: How Did We Miss It?," *British Journalism Review,* 20/1: 19–26.

Shapiro, S. (1987). "The Social Control of Impersonal Trust," *American Journal of Sociology,* 93/3: 622–58.

Sim, S. (2010). *The End of Modernity: What the Financial and Environmental Crisis Is Really Telling Us.* Edinburgh: Edinburgh University Press.

Simmell, G. (1978). *The Philosophy of Money.* London: Routledge and Kegan Paul.

Sparks, C. (2007). "What's Wrong with Globalization?" *Global Media and Communication,* 3/2: 133–55.

Spiegel (23011). "Brussels' Fear of the True Finns: Rise of Populist Parties Pushes Europe to the Right ," *Spiegel Online,* Apr. 25 http://www.spiegel.de/international/europe/0,1518,758883,00.html (accessed July 1, 2011).

Taibbi, M. (2010). *Griftopia: Bubble Machines, Vampire Squids and the Long Con that Is Breaking America.* New York: Spiegel & Grau.

Tett, G. (2010). *Fool's Gold: How Unrestrained Greed Corrupted a Dream, Shattered Global Markets and Unleashed a Catastrophe*. London: Little Brown.

Thompson, G. (2009). "What's in the Frame? How the Financial Crisis is being Packaged for Public Consumption," *Economy and Society*, 38/3: 520–4.

Zhang, H. (2009). "The Globalisation of Chinese Television: Internationalisation, Transnationalisation and Re-Nationalisation." Unpublished Ph.D. thesis. Department of Media and Communications, London School of Economics and Political Science.

Chapter 7

Crisis, Identity, and the Welfare State

Pekka Himanen

What is going on? A look at the crisis in summer 2011

Who would have believed in 2008 that we would soon be witnessing countries in the European Union (EU) on the brink of collapse? Who would have thought that the exceptionally popular new US President, who rose to power with the message of "Hope" and "Yes We Can"—and who was even awarded a Nobel peace prize during the first year of his presidency—would three years later have fallen to the lowest of approval ratings because of the crisis in the US economy, which has completely overwhelmed everything else?

But here we are as a result of the greatest depression since the Great Depression of 1929—a deep recession that some have dubbed the Great Recession. Its core is not only economic but is the interplay between the economic crisis, the welfare state, and cultural identity.

Let us anchor this key analytical conclusion strongly on empirical facts. So, what is going on?

Right at this moment, in June 2011 in Spain, 200,000 demonstrators are on the streets of Madrid, Barcelona, and other major cities protesting the way the economic and political elite has led the country into an economic crisis and how they have handled it by primarily cutting public expenditure. They call themselves *Los Indignados*, "The Indignants." Since the pre-crisis year of 2007, unemployment has tripled to over 20 percent and to 50 percent for those under 25 years old (nearing five million unemployed, which is equivalent to the whole population of Finland or more unemployed than there are in France and Italy combined, and therefore the young "ni–ni" or "neither–nor" generation that is neither studying nor working has become one of the biggest subgroups of the movement).

In Barcelona, the demonstration against the cuts in public expenditure forced the Catalonian government representatives to fly to their meeting by helicopter, secured by a chain of police cars and policemen. This was after an earlier demonstration at the Plaça Catalunya had been dispersed by the police with rubber bullets and 121 people had been wounded.

And yet Spain is not even one of the countries that has requested bailout packages from the EU. It is, however, mentioned as a country facing the threat of falling on the bailout track: it feels the pressure, with its exceptionally high level of unemployment combined with a dangerously high public deficit of around 10 percent of the country's GDP.

In the EU the public debt crisis phase started with Greece. Greece confirmed its request for an emergency bailout package of €110 billion from the EU and the International Monetary Fund (IMF) in May 2009. This amount of money did not come without conditions.

Greece has been forced significantly to cut public spending and to privatize. As I am writing this, Greece is looking for an additional bailout package that could surpass even the original €110 billion. It needs €12 billion urgently, as it has a loan payment due in mid-July.

Greece is facing the worst debt crisis in the whole EU: its public debt is at over 120 percent of the GDP and the public deficit is over 13 percent. At the same time, the unemployment rate has more than doubled to 16 percent and to almost 50 percent for those under 25 years old. As a response, labor unions have organized a series of general strikes.

Angry demonstrators at the Syntagma Square in front of the parliament house have become a familiar image on the TV news. Demonstrators have thrown stones and fire bombs at the police, who have used tear gas against them. Buildings have been set on fire. In one of these demonstrations a banner read: "You have a disease for which we have the medicine: Revolution." Three people have died in the demonstrations so far.

Recently, the protestors have started calling themselves the "Indignant Citizens Movement" (in Greek, *Kinema Aganaktismenon Politon, Κίνημα Αγανακτισμένων Πολιτών*). It is connected with the Spanish protests and has likewise been organized through social networking sites, which is why some have also given the movement the nickname "May of Facebook" (also referring to the ongoing "Arab Spring" movement, and in both of them the young generation's voice about an alternative future is central, linked to a key statistic that is still without real representative voice: currently 50 percent of the world's population is under 27 years old). What is significant is that this movement is no longer organized by traditional political parties or labor unions. There are 150,000 people from all backgrounds signed in on the "Indignants at Syntagma" Facebook page and more from other Greek locations. The most popular slogans at the demonstrations include: "Error 404—Democracy not found" and "Oust!" (Greek for "Leave!"). They also send messages to people in other countries in Europe. For example, as a reply to a slogan of the Spanish protestors, "Be quiet, the Greeks are sleeping," they raised a banner at the Spanish Embassy in Athens saying: "¡Estamos despiertos! ¿Que hora es? ¡Ya es hora de que se vayan!" (We've woken up! What time is it? It's time they left!). They also established a live link via Skype between the demonstrations in Madrid and Athens. And now the movement is already sending a message to the people of Italy and France with new banners: "Zitti che svegliamo gli Italiani" (Be quiet or you'll wake up the Italians) and "Silence! Les Français dorment! Ils rêvent de '68" (Silence! The French are sleeping! They are dreaming of May '68).

Of course, in the other corner of Europe, Ireland received an €85 billion bailout package from the EU and the IMF in November 2010. This was after its public deficit had exploded to almost 15 percent and its unemployment rate had tripled to 15 percent.

And then there is Portugal, the country in which our research group has gathered since 2009. In Portugal, the public debt has reached a record level of almost 100 percent of the GDP. The budget deficit is nearing 10 percent of the GDP. And the government of Portugal is paying almost 10 percent interest rates for ten-year loans. Unemployment has nearly doubled to 13 percent from the pre-crisis level.

Within Portugal the reaction may have been more peaceful than in Greece and Spain, yet the situation has triggered mass demonstrations, in particular the March 12 protests of the so-called Geração à Rasca, "The Junk

Generation" (or *quinhentoseuristas*, "the 500-euroists"), which were also one inspiration for the Spanish demonstrations. The Portuguese protest gathered over 200,000 people to demonstrate on the Avenida da Liberdade in Lisbon and elsewhere in the country—again organized using social media from Facebook to Twitter. The soundtrack for the protests was Deolinda's song "Parva que sou" about the poor working conditions of the young, especially the university graduates: "Que mundo tão parvo | Onde para ser escravo é preciso estudar" ("What kind of a world is so silly | Where you have to study to be a slave").

Even if we have theoretically understood for a long time how interconnected the global network society is—including the "network state" of the EU—the actual series of events surrounding Portugal still cannot but strike the observer. Or how did Portugal and Finland—two previously friendly small countries at the opposite ends of Europe—suddenly become key opponents in a drama that held the whole EU hostage?

This is what happened in this unexpected unfolding of events: on April 7, 2011, Portugal requested a €78 billion bailout package from the EU, which became the final trigger for the huge election victory of the nationalist and anti-euro and anti-EU party "True Finns" in the Finnish parliamentary election of April 17. The Finnish national election became essentially a debate over the Portuguese credit situation! After the election, Finland, the former model student of the EU, kept Portugal—and the rest of the eurozone—holding their breath for six weeks during its complicated government negotiations until Finland finally confirmed its participation in the bailout on May 25, just in time for Portugal's €5 billion debt rollout date. In the meanwhile, there was even a YouTube "battle" between Portugal and Finland, something that also became well known in the mainstream media. To influence Finnish decision-making, the Portuguese created a YouTube campaign recapitulating the great achievements of Portugal throughout history and reminding Finns of the Portuguese support for Finland during its hardships in the Second World War. And, if we can talk about the ultimate irony of history, it is probably here: Finland, which was now refusing to save Portugal from defaulting, had itself been only a few days away from default and falling under the control of the IMF during its own financial and economic crisis of the early 1990s.

Of course, the original primus motor of the crisis was the financial crisis of the USA in autumn 2008, symbolized by the collapse of Lehman Brothers on September 15 of that year. The USA shares the top rank in public debt with Greece, Ireland, and Italy: the US public debt has reached the level of

100 percent of the GDP and the public deficit is over 10 percent. Unemployment is almost 10 percent.

The IMF has estimated that overall the US banks have lost over $1 trillion. The cost of the public stimulus plan has risen from the original $1 trillion to more than $3 trillion. According to the Federal Reserve, the fall in housing prices, retirement assets, and other savings and investment assets has further wiped out more than a staggering $14 trillion of household wealth.

However, despite all this, up to the very end of our research group's meetings, there had been only limited protests in the USA—one of the few exceptions being the Berkeley campus demonstrations at Sproul Hall and other history-laden places (see the analysis of Rosalind Williams, Chapter 1, this volume). Then finally, in September 2011, a similar pressure caused those who had been excluded to start the Occupy Wall Street movement, rapidly spreading throughout the US and beyond with the slogan "We are the 99%."

Analytical context

All of this has significant analytical consequences. But, before jumping to the main analytical conclusions, let us also be conceptually a bit clearer about what we refer to by this crisis. As has been stated also by virtually every other author in this book, the first thing that we face is the need to clarify what specifically we mean by this crisis. There is no need to go through all the details again, so let me just express succinctly how I define the nature of the current crisis. Based on analytical reasons, I prefer to use the expression "the Great Recession," because this conveys the sense of a broad multidimensional crisis without claiming falsely that it has been literally global—because, strictly speaking, if one looks at the map of the crisis, it has not been a "global financial and economic crisis." As can be seen if one looks at the map, the concept that expresses the geography of this economic crisis most closely is "the industrial countries' crisis," because the collapse in GDP spans from North America to Europe and from the former Soviet Union to the Asian fully industrialized countries of Japan and the "Tigers," but this economic crisis has not occurred in most of Latin America, Africa, the Middle East, and Asia, as is well illustrated, for example, by the emerging economies of China, India, and Brazil.

And yet the financial and economic crisis has been global in the sense that it has impacted on all countries: no country has been able to ignore it or to afford not to form any reaction to it. This global impact applies both to the financial part of the crisis—as we really have one global financial market—and to the economic part, at least through the global export markets. This is simultaneously the reason why, if we want to be precise, calling this "the American–European crisis" would also not be completely correct. This is first because of the actual geography just described above: even if the crisis started in the USA and then spread to Europe in particular, one can hardly ignore the other major world economies that have been directly affected. The second reason is this larger impact.

The final reason for preferring the expression "the Great Recession" is the most important—namely that the analytical consequences of the crisis have not been limited to the financial and economic spheres. Just as in the Great Depression, the crisis has much broader and deeper social and cultural consequences, which is the very premiss of this book—that we need to understand these larger social and cultural implications. Ultimately, it can be argued, it will require a political and cultural response that is equivalent to the New Deal—that is, a new social contract.

Summa

So, after clarifying the concept of the crisis, what is the analytical meaning of the empirical developments described above?

The key analytical observation is that the current crisis has produced strong resistance identities against not only the measures used to treat the crisis but more deeply against the very development model that led to the crisis and from which the current attempts to rectify the situation derive. Therefore, there is an explicit tension between identity and the global network society as it is expressed in its currently dominating form.

Furthermore, the crisis described above is not limited to the acute situation of those economies that are on the brink of collapsing. We can make a further argument: the root of the current crisis is the fact that the generally dominant model for development has been based on systematic debt-taking. This goes for economic debt, but it also applies to other spheres. In relation to the environment, we have lived by taking an ecological debt from future generations. In terms of global social inclusion, our well-being has been based on a social debt taken from others.

It is this overall development model based on systematic debt that is in crisis now: living with money that does not exist or living with someone else's money (or resources, more generally).

Therefore, to use a metaphor, our world is like a patient who is suffering a heart attack in the form of the economic crisis that requires immediate action to stimulate the patient back to life. But, after a closer examination, it turns out that the same patient also suffers from other deathly diseases that need equal attention: lung cancer in the form of the climate crisis and diabetes in the form of the social crisis, where the obesity of the upper body threatens to cause the death of a lower limb.

There is a further level to this: analytically speaking, here the problem is the solution—or, the solution is the problem! That is, the cure that is used to treat the crisis further worsens the crisis. It is like the medicine killing the patient. This is because of the following analytical link: analytically speaking, there is only one sustainable way out if the public investment to an inclusive welfare state is to be maintained—that is, creating conditions for growth. However, cutting the public investments into these conditions for growth—such as education, research, and development—decreases growth even further, which again forces additional cuts in public investments. This is a vicious circle.

The analytical alternative would be to invest in creating a virtuous circle. In this virtuous circle, investments in creating growth make it possible to continue funding the public investments. This model would mean forming a virtuous circle where the growth of the economy makes it possible to continue to fund the inclusive welfare state and the welfare state then provides new, well-educated people in good health and basic security to continue the success of the economy.

This kind of a model links informational development with human development—in a deeper sense than simply having a successful informational economy and an inclusive welfare state behind human development. The core of the concept of a virtuous circle is the way it links informationalism with human development, the informational economy with the welfare state. It is not so that the success of the informational economy simply makes it possible to fund the costs of the welfare society. The welfare society provides the basis for the success of the informational economy and is therefore an investment. The welfare state produces highly educated people in good health and with a sense of security to create the further success of the informational economy. The model means a virtuous circle between the information society and the welfare state, or informational development and human development, in which they support each other.

But, finally, there is also a third key analytical concept determining the virtuous/vicious circle. This is identity. As Manuel Castells has argued in his trilogy *The Information Age* (Castells, 2000–4), the key tension of the information age is that between the global network society and identity. The theoretical challenge is how to build a project identity that supports the above virtuous circle. And, at the time of a crisis, the risk is that the identity turns into a resistance identity, coupled with the vicious circle.

The above examples of the Indignants movement in southern Europe, from Greece to Spain to Portugal—and its continuation the Occupy movement—are examples so far of an identity of resistance that has sometimes even turned into expressions of violence. So far the movement is without a new project identity to propose, although naturally this can change and a project identity can evolve, perhaps coupled with a call for some form of the above idea of a virtuous circle to replace the current vicious circle.

Another very strong form of resistance identity that we are presently observing in Europe is extreme nationalist identity. This is especially true about the developments in Northern Europe. In France, the National Front, led by Marine Le Pen, has continued to enjoy a 15 percent rate of support in national elections. In the Presidential election polls of 2011, Ms Le Pen had even been a frontrunner before President Sarkozy, which would take her to the second round with the Socialist candidate.

In the Netherlands, the Dutch Freedom Party achieved 15.5 percent of the vote in the general election of 2010. In Switzerland, the Swiss People's Party had a 28.9 percent rate of support in 2011.

In the Nordic countries, extreme nationalist parties even had a 20 percent rate of support in 2011. In Norway, the Progress Party had 22.9 percent of the vote in the parliamentary elections of 2009 (the second biggest share of the vote), and nationalist extremism exploded into violence when a horrible terrorist attack by a right-wing extremist killed seventy-seven people.

In Denmark, the Danish People's Party had a 13.9 percent rate of support in 2011; and the Sweden Democrats enjoyed 5.7 percent of the vote in the general election of 2010. And then there is the case of Finland—the True Finns received 19.1 percent of the vote in the parliamentary elections of spring 2011.

Pekka Himanen

Linking the theoretical model with empirical reality

Let us deepen the above theoretical discussion by linking it with a real empirical case so that we can test the general hypothesis through an illustrative example. I will use the empirical case of Finland, as it shows especially strongly the above links between economic crisis, welfare state, and cultural identity.

We have already analyzed the Finnish model (see Castells and Himanen, 2002). So what is the empirical realism of now defending a virtuous circle between informational economy, the welfare state, and cultural identity in the context of the crisis?

The first empirical observation is that Finland has been able to weather the economic storm better than most other advanced countries. First of all, it is one of the few countries that have maintained their highest AAA credit ratings. In fact, the main elements of the Finnish model have continued to stand. So, in contrast to the widespread idea that Silicon Valley represented the only successful model for informational development in the Information Age, Finland has been able to combine successful informational development with human development. In fact, for years Finland ranked as the most competitive economy in the world, with its highest rankings in innovation, producing things like the mobile phone giant Nokia (which had a 40 percent share of the global market) or the Linux open-source operating system (which is used to run one-third of the whole Web). But what made it different from Silicon Valley was the fact that, at the same time, Finland had one of the most inclusive welfare societies, providing one of the highest levels of human development in the world, including the lowest levels of poverty and income inequality as well as the highest-quality all-inclusive public health care system and social security for unemployment and retirement. This also included the highest-quality free public education system for all, which topped international comparisons on student performance, such as the OECD's PISA studies (where Finland was No. 1 in all categories: literacy, mathematics, natural sciences, and general problem-solving skills).

All of the main elements here continue to work, even after the impact of the Great Recession. In spite of the fact that the Finnish economy suffered from the crisis, it bounced back quickly. So, after a reduction of the GDP by 8.2 percent in 2009, the Finnish economy recovered in 2010 with a growth of 3.1 percent and, at the time of writing, an estimated growth of 3.6 percent for 2011, so there is currently no economic crisis in Finland. The Finnish banking sector has not been affected by the crisis either. The same applies to employment, which has not been shaken. The unemployment rates for recent years have been: 6.4 percent in 2008; up to 8.4 percent in 2009; 8.5 percent in 2010; and an estimated decrease to 7.7 percent for 2011. These figures are all below the levels of unemployment at the time when we wrote our original analysis of the Finnish model (see Castells and Himanen, 2002). Also, the policy of increasing the investment in the innovation system has continued, and in 2011 Finland is reaching the target of 4 percent of GDP going to R&D, which is the highest level in the world—a target confirmed by the new Government Program.

The welfare state continues in its earlier generously inclusive form. There have not been cuts in the welfare state since we wrote our 2002 book. In fact, the new Government Program of the coalition led by the Conservatives and the Social Democrats has introduced several measures to promote social inclusion: from increasing the minimum social security by €100 per month to reforming taxation to reduce income inequality and to move the general emphasis from taxing work to taxing consumption that is bad for the environment or for well-being (in a shift that some call "the green tax reform").

And, especially, the funding of education has not been put at risk; instead there have been further investments, especially at the university level. The education system has continued to perform at the top of international comparisons.

So the core of the Finnish model, in which the informational economy and the welfare state form a virtuous circle, continues.

Challenges of the Finnish model

However, if we are to discuss a serious real-life alternative to the development model that has been called to crisis, we also have to see the challenges of the alternative model. These are even more important because the following are also the key analytical challenges for the development models in general when a way forward from the crisis is being reconstructed.

Expanding the innovation-based economy's productivity growth

The Finnish model—just like the general concept of a virtuous circle—depends on creating conditions for growth. For this growth to be sustainable over the long run, the informational economy itself needs to expand and diversify to create a broad basis for innovation-based productivity growth. In 2002, Nokia was largely dominating the Finnish ICT sector. In order to achieve sustainable growth, Finland had to find a way for the informational economy to expand to other ICT successes as well as into other sectors, combining innovativeness in all fields with new entrepreneurialism. In general, the deepest European crisis is the crisis of a too narrowly innovation-based productivity growth, especially in the countries that have been worst affected by the crisis.

Innovation-based reformation of the welfare state in the information age

The long-term sustainability of the virtuous circle can also not be based on just the economy reforming itself and thus continuing to fund human development through the welfare state; it must also mean informational reformation of the welfare state itself and thus the development of the "welfare state 2.0"—that is, the welfare state in the Information Age. In 2002 the Finnish welfare state was already facing these pressures to renew itself, among other factors because of the aging of the population that was changing the dependency ratio. So, even if the welfare state was not just an expense that was possible to fund with the success of the informational economy but instead was an investment for the informational economy, it had still to go through a reformation of productivity and structures based on innovative informational development. This challenge was becoming bigger with the aging population, who would soon be starting to retire in large numbers. This challenge of creating the welfare state for the information age is also a general challenge for all countries.

The culture of multiculturalism

Finally, any development model must find a sustainable link between informationalism, human development, and identity. In our 2002 book, we noted how Finland had been able to create a positive link between its special version of being a global network society and the Finnish identity. However, we also identified a potential big problem: we showed that beneath its information society project identity, the Finnish identity was relying on the homogeneous Finnish culture. And this created the risk of it becoming a resistance identity based on closed nationalism. In such a scenario, the resistance identity would become a counterforce for the very Finnish model. This included, but was not limited to, the model's long-term need of tapping into the "brain circulation" of the global talent in the global network society (to use AnnaLee Saxenian's term (2007) in her analysis of Silicon Valley).

So where is the Finnish model now regarding these challenges?

Expanding the innovation-based economy's productivity growth

First, in terms of the economy, the answer is that, even if the growth rates mean that Finland has so far succeeded in creating growth based on the broader informational economy, it is also true that Finland has still not really addressed the challenge we mentioned in our earlier publication. So, even if Nokia continues to have the largest share of the global mobile phone market (about 25 percent in 2011) and is making big profits, it has been strongly challenged by the change in its market environment, and by the rise of companies such as Apple and Google, and this has been reflected in the decrease of Nokia's market value. The competition is now about designing the mobile Internet and applications, rather than just engineering hardware. So a new type of innovation is needed compared to Nokia's origins, as we pointed out in our previous book.

Nor has the ICT sector expanded so as to be less dependent on Nokia in any major way either. It is true that the mobile game industry has exploded in Finland, with such icons as Rovio Mobile's *Angry Birds* game, which has been a huge smart phone app hit, with over 500 million downloads in 2011. This makes it the most popular computer game in history and is turning the computer games characters into a Disney type world of movies, theme parks, and merchandise—and the big future aim is to become the first entertainment brand with over a billion fans and then to list it on the stock market. (The CEO of the company, Peter Vesterbacka, was listed by *Time* magazine as the seventh most influential person in the world in 2011: this can easily be said to be an exaggeration of his influence, but the magazine is probably thinking of him more as a face for the new open-innovation age, in which young people around the world can start implementing their creative ideas on open platforms, a shift that could have major consequences in the future.) However, for now, the revenues of the mobile game industry are still modest on the scale of the whole Finnish economy. The future may be good, but it depends on how the larger innovation and entrepreneurial environment develops to support this. In this larger picture, the future of the Finnish ICT sector is very much linked to how Nokia's restructuring in the new competition environment will take place. It is known that Nokia's new alliance with Microsoft to shift to the Windows operating system as the platform for its phones will mean laying off up to several thousand R&D professionals who were developing Nokia's own Symbian operating system. The critical question is: can this be translated into a new wave of innovation and entrepreneurialism, with thousands of the world's top developers starting businesses around their ideas in a supportive innovation environment? If so, then the principle "never let a good crisis go to waste" could open a new chapter in the story of the Finnish ICT sector.

Finally, looking at the present situation, even if we note that the Finnish economy is continuing to grow at good levels, these growth rates are much less than those we were witnessing at the turn of the millennium. This means that some of the strong dynamism of the Finnish model has been lost and the only way forward would be to expand and diversify the informational economy, as we have outlined.

Innovation-based reformation of the welfare state in the information age

As for the welfare state, the situation is similar: the welfare state has stayed strong without major cuts, but nor has there been an innovation-based informational transformation of its productivity and structures. Now, with the aging population literally stepping away from the workforce in the next few years, this is becoming a huge challenge, because, in addition to opening up for immigration, innovation-based productivity growth is the only way to relieve the public funding pressures. As we have pointed out, changes need to start immediately in order for the welfare state to continue without big cuts. And this would imply showing what the welfare state 2.0, or the welfare state in the Information Age, can be.

The only major exception is the very important investment in the renewal of the education system that is currently under way in Finland, especially at the university level, where it is most directly linked to the innovation system. There has been a significant increase in the funding of the universities and a change in their structure. Whereas earlier the university funding was split between twenty universities in a small country, there is now a development in which some of the universities have been merged and a division of specialization has been clarified, so that these universities can have sufficient resources to be at the top level in the world in their areas of specialization.

The most important of these structural renewals has been the merging of the Helsinki University of Technology with the Helsinki School of Economics and the University of Art and Design, forming a new Aalto University (named after the famous Finnish functionalist architect Alvar Aalto, whose work spanned all of these areas). The idea is to bring together three types of innovation that are needed to succeed in our time: technological, business, and design. Of course, the core goal of the universities is still to remain top-ranked in terms of pure research and arts. The applied aspect is only one dimension of Aalto University, and it is acknowledged that it can have real value to the innovation system only if its pure research and arts core remains intact, original, and at the top. Therefore the self-description of Aalto University is: "Where science and arts meet technology, business and design." Funding for the university has been significantly increased.

The strong public investment in the education system is a very important difference to the responses of most other countries during the crisis. Whereas in most other places the response has been to cut university funding along with other public expenditure, the Finnish model considers it a public investment in an intrinsic value as well as in the conditions for growth—and therefore in the virtuous circle. So, whereas in the USA, the government has responded to the crisis with a decrease in funding for education, the Finnish government has increased university funding during the same time period by channeling financing to its foundations. As shown by Rosalind Williams (Chapter 1, this volume), in the more generally illustrative case of the University of California at Berkeley, which is one of the very leading academic institutions as well as an important engine of Silicon Valley, state funding has been halved from $450 million in 2008 to $225 million in 2011, with tuition and fees rising by over 50 percent at the same time. As a contrast, the Finnish government has increased the university funding during the same time period—for example, by increasing public funding for the new "spearhead" Aalto University by €500 million (for its endowment) and holding to the principle that all higher education must be free so that it advances social inclusion.

This strengthens the university concentration in the Greater Helsinki area, where the leading basic research university, University of Helsinki, is also situated. From the viewpoint of the innovation system, the goal is for the Greater Helsinki Area to become a "spike on the map" in a global innovation economy, where the world is not flat but led by glocal concentrations of innovation. This "spike on the map" is being formed particularly in the physical environment of Aalto University, located in Otaniemi, Espoo, next to Keilaniemi, where Nokia and other leading ICT companies, as well as leading companies in many other fields (such as the energy field, with its biggest companies Fortum and Neste, and Kone, which is now headed by the person who led the most successful phase of the Nokia mobile phones) are situated. The plan that is being executed is for these to form an entrepreneurial and innovative environment, driven by the spirit of creative passion and enriching interaction.

There is both a national governmental plan as well as a city-level plan related to fostering the development of this entrepreneurial innovation environment. The construction plans for transportation and building in this area in the next few years alone amount to about €10 billion. It is the biggest concentration of R&D funding and professionals in Finland. For example, since the early 1990s Nokia alone has invested €43 billion in R&D. Making all these investments in a wise way to form an enriching innovation environment will be decisive for the next chapters in the Finnish informational innovation economy story.

Identity and the global network society

Finally, the third critical challenge we raised has also become newly relevant, both for Finland and more generally, and this is why the Finnish case is here especially raised. This is the link between identity and the global network society, where Finland was earlier able to relieve the tension by making the information society a national identity project. The times of crises are especially prone to producing strong resistance identities. And now, at the moment of the current crisis, we have witnessed this tendency both in Finland and elsewhere, including the cases I have described above.

The big global question is: can more constructive project identities be built in answer to the issues raised by the resistance identities?

In the Finnish case, the resistance identity is being expressed in a very different form to that of the current south European Indignants movement or the Occupy movement that has been very visible in some other countries. Yes, the end result of the 2011 election was that a coalition government was formed, led by the Conservatives and the Social Democrats, who became the two biggest parties. And in this sense a choice was made by the Finns—to use the Government Program's title—for an "open, just, and courageous Finland."

But the title was a conscious reference to another strong development in the election, which was the rise of the resistance identity represented by the nationalist party True Finns. It is this very fact that has forced the winning parties to emphasize how pro-EU, pro-Euro, and pro-immigration they are—including the new Prime Minister, who has emphasized that Finland's fundamental position of being open and part of the global network society will not change.

So there is a real battle between a more open global network society project identity and a closed resistance identity. And, unless it is possible to give new content to what is the renewed constructive project identity for the global network society by truly addressing the issues that have produced the resistance identity, it is a victory only for now and the resistance identity will keep growing stronger.

Furthermore, the form this identity takes is finally a key factor defining how that society is going to be able to handle the time of the crisis. In the case of Finland, as in so many other cases of advanced economies, the future of the welfare society is dependent on both its innovative informational transformation and immigration. In fact, the reality is that, without immigration, the welfare state will have to be cut when the population ages. So, the actual fact is that, in contrast to the idea that is connected with xenophobic identity according to which the immigrants come and take our welfare, the immigrants bring our welfare. So being against immigration is actually the same as being against the welfare state. The same goes for retirement age: the less immigration there is, the later the retirement age becomes. So being against immigration means calling for a radically later retirement age for people.

However, even if this is the analytical connection, the time of crisis highlights the key role that identity plays. The Finnish parliamentary election on

April 17, 2011 highlighted this topic directly. Let us be very empirical again and describe what exactly happened in this election.

In the election, Finland followed the trend of rising nationalist resistance identity seen earlier in many other European countries: the nationalist party of the True Finns gained a huge election achievement, with the support of 19 percent of the votes, becoming the third biggest party in Finland. Table 7.1 shows the shift between the parliamentary elections in 2007 and 2011. As one can see, the support for the nationalist True Finns has grown dramatically. In fact, this is the biggest single election shift in the Finnish parliament in decades.

So what happened? What is feeding the rise of the True Finns? The key to understanding their rapid growth is to see that just four years previously they were still a very marginal party with only 4 percent support. The party started as an anti-immigration and xenophobic movement emphasizing national Finnish identity, which is where their name also comes from. (The True Finns even included an art program in their official election campaign program, which basically stated that only art that supports national identity should be publically funded and "postmodern art" should find its own funding!)

But it would be overly simplistic to understand this tension between identity and the global network society only in terms of anti-immigration and xenophobic sentiments. This is the origin of True Finns but this is not why they received a further 15 percent points of support in the next election. The support for the party started growing dramatically in the context of the crisis as it escalated to a eurozone debt crisis in Greece, Ireland, and, at the same time as the election, Portugal.

Therefore, the core of the rise of the True Finns is that they came to represent a broader protest against the global network society in its current form, which led to the crisis and seemed not to offer a way forward from the crisis. The most important actual reason for the current rise of the True Finns

Table 7.1 Shift in party support, parliamentary elections, 2007–2011 (%)

Party	2011	2007	Percentage change
Conservatives	20.4	22.3	− 1.9
Social Democrats	19.1	21.4	− 2.3
True Finns	19.1	4.1	+15.0
Centre Party	15.8	23.1	− 7.3

was their rejection of the euro debt instruments for bailing out other countries; the eurozone became the symbol of the global network society.

We now know this through comprehensive empirical research. Juho Rahkonen has made an empirical study based on a sample of 4,000 voters. This shows that the vote for the True Finns was by no means from just one marginalized class of society. It grew into a general protest. In fact, 40 percent of the supporters identify themselves as being part of labor (whereas only 31 percent of the supporters of the Social Democratic Party identify themselves as labor). It is the party with the second highest proportion of entrepreneurs as supporters, coming only after the Conservatives. And, with a 12 percent rate of support, it is the second most popular party among students, coming right after the Green Party (18 percent). Table 7.2 gives a breakdown of party identification by profession.

Furthermore, the income level of the supporters of the True Finns matches the average Finnish income—and 5 percent of the supporters even reported an annual high-level income of over €90,000. The True Finns have support across different social classes as well as throughout the country. What unites them are the key themes of protest, especially in the form of being anti-euro and anti-EU and against the current ruling elite.

So the True Finns have grown into a general protest against the global network society in its current form (including, like elsewhere, against its current leaders, who led us into the economic crisis). So, in addition to being an expression of the tension between identity and the global network society (represented by the EU), the increase in votes was also a reaction

Table 7.2 Breakdown of party identification by profession group, 2011 (%)

Profession	True Finns	Conservatives	Social Democrats	Centre
Labor	40	10	31	22
Clerk	14	30	19	16
Entrepreneur	7	11	4	6
Manager	4	12	2	4
Farmer	2	2	0	7
Student	12	10	9	11
Housewife	1	3	1	2
Pensioner	16	21	32	29

Source: Rahkonen (2011) based on the survey by the Economic Research.

against the current establishment. It was more a vote against the current form than for anything new offered to replace it. At best, there was a vague conglomeration of loosely related goals.

In the end, one still needs to put the protest in context. The True Finns are still only the third biggest party in Finland, with less than 20 percent support, which means that they will not be able to dictate the future Finnish policy. This has been made especially clear by the winning party, the Conservatives, who have continued open global network society policies.

Summa summarum

However, globally—and on the general analytical level—we should pay much more attention to this social and cultural dimension of the crisis. It is not only the nationalist identity movements in different countries. It is not only the people participating in the demonstrations of the Indignants in Southern Europe or the expanding Occupy movement. The resistance identities have reached the mainstream population, which is more and more strongly against the current development model for the global network society that landed us in this crisis and yet is being used as a way out.

An increasing number of people disagree, and they are calling for an alternative development model to go forward. They may not have the answers themselves. Yet the situation will not be solved by ignoring them, which is simply a way of strengthening the resistance identities against the global network society.

Therefore, the ultimate—and generally critical analytical and practical—policy question is: can we formulate a more constructive project identity for a more sustainable development model in the global network society as a way forward? Or, will the crisis translate into a violent social and cultural crisis between the attempt to continue the global network society's development as it was and people's increasingly strong expression of a resistance identity because they cannot associate themselves with the old development model? There is an urgent call for a more sustainable form of global network society development that would combine informational development with human development from well-being to environment, supported by a more constructive project identity. That is, a call for dignified life—or, if you want to put it in these terms, a New Social Contract answering to the Great Recession with more Dignity.

References

Castells, Manuel (2000). *The Rise of the Network Society.* The Information Age: Economy, Society and Culture, vol. I. 2nd edn. Oxford: Blackwell.

—— (2004). *The Power of Identity.* The Information Age: Economy, Society and Culture, vol. II. 2nd edn. Oxford: Blackwell.

—— (2004). *End of Millennium.* The Information Age: Economy, Society and Culture, vol. III. 2nd edn. Oxford: Blackwell.

—— and Himanen, Pekka (2002). *The Information Society and the Welfare State: The Finnish Model.* Oxford: Oxford University Press.

Rahkonen, Juho (2011). "Perussuomalaisten ruumiinavaus" (Dissection of the True Finns), *Yhteiskuntapolitiikka,* 76: 4.

Saxenian, AnnaLee (2007). *The New Argonauts: Regional Advantage in a Global Economy.* Cambridge, MA: Harvard University Press.

PART FOUR

Beyond the Crisis

As well as examining the cultural and social behavior that led to the 2008 crisis, it is crucial to assess the social productivity of different cultures emerging in its aftermath.

The cultures that led to the crisis of the network society were fostered in practices of network individualism (a "networked self-interest") epitomized by the financial and managerial elites, institutionally backed by business school ethos and disseminated under a traditional model of communication based in mass communication and the building of reference groups.

An opposing perspective is emerging from the findings of the projects of empirical research presented in this part of the volume. To look beyond the crisis is to look at what is breeding out of the crisis. The different examples, ranging from Europe to North Africa, the Americas, and Asia, suggest that, although born of the pre-crisis experimentation of digital technologies and allowed by the dissemination of the Internet, these new cultures are fueled not by any identifiable professional elite but rather by very geographically diverse and heterogeneous networks of individuals. Those cultures propose new perspectives on how to look at ownership, production, distribution, and identity-building. Theirs are cultures of "networked belonging" built also out of network individualism but adopting a communal practice and seemingly able to contaminate virally non-digital areas of daily experience, production, and power relationships.

Examples of collective economic practices based on non-capitalist forms of production, consumption, and exchange can be found all around the more developed countries. The analysis presented here on Catalonia suggests that between 20 percent and 60 percent of the population at large, and a much higher proportion of people under 40 years of age, are engaged in some form of solidarity-based, life value economy. While many of these practices preceded the crisis, particularly in their most culturally conscious forms, the crisis seems to have increased their popularity and appreciation. In many different ways, probably as many as the diverse ways in which the alternative practices are present in people's lives, we can argue that they have laid the path to the rise and organization of political movements such as "The Indignants."

Understanding what lies ahead of the crisis and its aftermaths means looking deep into the cultures of networked belonging and into alternative economic practices, because it might be from their improbable remixes and mash-ups that we will witness a new politics able to foster a new social organization of life in the years after the crisis.

Chapter 8

Surfing the Crisis: Cultures of Belonging and Networked Social Change

Gustavo Cardoso and Pedro Jacobetty

Introduction

In the opening images of the documentary *The Chicago Sessions*, produced by the Dutch Broadcaster VPRO in 2009, Naomi Klein states that "class" had returned to America with a vengeance. This statement refers to the recent opposition between "Main Street" and "Wall Street," and Klein argues that Milton Friedman's views on the end of classes, by generalizing ownership of capital built on mass access to shares and real estate, had failed.

Although Klein might have spotted a true opposition of forces between those who own companies, "Wall Street," and those who have had access to credit in order to emulate capitalist ownership, "Main Street," we would argue that the fundamental opposition rising from the crisis is built not around ownership but between the very values that sustain those practices. These values are the cultures of "networked self-interest," which have been the basis of the very deployment of the crisis, versus the cultures of "networked belonging," which are currently being built.

What this analysis will try to unveil are the foundations of the cultures of networked belonging, the set of values and beliefs orienting material practices that have been taking shape in the first years of the twenty-first century, all of them attempts to promote social change, sometimes organized and with clear objectives, other times the hazardous product of networked serendipities of everyday life choices. Examples can be found in diverse geographies around the world, but here we choose to look more closely at a specific set of movements and organizations, including: the MBA oath movement toward the ethical professionalization of management; the International Pirate Party; WikiLeaks; the loose network of individuals referred to as Anonymous; the "Twitter" and "Facebook" revolutions in northern Africa; the "à rasca" generation movement in Portugal; and the #spanishrevolution.[1]

In this analysis we will try to look at how people are surfing the crisis. That is, who are the ones trying to achieve social change and what cultures (values and beliefs) seem to be behind such practices? Our overall objective is to discuss how experimentation is fueling new cultures and at what stage of proposing alternatives to the current political and economic system are we in.

In order to understand the true opposing values in action in our network societies we must look first at the cultures that have led us to the current crisis and, then, to the ones that are emerging through the crisis, allowing us to surf it and not drown ourselves in its tidal waves of social and economic disruption.

Crisis, networked individualism, and self-interest

The crisis that started in 2007 was a crisis that was rooted in very material assets—the housing market—but that unfolded globally within the virtual global financial networks, and from them into the world at large of which our daily lives are part. So we are now sure that this has been a crisis born out of the social system we have massively adopted as our own in the interdependence of the realm of networks, both mediated and non-mediated, that constitute our experience—that is, the network society (Castells, 2000). But at the same

---

[1] #spanishrevolution was the common online identifier for the group of Spanish people taking to the squares in Madrid, Barcelona, and other cities around the country during the first days of the movement in 2011. Although the use of # is associated directly to a Twitter identifier, it was adopted for ease of online search for news of the ongoing events promoted by those later to be labeled as "The Indignants".

time we can argue that this was not a crisis of the network society. Why? Because the network society is a model of organization of our lives—organization of production, power, and experience—all working toward a culture that defines our civilization. Therefore, although the organizational model might favor more a given trend of choices, in the end it will be our individual and collective choice of values that will inform our practices. So we should argue that, more than a crisis born out of the network society, the current crisis is born out of a set of values that were perceived, at a given moment in time, as dominant and therefore shared through the dominant mediation system (Hope, 2010). The argument put forward here is that, in the network society, power is built essentially through the use of mediated communication (Castells, 2009). Communication is power, but power can be exercised only as long as the values and practices that underlie communication are perceived as useful to the framing of the experience in everyday life (Silverstone, 1999). When those conditions change, power is no longer recognized by the social actors involved in those communication processes. When a crisis unfolds, doubts surface, along with the conditions for questioning the validity of the overall economic system. Those are the moments when spaces for alternative views of reality tend to surface, and this seems to be the point we have reached—a time when values and beliefs that used to be perceived as fundamental for the organization of our experience no longer seem to be perceived as such. What we are here calling the cultures of the crisis—that is, values and beliefs that influenced the practices that led to the crisis—are cultures fostered in practices of network individualism (Wellman, 2002). Such practices are forged under a culture of "networked self-interest," epitomized by the financial and managerial elites, institutionally backed by management school ethos, and disseminated under a traditional model of communication based in mass communication and the building of reference groups.

Network individualism and the new managerial elites

In the network society, the social and organizational paradigm of the network has given rise to new processes of individual and institutional connectedness where broadly embracing groups (Wellman, 2002) are now being replaced by diffuse social networks. As Wellman (2002) suggests, boundaries have become more permeable, interactions are multiplied, linkages switch between multiple networks, and hierarchies tend to be more flat and, at the same time, more complex in their structures. Although the transformation from a social organization based in groups into networks can be witnessed in multiple dimensions of our societies, from the political to the economic, we are here mainly interested in the ways in which the possibilities offered by networking individualism were appropriated by a small professional elite—the managers—and how such appropriation allowed for the spread of role models with values and beliefs based in an extremely self-centered and individualist culture of what we can designate as "networked self-interest." The network society is as much a social construct as it is a material infrastructure and an organizational process, but being the sum of all those parts allows it also to give rise to a new dimension of capital, network capital (Wellman, 2002), which can be best described as the networking and interaction of different kinds of capital, from the financial to the human and from the organizational to the cultural—developed through the use of mobile phones, tablets, computers, televisions, and so on, that allow social mediation to occur through and with the Internet. So the network capital can be thought of as a 2.0 version of what we used to define as social capital in a pre-network society environment. Network capital is the virtual melting pot and meeting point of resources such as "information, knowledge, material aid, financial aid, alliances, emotional support, and a sense of being connected" (Wellman, 2002: 20). Network individualism relies on the tools—hardware and software—available at a given time and also on how people choose to drive its use through social appropriation. For example, tools such as MySpace, QQ, and Facebook have allowed a different kind of experimentation that, in turn, has allowed different cultural developments through the practices of network individualism. Network individualism is not the direct product of a choice of how to live our lives, but a consequence of accepting the increasing role of mediation over networks in our societies, from the dimensions of friendship and family to the adoption of organizational information-based work.

Examples of such information-based work are many, but here we would like to center our attention on the financial and investment banking system and its managerial elites. The 2008 crisis had its epicenter in the financial system and, given that the financial systems are the product of both a technological and social interdependence and interaction, we can also find in them an underlying core set of values and beliefs that provided the guidelines for the culture shared within the financial system and disseminated outside of it—a culture that we have here defined as "networked self-interest." If the technological dimension of the financial system was—and is—based on the existence of a global network of nodes of financial hubs and servers, its social dimension is based on a network of managers at different levels and geographies, embracing network individualism practices and sharing among them a given culture. While studying a given crisis, we can choose to look at its outputs or its causes; we can also choose to look at very material manifestations (numbers and indexes in the stock or housing markets, and so on) or at its cultural manifestations. To follow cultural approaches to a crisis means also identifying and analyzing the underlying features of a given set of values, beliefs, and practices—that is, the way people think and act, but also who those people are and why they operate in a given cultural set.

Although much has been published on the sociological and political economy approaches toward the crisis, the study of managers, management, and managerial culture has been the aim of few analyses. One such exception is the work of Khurana (2007), which argues that the study of business school practices has a fundamental role in allowing us to understand the foundation of the crisis unleashed over the second half of the last decade. For Khurana (2007) the ideas of professionalism and morality, which once inspired the formation of business schools in the early twentieth century, were conquered by a perspective of managers as mere agents of shareholders, whose function is to act as facilitators of profit-sharing. During the major part of the twentieth century, managers operated under a system of managerial capitalism, one in which the scope for choice was considerable. But, after the crisis of the 1970s (Castells, 2000), de-regulation was adopted in order to improve both the productivity of labor and the profitability of capital. De-regulation also had a strong impact on managerial capitalism, because managers were seen as part of the problem that de-regulation was trying to solve.

The next step in order to address what could be described as "potential shortcomings for the remuneration of the capital invested" would be the creation of global markets destined to enhance the ability for profit maximization. In such a process, managers lost power to shareholders, giving birth to a profound change in the relations between executives, companies, and shareholders. This transformation of power relations, in order to maximize profit, led to the development of a new kind of corporate model: investor capitalism (Khurana, 2007). Other analysis suggests that we witnessed not only that, but also a change through the emergence of a new Wall Street system (Gowan, 2009), a system where investment banks no longer engaged only in lending, funds management, or trading on behalf of clients but also undertook proprietary trading in financial and other assets, lending to others in order to buy and sell financial and commodities derivatives in order to manage price differentials (for example, hedge funds, private equity groups, and special investment vehicles).

As in many other professional areas established during modernity, management relies on the acceptance of symbolic guaranties and expert systems (Giddens, 1990). But the legitimacy and authority of such groups within society and the needed trust for their action are university based. In the case of management, such legitimacy is rooted in business schools within universities and, more particularly, in the MBA degrees they offer. It is within the universities, through the relationships established with corporations in the exchange of human resources—both of teachers and students—that the objectives and models of performance and management have been shaped in the most developed capitalist societies around the world—usually departing from the core centers in the USA and later disseminated to the hubs of the managerial MBA in Europe and Asia.

In the pre-2007 period, the purpose of management was delineated as being equal to the maximization of shareholder value, legitimating the focus on share price as the measure of value and social perception of the success of both corporations and managers (Khurana, 2007). Such legitimization processes, developed within MBA courses, were not the mere product of taught competences or skills, but overall encompassing micro and macro economic theories that became the dominant paradigm within business schools for the nature and purpose of management (Khurana, 2007).

The arrival of management to the university world followed a common process of legitimization in modernity. In the process of achieving higher social recognition, and only after they had been established as scientific fields, management, and other professional fields, such as journalism (Eco, n.d.), which had first established themselves outside of the realm of the university, have in common an unresolved conflict between the economic dimension of the use of their instruments and the cultural dimension of norms and values that should work as ethical boundaries in the relationship between individual power and societal trust. In management, the de-regulation processes anchored in their generalized acceptance by the great majority of business schools produced a given cultural construct of success, one that was measured through perceived market share value. Such a theoretical definition of success created the conditions for outsized executive pay and stock option policies. Those cultural constructs, when applied to the financial realm of management, created in turn the cultural conditions for the formation of the array of financial innovation special purpose vehicles that, in turn, opened up the way for the subprime crisis and the subsequent quasi-collapse of the US financial system and of the remaining nodes of the world financial system. But more importantly, for our analysis, they created the conditions for a culture anchored in the power of digital networks and a perception of individualism as equal to self-interest. The ethos of business schools over the last thirty years has paved the way for a *culture of networked self-interest,* where social actors tend to favor the increase of individual power and the demise of societal trust by ascribing a much lower value to norms of fairness, equity, and allegiances to institutions, creating the conditions for practices where commitments and social loyalties might be valued less than the pursual of opportunities according to their current availability (Nisbet, 1988; Bauman, 2000; Khurana, 2009). We must also acknowledge, as Savage and Williams (2008) argue, that, given present-day capitalism, a new research agenda connecting "elite theory with a social analysis of money, finance and power" is a needed condition in the understanding of current social transformations. The managerial elites, particularly the ones acting in the financial system, can be characterized as being, by nature of their trade, mediators of business but also able to move between different fields of the economy, and thereby able to network and connect otherwise disconnected realms of value creation. Financial managerial elites, by doing so, forge a cohesive identity as a "wide-ranging" social elite (Savage and Williams, 2008) and establish themselves as core elements in the building of network capital in the global economic system. It is precisely this ability of financial management, by building networks beyond those networks of early life (for example, school, family), that gives them such a central role in the global economy and, therefore, the power that makes them recognizable as elites. Of specific interest for our analysis, on the role of financial managerial elites in the crisis, are the ways in which those very same elites became global role models of a given culture that validated and encouraged the participation of a large portion of the global population in dangerous practices of consumption and investment. For such a path, we need also to acknowledge not only that the exercise of power is associated with a given institutional set, such as an investment bank or private equity company, but that it is derived from the potential to influence or facilitate something, which is based on cultural constructions (Scott, 2008). It is what Giddens (1979) called the ability of "authorization," derived from the internalization of prevailing cultural values and identification with those who occupy the dominant positions in terms of these values. Power comes from legitimacy, and the latter is dependent on the belief that a given pattern of domination is right, correct, justified, or valid (Held, 1989; Beetham, 1991; Scott, 2008). Such validity is also the product of the recognition of a unique set of expertise, based on symbols and social meanings, which they monopolize as a group or network of individuals. But their power, as elites, is also limited to the ways in which visibility is given to those sets of expertise—that is, its power also depends on the communication model of a given society.

Networked self-interest under mass media coverage

Although the mid-1990s witnessed the beginning of a profound change in the way in which we communicated, until very recently we have been mainly living under a mass-communication and mass-media mediation model. Such logic fosters mainly the integration of the individual in the already existing institutions of society and not the building, through experimentation, of new institutional settings. The main novelty of the birth and development of the cultures of networked self-interest during the 1990s and early 2000s was their hybridism, in the sense that they are the products not only of network individualism, possible through the centrality of networks like the Internet in our lives, but also of the old mass media technologies, instrumental in the dissemination of values and beliefs, centered in the valorization of individual power and demise of the value of social trust. If financial managerial elites were the central actors in the construction of a culture of networked self-interest, how was their communicative power achieved in order to have disseminated these cultural practices? Drawing on Castells (2000) and Hope (2010), we must first remember that the dissemination of this given culture occurred in a period of emergence and proliferation of de-regulation policies, globalization of financial activity, financialization of capitalism, and the increasing networking of mass media, telecommunications, and computers. These very same elements have not only induced extraordinary economic growth but also been instrumental in the accumulation of financial dangers that led to the 2008 crisis. As Hope (2010) points out, the power of investment banks, the securitization of household debt, the spread of mortgage derivatives, and the role of global computer networks and the news media all had an important role in creating the underlying conditions for the implosion of the crisis and also its extremely rapid worldwide spread. But, if we turn our attention to the period between the fall of the Berlin Wall in 1989 and the fall of the Twin Towers in 2001, we would also find a timeframe where the combination of 24/7 global news broadcasting, the global emergence of financial networks, and the spread of online trading gave rise to the transformation in the way in which business news media worked. Business news media started building their own expert system of people knowledgeable in markets during that very same decade. As entertainment media have their celebrity system, or as Hollywood had its star system, business news media developed what we can call an *analyst system*. Such a system of news commentators had, before the 1980s, been characterized by the use of academics and private-sector economists, combined with some public servants (Hope, 2010). Such a news analyst system relied heavily on macro analysis of national statistical indicators, trade balances, economic growth, and employment outlooks—all usually produced by government or academic institutions. Under a de-regulation model based on "investor" capitalism and a "new Wall Street" system, general purpose and business news media evolved toward creating panels of commentators for the analysis of the global financial environment. In doing so, the business news media assumed the nature of a system based in the financial managerial elite of bankers, traders, investors, stockbrokers, and so on. The rule of commentators became increasingly the individual opinion and interpretation of real-time data originated in financial markets. The natural outcome of such an evolution was the rise of an interdependent system where the analysis of data produced in financial networks is itself an inductor of information for the trader's decision on what to buy or sell, creating constant realignments of trade decisions based in news media analysis and a global turbulence interdependent system between business news media and markets. A system where the financial managerial elite, both through their professional decisions on markets and their embedded values and beliefs on news commenting, gave rise to the global diffusion of role models based on a culture of networked self-interest.

The rise of the managerial financial elite to the news media circuit, and the generalization of such types of commentators, led also to the transformation of business journalism, making it also much more permeable to the values of networked self-interest cultures (Tambini, 2010). The dissemination of the material conditions that gave rise to network individualism, its appropriation by the financial managerial elite, and the transformation of the business news media allowed for the dissemination of a culture where social actors tended to favour the increase of individual power, the demise of societal trust, and the adoption of networked self-interest as a role model for many of the power holders—with long-lasting effects in policy, economy, and culture. But we have also argued that values and beliefs hold only as long as they are useful for people. After the 2008 crisis, the practices framed under a culture of networked self-interest came largely under fire and criticism. So the question we must ask ourselves now is, are we able to find signs of change—signs that might be seen as indicating the formation of a new set of practices, informed by different values, that might constitute themselves as new role models in society at large?

Mediated belonging and social change

Five years past the very first signs of crisis, it seems to be time to assume that this crisis is not identical to the ones with which we have been living in capitalism since the 1973 oil crisis. This is a different crisis, because it occurred under a globalized world, where China had become a central player in the economy and diplomacy and the USA and Europe had become weaker. This crisis is also different because European and American power has been consumed by two wars and a financial sector that, as a product of its own choices, imploded, and afterwards, in order to survive, dried up the financial assets of sovereign states. Last but not least, this is a crisis where future growth and creation of wealth no longer directly imply the creation of more jobs. All crises have conflicts, but not many are led by the masses. Conflicts are normally the product of potential elites, the ones who aspire to exercise power but who are not allowed to by the current elites. In moments of economic growth, the mechanisms of social mobility and democracy are instruments used in the symbolic fight between potential and current power elites. But, when crisis persists, those mechanisms tend to lose their efficacy. Our society is a society based on the role of knowledge and information, a network society that links all domains from the social to the economic and political with value for the global economic system. Therefore, the ones who are able to exercise power, but who are left out by the crisis, are today the informational professionals with university degrees, the ones who cannot find a job in accordance with their expectations of social mobility, or who simply cannot find a job at all. It is among those that we will find the actors of new social conflicts. And who and what are their targets? New social conflicts are the products of individualized but at the same time networked action. Many times their actions are anonymous but seek support in online social networks. The elites promoting social change through their actions (and early adopters of what seem to be new networked cultures) are radically different from the financial managerial elites and their networked self-interest cultures. The elites challenging the current powers are what we can designate as *elites by objectives*, because they are recognized as such by their peers as long as they are able to attract others' attention and participation in the actions they promote through digital networks, but with a concrete impact on places and institutions. Their power is built in the networks and expressed symbolically both in online social networks and in the streets, based on their ability to update perpetually their actions and objectives, and to sustain a network of sharing ideas and actions under a logic of permanent access among their members. We know of the communication power (Castells, 2009) behind the new networked communication model (Cardoso, 2011), but we still need to build new knowledge of the future consequences of the power struggles lying ahead. Those struggles seem to be fought around the issues that people consider more important in times of crisis and, as we will see in the following examples, they will many times depart from the need for change within the political system, but also from the search for economical change and, even, a change in the way we perceive business and our very own lives. In the pages ahead we will explore the transformation of practices during a time of crisis, fueled by the cultural change within a network society where young and old have adopted the digital realm of networking and, by doing so, are learning to surf the crisis and experiment with social change. These people are the ones assuming the role of innovators in a network society, sometimes experimenting in traditional institutional settings such as universities, political parties, NGOs, and special interest groups, and other times moving to the streets and squares and assuming their identity of *network individuals.*

Pledges towards change: the global business oath

The first example of mediated belonging toward social change analyzed here is one that derives from the actions of a small group of MBA students and young managers around the world to change the ethics of a profession—that is, the ethics of management. As we know, despite attempts to turn management into a profession when business schools emerged, ethical concerns in this area have been put aside in favour of profit maximization and economic efficiency. A 2008 article in the *Harvard Business Review* by Rakesh Khurana and Nitin Nohria contained guidelines for a professional management code. Following this article, a few attempts have been made to formalize desirable norms of conduct for those who have studied at business schools. After such experiments at the level of business schools, an international initiative to create a standard global business oath was undertaken by the World Economic Forum's (WEF) Young Global Leaders, the MBA Oath, the Aspen Institute, the Principles for Responsible Management Education, the UN Global Compact, the Association of Professionals in Business Management, Net Impact, and the Canadian MBA Oath (The Oath Project, n.d.). Together they have founded The Oath Project. The strength of social media is illustrated here in a management grass-roots movement started by business school students that defies the established shareholder value as the absolute end for business activity. It has spread rapidly through partially overlapping individual social networks and organizations, aided by the involved individuals' commitment to extending the oath to a broader audience and private social networks such as the WELCOM of the WEF. The Oath Project and its global business oath is an example of the recognition of the failure of the values and beliefs epitomized in the culture of networked self-interest and the realization that social change can be promoted through peer groups who perceive that there are tools that can be used in order to change business culture and, in the process, change society.

Public policy towards change: the Pirate Party

The second example of the search for social change through cultural change is one in which the perception of change in the distribution practices of fan and popular culture goods has led to the use of the political party system as an engine of societal transformation. The *Piratpartiet*, or Pirate Party, is a Swedish political party that started as a movement revolving around file-sharing and anti-copyright activities. The Pirate Party has successfully spread across various countries—achieving in 2011 in the regional elections in Berlin 9 percent of the vote and fifteen seats in parliament. Despite the fact that officially registered Pirate Parties can be found only in Europe and Canada, this might be considered an extremely successful international political movement. Furthermore, Tunisian Pirate Party activist Slim Amamou was appointed Secretary of State for Sport and Youth in the new Tunisian government (BBC News, 2011a). The analysis of several charters of Pirate Parties around the world shows that this movement's shared ideology revolves around a technological emancipation of the individual, in relation to what is believed to be an artificial scarcity of information in the digital era for the protection of vested interests, whilst adapting to the variations in national contexts where it emerges. But the focus on shared ideas amongst the parties of different countries must not obscure the fact that we find many new ideas being tested. In the UK, for instance, one of the main goals set by the party is to make patented drugs available generically, which the party claims would save the National Health System (NHS) millions of pounds (BBC News, 2010). In Spain, they advocate for a real-time participatory platform so that citizens can take part in political decisions (Partido Pirata, n.d.). The Italian party clearly states that it aims to promote research on participatory democracy, culture, and privacy, and also disseminate the resulting knowledge to the scientific community. The creation of Pirate Parties departing from the sharing of a small number of principles—privacy, freedom of speech, and abolition of copyright—and the evolution of their political discourse toward several other areas of life, from health to education, shows us the power of values and beliefs rooted in generalized practices in society—even if many times these are considered outside the law—and how they can move beyond a small group of loose individuals and into an institutionalized network of parties around the world trying to influence public policy and promote social change.

Openness towards change: WikiLeaks

WikiLeaks, in spite of all its controversies, is probably the best-known example of the appropriation of a networked culture toward change. The rule underlying its actions is that, if someone has produced information for someone else that might be considered of general interest, then such information is worth sharing. WikiLeaks is also based on an openness culture, as it is a crowd-sourced, crowd-funded non-profit organization operating internationally (Sreedharan, Thorsen, and Allan, 2012). Since its launch in 2007, according to the organization's website, "WikiLeaks has released more classified intelligence documents than the rest of the world press combined." Jay Rosen (2010) noted that WikiLeaks was the world's first stateless news organization, reversing the historical trend of media holding the powerful responsible while functioning under, and protected by, the laws of a given nation—making use of the global stateless logic of the Internet (see also Sreedharan, Thorsen, and Allan, 2012). Its impact is changing not only the relationship between media and the state but also the very rules of the game, undermining state authority in controlling access to information while influencing the established media's coverage stories. This innovative organization, founded on social media and public-service principles, publishes sensitive material in the name of public interest, destabilizing traditional power balances and empowering individuals. "WikiLeaks shifts the source of potential threat from a few, dangerous hackers and a larger group of mostly harmless activists—both outsiders to an organization—to those who are on the inside" (Bodó, 2011). The US Embassy cables and the alliance made by WikiLeaks, the *Guardian*, *El País*, the *New York Times*, *Der Spiegel*, and *Le Monde* surfaces as an example not only of the Networked Communication Model (Cardoso, 2011) but also of the culture of openness and how its appropriation changes more than just the digital realm of the newspaper business. WikiLeaks' practices have had strong impacts on the discussions of business ethics, international relations ethics, the role of journalists and journalism in our societies, and even the existing contradictions and possible mismatches between the social perception of reserve and privacy, the ones practiced by businesses and governments, and the ones defined by national and international law. Given its wide dissemination, as a well-known case study, WikiLeaks is today a strong example of how small non-profit organizations that place their core attentions on the role of information in our societies might achieve social change through new cultural perceptions of power.

Literacy towards change: the entity known as Anonymous

Hackers can also network themselves, and when they do so they become another kind of special interest group; such is the case behind "Anonymous," a networked "non-organization" that, until the WikiLeaks public presentation of the War Logs and Embassy Cables, was mainly an unknown cultural center of the Internet (Blair, 2008). Websites such as the 4chan image board, where people interact by uploading images and writing comments in threads, do not require user registration. The lack of user names meant most activity presented on the site was signed by "Anonymous," in a setting where culture "is constantly changing due to the uncontrolled growth of memes" (Blair, 2008). It is not really a group of dangerous skillful hackers, despite the media's description, but a collective name adopted by like-minded individuals who occasionally act together in activities usually referred to as "operations." Membership in this group is ad hoc. Underwood and Welser (2011) observed the public online sources used by Anonymous "to plan, discuss, coordinate, and execute Project Chanology," which consisted of both online and offline protests against the Church of Scientology. In this quest to protest the religion's alleged violation of human rights and freedom of speech, participants saw themselves as "tricksters," and regarded participation in these protests mostly as "fun." But, it was "Operation Payback" that gave Anonymous public recognition through mass media coverage. Those behind Operation Payback retaliated in support of WikiLeaks by launching DDoS attacks against companies including PayPal, MasterCard, Visa, and Amazon (Amorosi, 2011). One of the strengths of Anonymous is its lack of typical group structures. Individuals are seen as responsible for their actions. The actions of Anonymous are developed under a social media cultural approach around particular interests. The participants' identification with the satirical faceless collective-turned-archetype is the sole recruitment requirement. Because of its very nature, one can never claim to be part of Anonymous unless acting with others under this "banner." Anonymous shows us how people with high digital skills and literacy, when moved by a common purpose, can act upon changing what they deem as wrong. Although their very nature can induce organized vigilant actions, very much in the same way that Alan Moore depicted his *V for Vendetta* masked avenger—which is also used as an icon by Anonymous—their actions also show us that, in the digital realm of highly skilled hackers' individualism, mobilization toward collective action and social change might be taking new forms.

Social Media towards change: the Arab Spring

On December 17, 2011, a shocking event took place in the city of Sidi Bouzaid, Tunisia. Mohamed Bouazizi, a 26-year-old street trader, set himself on fire at the gates of the local governor's office in protest for being beaten and humiliated by authorities (*New York Times*, 2011). The public regarded him as a victim of Ben Ali's dictatorship, which led to protests throughout the nation, culminating in a revolution. The success of the Jasmine Revolution in Tunisia was the first of a series of popular uprisings felt throughout North Africa and the Middle East that became known as the "Arab Spring" of 2011. In Egypt, on January 25, organized protests took to the streets of Cairo, leading to the fall of President Hosni Mubarak's regime on February 11 (*Guardian*, 2011). By the end of January 2011 the

Gustavo Cardoso and Pedro Jacobetty

protests had spread to Yemen, Lebanon, Syria, Morocco, Oman, Jordan, and Palestine, and, by February, to Bahrain, Iran, Libya, and Iraq. The identified reasons for these uprisings are related to the impact of the global economic crisis in North Africa and the Middle East but also to "the decades in which people were denied political rights" and "corrupt governments and persistent (now well documented) human rights abuses" (Hanelt and Möller, 2011). These events can also be looked at from the lenses of the Internet and social media. WikiLeaks did, in fact, release a cable in which a US diplomat denounced Ben Ali's corruption. About 40 percent of Tunisians were connected to the Internet, half of whom were on Facebook and were under the age of 30 (Mourtada and Salem, 2011). It is important to state that this is a "newly media-literate population" that used these technologies to express public defiance and displays of popular anger, while disseminating information about the protests (Harb, 2011). It is true that social network sites are the basis of much of today's social organization, effectively connecting people and allowing information exchange. But to claim they are the reason for the revolts in North Africa and the Middle East is a misconception. It is very important to address the issue of new forms of communication in revolutionary processes, but they must not be taken as revolutionary elements themselves. In fact, the communicative context of societies depends on much more than access to different communication platforms. During the protests, Egyptian authorities shut down the Internet in the country for a few days, as well as mobile communications, which, according to Thomas M. Chen (2011), "incited the protesters even more." In Tunisia, the government blocked particular news sites and blogs, and began arresting bloggers and stealing Facebook login passwords (Chen, 2011). Google, for instance, created a service to allow people in Egypt to send Twitter messages by calling a phone number and leaving a voice message (Oreskovic, 2011). Another interesting fact resides in the articulation between social media and mass media, especially television, where the TV channel Al-Jazeera played a central role in constructing shared revolutionary narratives and life meanings. Its coverage of Tahrir Square during the protests, which included footage taken by citizens, led to the blocking of the channel in Egypt, just as it had happened in Tunisia. Nonetheless, it continued to re-broadcast user-generated content: citizens' footage (Harb, 2011). The influence of this international TV news channel is felt in the impact of the protests on international support and on political change, leading to the idea that the communication context for popular uprisings are important but multidimensional, and that new media alone cannot do much for broad societal change. The Arab Spring movements and their successes are connected to the use of the Internet and mobile phones as tools of organization toward autonomy. But they are also of interest for us in our analysis, because they show us how the desire and ability to circumvent censorship tools deployed by governments, originally designed to control access not only to political information but also to entertainment, has led the younger population in those countries to lead the protests. They show in practice how the theoretical approaches to the contamination of practices developed toward access to popular culture also become central to supporting the fight for democracy.

Music toward change: the "à rasca" Generation

On January 22, 2011, "Deolinda," a Portuguese band, was performing at the Oporto Coliseum when it began playing a new song, not yet released to the public, called "How Stupid I Am." The song described the current lives of young people in Portugal and the difficulties of attaining professional success and earning enough to be independent from their families. The performance was recorded by a mobile phone and posted online and then shared through YouTube and Facebook, becoming the springboard of the "à rasca" generation movement. The "à rasca" movement was launched on February 5, 2011, by four people on Facebook, and described itself and its objectives in its online manifesto:

We, the unemployed, 'five hundred Euros people', others who are being underpaid for their work, slaves in disguise, working without contracts, with short term contracts, working students, people with scholarships, students, mothers, fathers and sons of Portugal. We that up until now have lived like this are here today to give our contribution to unleash a qualitative change in our country. (Precarious Manifest, n.d.)

The *Geração à rasca* demonstrations that took place in several Portuguese cities on March 12, 2011, were chronicled via Facebook and disseminated through TV and press coverage. These protests were spurred on by a movement that claims to be non-partisan, secular, and peaceful. It intended to pressure the government to fight unemployment, to improve working conditions, and to ensure the widespread valuation of academic qualifications. These are the demands of a young Portuguese generation that is highly affected by unemployment and that takes part in the labor market mostly as short-term workers or trainees. Social network sites were the movement's main communication and organization platforms. The movement's success was partially due to the high penetration rates of these websites in younger generations, where it could rapidly disseminate and gather new supporters. News coverage of the upcoming protest also played an important role in the unfolding of events. The memory of the uprisings in North Africa and the Middle East, which had shown how overlapping networks changed the interconnection between traditional news media and new social media, was still fresh. When the protest began to gain momentum on the social network sites, public and journalistic interest turned its attention toward what could be the next big protests to break the barrier between the online world and the offline urban centers. In Lisbon and Porto, a large crowd of demonstrators took to the city centers. Their type of organization made it the perfect vehicle for non-institutionalized conflicts in Portuguese society. Hundreds of thousands of demonstrators throughout the country brought homemade posters to the streets with their own slogans. Unlike most other protests, the social diversity became the key characteristic of the March 12 demonstrations. This diversity is identified when analyzing not just the protesters' social and political backgrounds, but also those of their targets: a very broad spectrum of politicians and public officials, on the one hand, and industrial and financial capitalists, on the other. The "à rasca" generation movement is, together with the Arab Spring movement, an example of the integration of the different cultures that comprise the networked cultures of belonging, both under authoritarian regimes and democracy, into facilitating social movements toward societal change. But the most interesting feature of this movement seems to have been the role of music in the unleashing of a shared sense of common objectives and of belonging to a common generation with shared problems. The music was shared on YouTube and Facebook like many other songs in these networks, which have replaced MTV as the core environment for listening to and seeing music. What was unique was the music's role in creating a necessary environment among Facebook users in Portugal. The sharing on Facebook of Deolinda's music video worked as a catalyst for the consciousness of a social belonging to a wider group with similar concerns on the political and economical Portuguese situation, paving the way for the second stage in the process of mobilization—the invitation to join the organized demonstration on March 12. Although different from the Arab Spring, where the skills developed to circumvent censorship of cultural goods were fundamental for creating the organizational environment for the uprising, popular culture was also instrumental to the mobilization in Portugal. What many of these movements depicted here have in common is the relationship established between cultural consumption of fan and popular culture and how those circuits, imagery and narratives, skill and tools, first developed in the entertainment realm, have influenced civic and political participation. The new networked cultures seem to flourish best where experimentation with fan and popular culture takes place; only then is such experience applied toward social change in civic and political movements.

Networking spaces and flows toward change: the #spanishrevolution Indignants

Not only in Portugal, but in Spain too, the economic, political, social, and cultural echoes of the crisis have been felt. Spain, with a 43 percent juvenile unemployment rate, is an example of how severe these impacts can be on a country (*Público*, 2011). The 2011 Spanish May protests, beginning on May 15, 2011 and summoned by the *Democracia Real YA* platform in fifty Spanish cities, were the start of what would become a network of European protests. The platform responsible for the protests had been in existence for only a few months, but, along with about 200 micro-associations that had joined the protests, showed that it was possible to mobilize a great number of people in a short amount of time without many resources through the use of social networks and "massive digital mouth-to-mouth" dissemination (*El País*, 2011a). Its inspirations were the protests in the Arab world (BBC News, 2011b), in Greece (*El País*, 2011a), in Portugal (*Jornal de Notícias*, 2011), and in Iceland. The manifesto behind the protests clearly states that it represents progressives and conservatives, believers and non-believers, people with defined ideologies and others who consider themselves apolitical, thereby making up a non-partisan movement claiming to be "concerned and angry about the political, economic and social outlook which we see around us: corruption among politicians, businessmen, bankers, leaving us helpless, without a voice" (Democracia Real Ya, n.d.). It goes on, stating that "the priorities of any advanced society must be equality, progress, solidarity, freedom of culture, sustainability and development, welfare and people's happiness" (Democracia Real Ya, n.d.). Furthermore, it advocates "the right to housing, employment, culture, health, education, political participation, free personal development, and consumer rights for a healthy and happy life" (Democracia Real Ya, n.d.). The protest gave birth to the 15-M movement, also known as the Spanish revolution or The Indignants. What is singular about this particular protest is not its message, which is similar to that of a series of protests of a new kind that have been spreading throughout Europe in reaction to the economic recession that followed the financial crisis, the announced austerity measures, and, in some cases, bailout programs that will greatly impact on the younger generations' lives. Nor is it its size, having fewer participants than the "à rasca" generation protests in the cities across neighbouring Portugal on March 12, 2011. What is fundamentally different is the fact that, instead of being a massive single day demonstration, protesters camped in the city centers, like Madrid's Puerta del Sol or Catalonia Square, and stayed there (*El País*, 2011b). Another striking feature of these protests has been their ability to gain an international dimension. As of May 24, there were protests inspired by the Spaniards in over 675 cities of the world. In the networked communication paradigm, increasingly overlapping networks spread across devices. The messages are not only sent through a diversity of media, which makes it easier for movements like the 15-M to reach ever broader audiences and for people to follow the unfolding of events more easily; they are also integrated in a simultaneous and global exchange by journalists, news readers, analysts, students, politicians, and the protesters themselves, all around the globe. Both by occupying the squares around Spain and by fostering similar movements outside the country, like the October 15, 2011 global democracy protest, the #spanish revolution movement of The Indignants has taken the social appropriation of the new networked cultures a step further. No longer are we merely witnessing the realm of demonstrations developing online and in the streets; we had already seen people gain permanent access to online spaces (where social identification and belonging are built through participation in event-organizing and decision-making), but now we are also beginning to find struggles for permanent access to spaces where people can gather, such as squares in cities or symbolic buildings, which is perceived as fundamental toward social change. In terms of social mobilization, we have accepted the non-dissociation between digital and physical spaces, because it is possible to belong to both simultaneously, and, more importantly, the #spanishrevolution movement showed that the only places where a discussion of the reform of the political system seemed to be possible where the squares and networks, given that even under democracies the current political parties and other institutions, such as universities, no longer seemed suitable. The movement showed that the languages spoken in power and on the streets are different and that there is a common cultural mismatch. The #spanishrevolution brought with it the clarification that we are witnessing the meeting of two very different cultures and two very different groups of social actors—one still the heir of the 1980s cultures of self-interest and the other born out of the cultures of the 2000s, centerd on belonging.

Networking social change

What do these examples tell us about the way in which people are using their power for social change? First, we would argue that they show us evidence that the practices we have identified are increasingly connected to a change in culture in our societies. We live in a network society under network individualism, but the underlying culture that frames our actions is moving toward the adoption of a paradigm centered less on self-interest and more on the ability to adopt common interests and belong to a group that shares objectives within a given network. Such a cultural move is fueled by a change in values and beliefs; a change that was built first through experimentation with digital cultural goods and that has influenced the ways in which we perceive production, distribution, ownership, and social networking with our peers in networks. Second, we would like to argue that, although the changes in our perception toward production, distribution, and ownership are fundamental in promoting engagement in social change, the core change is at the level of the way in which we perceive that social organization occurs, which is equivalent to stressing the role of mediated social networks such as Facebook and Twitter. Mediated social networks can be used for managing our personal networks, under a personal capital logic, or they can be used for the management of autonomy, as identified by Castells (Castells et al., 2003) in a multiplicity of projects as diverse as professional development, communicative autonomy, entrepreneurship, bodily autonomy, socio-political participation, and individual autonomy. In this context, autonomy should be taken as individual or collective projects built around an individual or shared definition of culture—a certain representation of society (Touraine, 2004). This autonomy is no longer just mainly related to the working or professional sphere, in an autonomous space or time, but is also increasingly linked to the recognition of how important it is to create a moral autonomy around the individual, his subjectivity, and his ability to act (Touraine, 2004). The spheres of autonomy discussed here mostly refer to objectives, which may be associated with situations of conflict and operate primarily in symbolic levels. As Stalder (2010) suggests, autonomy is increasingly constructed from semi-public networks that are structured by different dimensions of network communication and more or less frequent face-to-face meetings. In other words, mediation is now a central aspect for the development of autonomy. The establishment of autonomy, people's ability to live their lives according to their own plans, is something that occurs at different scales and that contains the diversity inherent to the human condition of creativity and difference. Such projects of autonomy are facilitated by communication protocols that are based upon already established trust amongst participants. Under a social network mediation environment, it is the connecting of individual projects that allows the creation of trust, without which collectively shared autonomy projects cannot be activated (Stalder, 2010). But the true power of social networking lies in its potential as an element of networked communication, linked to the networks in which we are already inserted and enhancing them as network communication structures, not limited to their usage as social media. Social networks entail shared spaces of creation that can lead to action and intervention spaces for social change. But this depends on the role we assign them within a wider strategy, which in turn should lead to action. When actors govern power creation following a *networked communication* model—that is, combining *interpersonal multimedia communication, one-to-many mediated communication, self-mass communication* (Castells, 2009) and *mass communication*—and, through the power of shared ideas, foster the contact between mediated and face-to-face communication, they create the conditions for social change in the context of the network society. The analysis by Neumayer and Raff (2008) of the protest "No More! No More Kidnapping! No More Lies! No More Murder! No More FARC!" points precisely to these processes. This protest was organized through Facebook in 2008 and gathered 100,000 participants within the mediated social network. But, in cooperation with newspapers and television, it led to a concentration of approximately 500,000 people in over 165 cities on February 4, 2008, creating a global social network of spaces and flows.

In this process, mediated social networks, which depend upon contemporary social media tools, play a fundamental role for creating sustainable bridges between social actors who share interests. Furthermore, they make them visible to each other. Mediated social networks carry with them the possibility of social change, but only if they are used to manage bridging social capital that reaches heterogeneous groups, and provided that the network's organizational logic takes into account the use of communication tools under the logics of the networked communication model. In order to achieve this, **programmers** and **switchers** that produce network power—that is, the actors who provide the network's organizational matrix and efficiency— must develop action-oriented strategies, manifested in discourse and ideas, which lead to change while operating in this new communication model.

New network actors and cultures

The mediation practices giving rise to networked communication are changing our media culture and, in the process, our values and beliefs as citizens of a global network society—that is, they are also changing the way in which we build our relationships with other people, with organizations, and with everyday life, by giving us the tools to design future institutions. As Jenkins (2006) suggests, the "traditional" convergence theory based on the birth of new technologies that will increasingly converge media does not find empirical support; rather than a convergence based on new patterns production, what we are witnessing are new patterns of consumption that foster a convergence culture. Such convergence culture is the product of old and new media intersection, a place where grass-roots and corporate media collide, where the power of the media producer and the power of the consumer interact in unpredictable ways (Jenkins, 2006). But this is also a space where the ways in which we produce fan and popular culture also seem to be influencing the very ways in which political and civic participation occurs. Such an influence can best be understood if we look, for example, at the *#18daysinegypt* project about the protests in Egypt, which led to the fall of Mubarak's regime. This documentary, as the title suggests, is about the Egyptian protests occurring between January 25 and February 11, 2011. But what makes this documentary different is its crowd-sourced strategy—that is, it is assembled from footage taken by the protest's participants or direct observers. This is possible only because of the proliferation of multifunctional handheld personal devices with video recording capabilities, such as cell phones. Furthermore, it is not based in just one collaborative platform, or on individual footage submission processes. Instead, it makes use of already popular websites such as Twitter, YouTube, and Flickr, by hashtag strategy. It seems clear that much of the experimentation being followed under the premisses of fan and popular culture is being increasingly used as role models of practices for civic and political engagement toward social change. It is as if some of those unpredictable ways, as stated by Jenkins (2008), in which the power of media producers and consumers is increasingly interacting, are giving rise to some already well-defined traits of what we can call the *cultures of networked belonging*, all of them present in the case studies previously analyzed and whose action has been aimed at social change. The networked cultures of belonging are the array of four different dimensions of practices that have been reshaping our values and beliefs and in doing so have created a culture still anchored in network individualism but no longer centered in self-interest. Those practices can be clustered in what we can call "cloud cultures" toward how we currently conceive ownership, "openness cultures" toward the ways in which we expect goods and services to be produced, "piracy cultures" toward the ways in which we expect goods and services to be distributed, and, finally, and probably the most influencing dimension for the change in values and beliefs, the "social networking cultures" toward the ways in which we build identity by combining the mediated environment and non-mediated experience in networks of relationships. In our daily lives, the sense of *belonging* shapes, at different degrees, our social and psychological processes of self and identity (re)construction. It describes not only social relationships but also a part of our contemporary relation with the media. In a social landscape where contemporary societies are increasingly characterized and produced by a communicational model built on the notion of network, networked belonging is a fundamental cultural trait of the experience of mediation. Networks can enhance, through mediation, social relationships and, consequently, nurture the sense of belonging in a community. In this scope, mediated belonging increases the extent of online imagined communities. We can find this sense of belonging both as a measure of communitarian involvement and as the fulfillment of personal needs for self-esteem. But belonging also stands as a descriptive possibility in framing the nature of our relation with technology, the ever more intricate forms of use that make it increasingly difficult to distinguish between the function of the medium and the social consequences of its appropriations. The cultures of belonging are expressed in many of the different social appropriations of mediation that occur in our daily lives, ranging from participation in social network sites, participation in online communities, political or civic participation, user-generated content, and its sharing among participants in content-producing networks, fan culture interactions, file-sharing communities and networks, and so on. But the reason why it has become such an important feature of our social interaction derives from the growing use, and individual significance, given by us in daily routines to social network media such as Facebook, making *social networking cultures* a fundamental trait of the new networked cultures of belonging.

The second dimension of the networked cultures of belonging can be found in the growing importance and visibility of *openness cultures*, products of three distinctive practices that are today central to the digital realm of production: remix and mashup; open source; and beta and updating practices. The combination of those three production practices has allowed the dissemination of a culture of production based on openness and by doing so we have increasingly taken for granted the fact that a significant part of production in our daily lives operates under such principles. This culture of production under openness has in turn influenced the way in which we produce actions and events toward social change. It is as if the way in which digital culture products, such as video, music, or software, are produced has become one of the components of a given "normality" of how we conceive production to be defined. That very conceptualization has virally contaminated how we expect production to occur not only under digital formats, but also for events and even hardware—for example, let us not forget Apple and its yearly hardware updates such as the iPhone. The openness dimensions of the networked cultures of belonging are ones where we find extremely low barriers of entry for whomever wants to join a given network of production with a common aim. It is also under such openness principles that we find a justification by which we can understand why such networks tend to be in such a permanent systemic mode of updating objectives and strategies for action. Openness as a core principle associated to production also means that these are cultures where continued innovation and the ability to surprise others and add novelty, while departing from previous experiences or concepts, tend to be a common signature.

The third dimension of the networked cultures of belonging can be found in the so-called "cloud cultures" and how their set of practices gave rise to beliefs and values that have been changing the way in which we currently conceive ownership. Ownership has been intimately related to individual or organizational possession, but, with the introduction of digital networks in our capitalist economies, the value of ownership seems to have moved toward an increasingly high correlation with access. Such a trend was at first visible mainly in the establishment of global financial markets, where trade is performed in digital networks and where the success of operations is ascribed not to one's ownership as a member of the network but rather to having permanent access and being able to trade permanently global financial assets. In financial networks, the ownership of assets is granted less by legal possession than through the permanent access that allows sustaining value through real-time decisions, because only access and trade interactions are what allow for the gain of financial advantages—that is, money. If access has become a central piece in the definition of ownership in financial networks, during the last few years we have witnessed a trend of business models that has led to the spread of this culture of ownership based increasingly on access as a needed condition for sustaining possession. Examples of such can be found in the way in which we appropriate mediation when we watch or listen to streaming media, or when we access documents saved in distant computer networks, or even when we use mail systems such as Gmail, Hotmail, or Yahoo. The use of computers and the storing of data have evolved from nearness to distance and in the process we have changed the way in which we perceive ownership of digital data, be it personal communication or movies or music. We began by storing our data possessions in local computer disks or keeping it close to ourselves, by using originally floppy disks and later USB sticks, but we are increasingly switching to storing personal data in data clouds far away from our physical locations. In a consistent cultural change in the perception of ownership, we have moved from needing to see where data were stored, to believing that, as long as we can access it somewhere in the world, we own it. Such a trait is the product of cultural change precipitated by the nature of communication itself and the ability to build it under a networked communicational model. Clouds have become the foundations of digital network cultures: for business, they have allowed new business models; for individuals, they are increasingly seen as facilitators of collective action. So *cloud cultures* have changed the way in which we value ownership, but in the process have also changed our culture of valorization toward access and have given us new foundations with which to view social mobilization as dependent on constant access of those involved. Cloud cultures and their valorization of access over possession make membership to a given organization less important than permanent contact with others and with the digital contents that are stored far away from us in cloud computing facilities.

The last dimension of the networked culture of belonging here analyzed are the so-called "piracy cultures" and the notion that, if something is available in the network, it should be shareable, which primarily questions under what circumstances, legal or other, can information be shared. Piracy cultures reflect the ways in which we expect to access digital goods and how such shared cultural construct influences our values and beliefs within society. In order to address what we are calling *piracy cultures* of networked communication, we need first to establish from where the very definition of piracy comes from. Usually we look at media consumption departing from a media industry definition. We look at TV, radio, newspapers, games, Internet, and media content in general, departing from the idea that access to those is made through the payment of a license fee, subscription, or simply because it is either paid or made available for free (being supported by advertisement)—that is, we look at content and the way people interact with it within a given system of thought that looks at content and its distribution channels as the product of relationships between media companies, organizations, and individuals effectively building a commercial relationship of a contractual kind with rights and obligations. But what if, for a moment, we turn our attention to the empirical evidence found not just in Asia, Africa, and South America but also all over Europe and North America? All over the world we are witnessing a growing number of people building media relationships outside of the institutionalized set of rules (Sundaram, 2001; Wang, 2003; Larkin, 2004; Yar, 2005; Athique, 2008; Lobato, 2009; Karaganis, 2010). The question presented by the building of these relationships toward access of cultural content and software is not so much whether we are dealing with legal or illegal practices, but how they are going to become fundamental to our understanding of a new view of entertainment media distribution and its consumption. Because we need a title to characterize those cultures in their diversity, but at the same time in their commonplaceness, we propose calling them "piracy cultures." The main point is that distribution of fan and popular culture has moved from distribution channels dominated by corporations into an environment where individuals have a primary role. The corporations themselves deem a large portion of those individualized distribution channels of popular culture illegal, but they exist and have moved from a marginal economic cluster on the mass communication model into an alternative system of distribution on the networked communication model.[2] Such a change in

---

[2] Digital copyright infringement is driven by technological change. The compact cassette allowed individuals to copy music and software during the early days of personal computing. Later, it was replaced by the floppy disk as the typical support

the growing dimension of individualized uses has led to the generalized perception in society at large that distribution channels no longer have to be dependent on organizations and can rely on the networking of individuals. The consequences of such a change are far beyond the economic losses of corporations with business in the popular and fan culture dimension. The generalization of the perceived piracy cultures' core values—that is, "what exists is shareable"—also makes the idea of one's participation in a network of sharing, not of files, but of ideas or the organization of events toward a common objective, much more plausible. Through the adoption of piracy practices one is also adopting the values of sharing and, in the process, the ethos of being part of a network of nodes within larger networks. Piracy cultures are constitutive of social change because they allow for the social construction of the value of being part of a wider network, where common values can be shared and autonomy is constructed.

The networked cultures of belonging are the products of the radical change of the media system from what Merton (1957) called in the late 1950s "reference groups" into "belonging groups," emulating social functions that for a long time were only an attribute of face-to-face interaction with family, friends, or school. The change in mediation (Silverstone, 2000) and the building of a new communicational model of networked communication (Castells, 2009; Cardoso, 2011) is allowing mediation, not only to play the role of reference group or organizer of actions toward autonomy, but to foster belonging as well. The overall premiss present in this analysis is that, if mass communication and mass media fostered mainly the integration of the individual in already existing institutions, networked communication fosters the building of new institutional settings through the social networking of individuals.

What the case studies here analyzed and what other events—such as the "Occupy Wall Street/We are the 99%" movement in the USA, Tent City in Tel Aviv for better housing and living conditions in Israel, or Chile's demonstrations by students and families to change the education system—seem to tell us is that people are questioning the status quo. In doing so, they also seem to be culturally valuing social trust more and the promotion of self-interest less. The role of the cultural changes in property, production, distribution, and socialization, produced by the appropriation of network

for piracy. The development of the Bulletin Board System (BBS) and the Internet enabled the dissemination of digital pirated contents throughout the world (Li, 2009: 284–5).

technologies and digital products, seems also to have had a fundamental influence on the way in which such movements and groups of people have decided to become, or have accomplished being, heard. We seem, therefore, to be at a time when people, rather than being interested in proposing alternatives to the current political and economic system, are more interested in understanding how can they improve their living conditions as a society or group. People are in search of places where they can ask new and old questions, in order to try out different answers. By doing so we are, through mediation, changing the cultures of our network society and fundamentally creating new departure points that might lead us toward new lives in the aftermath of this crisis—whenever it happens. We are witnessing the surfing of the crisis, using the power of sharing with others as a common ground for building a future to which people might feel they belong.

References

Amorosi, D. (2011). "WikiLeaks 'Cablegate' Dominates Year-End Headlines," *Infosecurity*, 8/1: 6–9.

Athique, A. (2008). "The 'Crossover' Audience: Mediated Multiculturalism and the Indian Film," *Continuum: Journal of Media and Cultural Studies*, 22/3: 299–311.

Bauman, Z. (2000). *Liquid Modernity*. Cambridge: Polity Press.

BBC News (2010). "Election: Can Pirate Party UK Emulate Sweden Success?," Apr. 27 <http://news.bbc.co.uk/2/hi/uk_news/politics/election_2010/8644834.stm> (accessed Sept., 2011).

BBC News (2011a). "Turmoil in Tunisia: As it Happened on Monday," Jan. 17 <http://news.bbc.co.uk/2/hi/africa/9363808.stm> (accessed Sept., 2011).

BBC News (2011b). "Spanish Youth Rally in Madrid Echoes Egypt Protests", May 18 <http://www.bbc.co.uk/go/em/fr/-/news/world-europe-13437819> (accessed Sept., 2011).

Beetham, D. (1991). *The Legitimation of Power*. Houndmills: Macmillan.

Blair, A. (2008). "'We are Legion': An Anthropological Perspective on Anonymous." The Impact of Technology on Culture, Senior Symposium in Anthropology, Idaho State University.

Bodó, Balázs (2011). "You have no Sovereignty where we Gather: Wikileaks and Freedom, Autonomy and Sovereignty in the Cloud," SSRN, Mar. 7 <http://ssrn.com/abstract=1780519> (accessed Sept., 2011).

Cardoso, G. (2008). "From Mass to Network Communication: Communicational Models and the Informational Society," *International Journal of Communication*, 2 <http://ijoc.org/ojs/index.php/ijoc/article/view/19/178>(accessed Sept., 2011).

Cardoso, G. (2011). "The Birth of Network Communication: Beyond Internet and Mass Media," *Revista TELOS (Cuadernos de Comunicación e Innovación)*, 88 <http://sociedadinformacion.fundacion.telefonica.com/seccion=1268&idioma=es_ES&id=2011012508180001&activo=6.do>.

Castells, M. (2000). *The Rise of the Network Society*: The Information Age: Economy, Society and Culture, vol. I. 2nd edn. Oxford: Blackwell.

—— (2009). *Communication Power*. Oxford: Oxford University Press.

—— Tubella, I., Sancho, T., Diaz de Isla, I., and Wellman, B. (2003). *La Societat Xarxa a Catalunya*. Barcelona: Random House Mondadori.

Chen, T. M. (2011). "Governments and the Executive 'Internet Kill Switch'," *IEEE Network*, Mar.–Apr. 25/2: 2–3.

Democracia Real Ya (n.d.). *Manifesto (English)* <http://democraciarealya.es/?page_id=814> (accessed Sept., 2011).

Eco, U. (n.d.). "University and Mass Media" <http://www.uni-weimar.de/medien/archiv/ws9899/eco/text3.html> (accessed July 2011).

El País (2011a). "15-M: los ciudadanos exigen reconstruir la política," May 17 <http://politica.elpais.com/politica/2011/05/16/actualidad/1305578500_751064.html> (accessed Sept., 2011).

—— (2011b). "Continúan protestas pacíficas en España tras cinco días de resistencia," May 19 <http://www.elpais.com.co/elpais/internacional/cientos-espanoles-asientan-van-cinco-dias-protestas> (accessed Sept., 2011).

Giddens, A. (1990). *The Consequences of Modernity*. Stanford, CA: Stanford University Press.

Gowan, P. (2009). "Crisis in the Heartland: Consequences of the New Wall Street System," *New Left Review*, 55: 5–2.

Guardian (2011). "Hosni Mubarak Resigns—and Egypt Celebrates a New Dawn," Feb. 11 <http://www.guardian.co.uk/world/2011/feb/11/hosni-mubarak-resigns-egypt-cairo?intcmp=239> (accessed Sept., 2011).

Hanelt, C. P., and Möller, A. (2011). "How the European Union can Support Change in North Africa," *spotlight europe*, #2011/01: 1–8.

Harb, Z. (2011). "Arab Revolutions and the Social Media Effect," *M/C Journal*, 14/2 <http://journal.media-culture.org.au/index.php/mcjournal/article/viewArticle/364> (accessed Sept., 2011).

Held, D. (1989). *Political Theory and the Modern State*. Cambridge: Polity Press.

Hope, W. (2010). "Time, Communication, and Financial Collapse," *International Journal of Communication*, 4: 649–69.

Jenkins, H. (2006). *Convergence Culture: Where Old and New Media Collide*. New York: New York University Press.

—— (2008). "The Cultural Logic of Media Convergence," *International Journal of Cultural Studies*, 7/1: 33–43.

Jornal de Notícias (2011). "Geração à rasca' é referência para Espanha", May 20 <http://www.jn.pt/PaginaInicial/Mundo/Interior.aspx?content_id=1857358> (accessed Sept., 2011).

Karaganis, J. (2010). "Media Piracy in Emerging Economies: Price, Market Structure and Consumer Behavior," World Intellectual Property Organization, Dec. 1–2 <http://www.wipo.int/edocs/mdocs/enforcement/en/wipo_ace_6/wipo_ace_6_5.pdf> (accessed Sept., 2011).

Khurana, R. (2007). *From Higher Aims to Hired Hands: The Social Transformation of Business Schools and the Unfulfilled Promise of Management as a Profession*. Princeton: Princeton University Press.

—— (2009). "MBAs Gone Wild," *American Interest*, July–Aug. 4/6: 46–52.

—— and Nohria, N. (2008). "It's Time to Make Management a True Profession," *Harvard Business Review*, Oct. 86/10: 40–77.

Larkin, B. (2004). "Degraded Images, Distorted Sounds: Nigerian Video and the Infrastructure of Piracy," *Public Culture*, 16/2: 289–314.

Li, M. (2009). "The Pirate Party and the Pirate Bay: How the Pirate Bay Influences Sweden and International Copyright Relations," *Pace International Law Review*, 21:1: 281–308.

Lobato, R. (2009). "Subcinema: Mapping Informal Film Distribution." Ph.D. thesis, School of Culture and Communication, University of Melbourne <http://repository.unimelb.edu.au/10187/8855> (accessed Sept., 2011).

Merton, R. K. (1957). "Continuities in the Theory of Reference Groups and Social Structure," in R. K. Merton (ed.), *Social Theory and Social Structure*. Glencoe, IL: Free Press.

Mourtada, R., and Salem, F. (2011). "Arab Social Media Report, Facebook Usage: Factors and Analysis, Arab Social Media Report," 1:1 <http://www.dsg.ae/portals/0/ASMR%20Final%20May%208%20high.pdf> (accessed Sept., 2011).

Neumayer, C., and Raff, C. (2008) "Facebook for Global Protest: The Potential and Limits of Social Software for Grassroots Activism," in Larry Stillman and Graeme Johanson (eds), *Proceedings of the 5th Prato Community Informatics & Development Informatics Conference 2008: ICTs for Social Inclusion: What is the Reality?* Caulfield, East Australia: Faculty of Information Technology, Monash University. CD-Rom.

New York Times (2011). "Slap to a Man's Pride Set off Tumult in Tunisia," Jan. 21 <http://www.nytimes.com/2011/01/22/world/africa/22sidi.html?pagewanted=1&_r=3&src=twrhp> (accessed Sept., 2011).

Nisbet, R. (1988). *The Present Age: Progress and Anarchy in Modern America*. New York: Harper & Row.

The Oath Project (n.d.). *Partners* <http://www.theoathproject.org/partners> (accessed Sept., 2011).

Gustavo Cardoso and Pedro Jacobetty

Oreskovic, A. (2011). "Google Launches Twitter Workaround for Egypt," *Reuters*, Feb. 1 <http://www.reuters.com/article/2011/02/01/us-egypt-protest-google-idUSTRE710 05F20110201> (accessed Sept., 2011).

Partido Pirata (n.d.). *Que Proponemos* <http://www.partidopirata.es/conocenos/que-proponemos> (accessed Sept., 2011).

Precarious Manifest (n.d.). "*The Precarious Generation Manifest*" <http://geracaoenras-cada.wordpress.com/manifesto/english/> (accessed Sept., 2011).

Público (2011). "Indignados: el porqué de la fatiga democrática", May 22 <http://www.publico.es/espana/377681/indignados-el-porque-de-la-fatiga-democratica-elecciones2011> (accessed Sept., 2011).

Rosen, J. (2010). "The Afghanistan War Logs Released by Wikileaks, the World's First Stateless News Organization" <http://archive.pressthink.org/2010/07/26/wikileaks_afghan.html> (accessed Sept., 2011).

Savage, M., and Williams, K. (2008). "Elites: Remembered in Capitalism and Forgotten by Social Sciences," in M. Savage and K. Williams (eds), *Remembering Elites*. Oxford: Blackwell.

Scott, J. (2008). "Modes of Power and the Re-Conceptualization of Elites," in M. Savage and K. Williams (eds), *Remembering Elites*. Oxford: Blackwell.

Silverstone, R. (1999). *Why Study the Media?* London: Sage.

—— (2000). "The Sociology of Mediation and Communication," in Craig Calhoun, Chris Rojek, and Bryan Turner (eds), *The SAGE Handbook of Sociology*. London: Sage.

Sreedharan, C., Thorsen, E., and Allan, S. (2012). "WikiLeaks and the Changing Forms of Information Politics in the 'Network Society,'" in E. Downey and M. A. Jones (eds), *Public Service, Governance and Web 2.0 Technologies: Future Trends in Social Media*. Hershey, PA : IGI Global.

Stalder, Felix (2010). "Autonomy and Control in the Era of Post-Privacy," *Open: Cahier on Art and the Public Domain. No. 19: Beyond Privacy. New Notions of the Private and Public Domains* <http://felix.openflows.com/node/143> (accessed Sept., 2011).

Sundaram, R. (2001). "Recycling Modernity: Pirate Electronic Cultures in India. Sarai Reader 1:93–9" <http://www.sarai.net/journal/pdf/093-099%20(piracy).pdf> (accessed Sept., 2011).

Tambini, D. (2010). "What Are Financial Journalists for?", *Journalism Studies*, 11/2: 158–74.

Touraine, A. (2004). "On the Frontier of Social Movements," *Current Sociology*, 52/4: 717–25.

Underwood, P., and Welser, H. T. (2011). " 'The Internet is here': Emergent Coordination and Innovation of Protest Forms in Digital Culture," iConference 2011, Seattle.

Wang, S. (2003). *Framing Piracy: Globalization and Film Distribution in Greater China*. Lanham, MA: Rowman and Littlefield.

Wellman, B. (2002). "Little Boxes, Glocalization, and Networked Individualism," in Makoto Tanabe, Peter van den Besselaar, and Toru Ishida (eds), *Digital Cities II: Computational and Sociological Approaches*. Berlin: Springer.

Yar, M. (2005). "The Global 'Epidemic' of Movie 'Piracy': Crime-Wave or Social Construction?" *Media, Culture and Society*, 27/5: 677–96.

Chapter 9

Beyond the Crisis: The Emergence of Alternative Economic Practices

Joana Conill, Manuel Castells, Amalia Cardenas, and Lisa Servon

Introduction

The economic crisis that has unfolded since 2008 has shaken the foundations of millions of lives in Europe and North America. Suddenly, employment became uncertain, credit was restricted to a few, consumption was
reduced to the essentials, social services were deeply cut, and a dark cloud
engulfed the future of their children, reversing the pattern of higher expectations for the next generation. The crisis did not come as a surprise for
those who did not expect much improvement in their lives from what they
labelled "capitalism," a shorthand expression for the dominant social and
economic organization. Not only did they distrust the facade of stability of a
system submitted to recurrent crisis, but they rejected its basic principles.
They objected to the destructive pace of life, and to the nonsense of working relentlessly to have enough money to consume meaningless goods
and services, eat chemical food, drug themselves, and compete with their

human fellows in an increasingly aggressive world. They resented the destruction of the environment that in their view was advancing the expiry date for the human adventure on the blue planet.

Those who dared to live alternative ways of life, based on a different set of economic practices rooted in the quest for the use value of life and for meaningful personal relationships, built networks of solidarity, support, and experimentation. They did not withdraw from society. Most of them had regular jobs and benefited from the safety net of the welfare state. Yet, while using resources available to them, they engaged in various forms of production, consumption, exchange, education, health care, housing, urban living, communication, and cultural expressions, which provided meaning to their lives. So doing, they looked for ways to improve their personal relationships, they learned how to work together and act together in a cooperative mode, and they gradually built their relative autonomy vis-à-vis the institutions of the capitalist market economy. And so, when the crisis hit, they were prepared for it. Indeed, rather than being distressed, the dramatic events that followed confirmed, from their perspective, what they had been saying all along. They were strengthened in their convictions, as they suddenly seemed to be the wise lot rather than the marginal counter-cultural types.

For many others who had accepted an existence sustained by the dream of consumption and the fear of departing from normality, when the crisis disrupted their lives, a window of hope appeared through examples that offered glimpses of a different life. Not so much because of a sudden ideological conversion but as a result of the impossibility of living by the rules of the market. Being jobless or credit-less stalled the avenues of consumption. Not being able to count for sure on the safety net of the welfare state increased uncertainty for the future. The perceived incapacity of the political elites to solve their problems destroyed trust in the institutions in charge of managing the crisis. The only safe place was home, but, with the possibility of mortgage foreclosure, even home could vanish at any time. Thus, the notion of reconstructing everyday life around autonomous economic practices that do not rely on the banks or government became more realistic than the traditional pattern of economic behavior. This is not to say that the masses of the world joined in the practice of an alternative economic culture. But the possibility of a convergence between cultural transformation and economic survival was opened. How much this actually took place we do not know. It depends on specific conditions of countries, localities, economic environments, and social groups. And the record can be set only by rigorous investigation. This is the purpose of the research whose findings we present in this chapter. We know that there are a great deal of alternative economic practices in the world at large, some of them survivors of pre-capitalist cultures, others conscious projects of reinvention of life, still others adapting to the uncertain contours of existing capitalism. There is also an increasingly abundant literature on these practices and their implications for social and economic change in a variety of contexts (Adaman and Madra, 2002; Gibson-Graham, 2002, 2006; Leyshon, Lee, and Williams, 2003; North, 2005; Miller, 2006).

In this chapter we focus on the observation of the rise of alternative economic practices focusing on a specific context: Catalonia. Whilst this is a country that has always been characterized by a rebellious, innovative culture, and by social movements challenging imposed orders, we are not claiming any special distinction for our field of study. Indeed, we believe that any other country (say Germany or Britain, for instance) would yield a similar harvest of alternative practices. We are simply taking advantage of the privilege of having direct access to transformative processes in the Catalan society in order to conduct an empirical investigation on practices that are relevant for the understanding of the new social dynamics in many European countries.

While embarking on our inquiry, we kept in mind the distinction between those alternative economic practices that consciously aim at creating a new way of being, and non-capitalist practices that permeate people's everyday life out of necessity or out of persistence of non-commodified social forms. Therefore, our study has two different foci that we will try to integrate in the analysis.

On the one hand, we have observed the networks, organizations, and individuals that, at least part time, consciously live apart from capitalist patterns of economic behaviour, and according to rules and values they find meaningful for themselves. On the other hand, we have investigated to which extent these practices are integrated in the behavior of the population at large during the time of crisis. Although our findings are preliminary, they suggest that there is more resonance than is usually acknowledged between a conscious alternative economic culture and the culture of a mainstream society shaken by the economic crisis.

This hypothesis explains our methodology, which we will briefly describe here, referring to the methodological appendix of this chapter for technical details. First of all, we have studied the universe of conscious alternative economic practices in Catalonia by a sequence of three research operations:

1. We identified networks and organizations involved in these practices and interviewed seventy individuals selected in terms of their strategic role and knowledge of the practices.

2. On the basis of these interviews, we made a documentary film (<www. homenatgeacatalunyaII.org>) that communicated our findings to a broad audience, both nationally and internationally.
3. We used the film to stimulate debate in eight focus groups that provided the opportunity for us to understand the formation of the consciousness of an alternative economic culture in the diversity of its expressions, and in contrast with individuals who do not share the culture.

Second, using the results from the qualitative research, we elaborated a questionnaire and conducted a survey of a representative sample of the population of Barcelona (800 interviews). The survey tried to measure the extent of diffusion of each one of the identified alternative economic practices in society at large, and determine the factors inducing or restraining the diffusion of these practices during the economic crisis. This chapter presents the results of these studies and tries to make sense of our observation.

The culture and organization of alternative economic practices

While economic practices that do not fit within the pattern structured by the rules of the capitalist market permeate throughout the entire society, in some cases there is a deliberate attempt to connect these practices to an alternative vision of the meaning of life. In this section we focus on the understanding of these conscious practices oriented toward a use value economy, and on the discourses that surround these practices. We will be referring to practices that are organized in various ways, be it in networks, associations, collectives, or organizations such as cooperatives of diverse legal status.

We will start by identifying practices related to organizations that exist in Catalonia. Whilst our observation focuses on the 2009–11 period, the time of the economic crisis, many of these organizations and related practices pre-date the crisis and seem to be related to the search for a more meaningful way of life by thousands of people—most of them, but not all, young adults (approximate average age: 35), and usually college educated.

For the sake of clarity we have grouped the diverse universe of these organizations, and their membership, in a typology presented in Figure 9.1 and Table 9.1.

We review these practices below.

Table 9.1 Typology of most active organizations involved in alternative economic practices in Catalonia, estimation of organizations and participating persons, 2008–2011

Organization	Number	Average number of persons	Total of persons involved
Agro-ecological production networks	12	22 families	264 x 4 = 1,056
Agro-ecological consumer cooperatives	120	30 families	3,600 x 4 = 14,400
Exchange networks	45	120	5,400
Social currency networks	15	50	750
Free universities	3	200	600
Hacklabs	1	150	150
Shared parenting cooperatives	10	25	250
Seed bank networks	4	20	80
Community-based urban orchards	40	15	600
Total*	**250**		**23,286**
+ Ethical banks**	4	71,138	284,554
	254		**307,840**

Notes: * Some of the people involved in these practices may overlap. ** Numbers of persons in ethical banks indicate members and clients of the financial cooperatives.

Production

The most important form of alternative production is in the area of *agro-ecological farming and food processing*. This is not just organic production but, according to the producers' definition, "a production system that maintains the health of soils, eco-systems, and people." There are dozens of agro-ecological farms and hundreds of farmers distributed all around Catalonia.

Agro-ecological production also has a presence in cities, some of the projects being supported by municipal governments. In Barcelona we counted fifteen urban community orchards cultivated and taken care of by neighbors, involving about 600 people. A significant agro-ecological activity is the organization and maintenance of seed banks, which preserve local

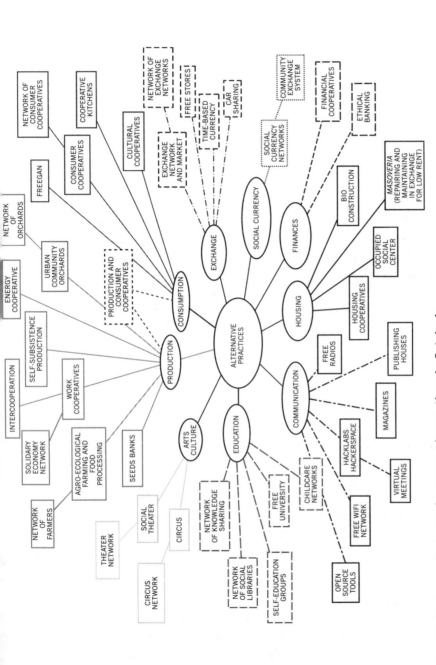

Fig. 9.1 Universe of alternative economic practices in Catalonia

Note: This diagram illustrates the structure of the alternative economic practices that were most pervasive in Catalonia in 2010–2011.

varieties of fruits and vegetables to slow down the global trend of original seed extinction. These are also organized in networks of seed banks.

In related non-farming activities, there is evidence of the growth of *self-subsistence production*, such as baking bread, raising poultry for eggs and meat, and cultivating vegetables in the terraces and gardens of private homes. There is also some artisanal production of domestic utensils. Many of these activities are integrated in networks of support, advice, and sharing.

Consumption

Agro-ecological consumer cooperatives have been growing fast in recent years. They usually organize only consumers, but in some cases they integrate both producers and consumers. Although the producer–consumer networks are still a small phenomenon in Catalonia, they are connected to similar associations in southern France, with the strong presence of the Association pour le Maintien de l'Agriculture Paysanne, and to Andalusia, where there are dynamic associations such as La Ortiga (Sevilla), La Breva (Malaga), and El Encinar (Granada). These associations are based on a stable commitment between producers and consumers bound by mutual solidarity. There are more than 100 consumer groups of agro-ecological products in Catalonia. There are complex internal debates to ensure that both consumers and producers find a fair balance between their interests. The expansion of these consumer groups, most of which were created in the 2000s, comes both from an alternative political culture, and from the growing concern about unhealthy food in a chemical production system. In 2008, a "meeting space" was organized to assemble around a debate amongst the people involved in the consumer cooperatives movement—over 10,000 persons at the time. The assembly, named La Repera, refused to organize a formal coordination, as they believed the groups should be autonomous and able to engage in an open debate about the forms and aims of the movement around common goals of an alternative form of food consumption. In the view of many participants, the instrumental dimension of the co-ops was only part of their collective project. The key was to build a network of conscious deliberation about how to live according to ecological and ethical values. As an extension of the consumer cooperatives, there have been a number of experiments of autonomous school canteens organized by parents to ensure that their children are fed with agro-ecological products.

There has also been a growing trend toward the establishment of agro-ecological restaurants cooperatively managed.

Exchange

There are a considerable number of *exchange markets and exchange networks that engage in barter of goods and services.* Most of these are organized weekly in public squares, and they serve primarily local residents. They do not use money, and they are based on voluntary valuation of the barter. Often they extend the barter process to email lists, sort of a Craigslist among local neighbors. One of the most active exchange networks, Xaingra, in the Gracia District of Barcelona, has over 1,000 members in its email list. Trust in a particular network is the prevailing characteristic of these exchange systems. Exchange of services is important, as people trade skills and time, as in the time bank systems that have proliferated around the world. We identified forty-six local exchange networks in Catalonia and fourteen in Barcelona.

Social currency and ethical banking

Social currency is a formal, printed note that indicates a value unit that is accepted only within a local network, or networks connected to the local network, for the purchase of goods and services. The goal is to remain linked to local production and distribution and to avoid accumulation, as the value depends on the participants in the network. In Catalonia the most developed social currency networks are the Ecoseny (from the Montseny area) and the Eco of Tarragona. In some cases, these currencies have been used in exchange networks in other areas, including Barcelona. Furthermore, these currencies are integrated in a worldwide community exchange system that, as of 2010, included 254 social currency networks present in 31 countries and 300 localities (including 51 networks in the USA). The key issue is to coordinate the local exchange with the broader reach of the social currency, ultimately aiming to develop an alternative currency system based on trust and equivalence, and excluding accumulation, inflation, and unfair exchange. Social currency proponents see its role in the broader context of the different levels of economic exchange. According to our interviewees:

We could see different economic levels here, like circles that go from small to large, that have to be set in motion with rules that are different, but complementary. The first level is free, it's what you have with your family, and friends, it's your closest circle of trust. And, without having to measure the value added by each person, just giving and receiving what you can is enough. The next level is direct exchange, also within a close-knit network but without the high level of trust found in a family unit. Then there's a circle that is further away, but is direct, that is, it allows for relationships that are direct and stable, which include, for example, something like a social currency. A social currency can help us substitute everything that currently functions with euros, which is a way of valuing things that we can't control, and which are handled by banks. We can use rules that are created in committee, in a participatory way, and that we try to adjust to certain relationships... that we believe in, which are socially and ecologically fair. So everyone contributes and receives in a balanced way. Of course, ideally, the first level ends up consuming all the others. Of course if we do it backward, if the social currency ends up consuming all of the lower levels, bad news! The social currency has to consume the upper levels, the euro economy. If we don't have much trust we'll accept less credit, and we'll create less currency, and if we are more trusting we'll accept more credit and create more currency. More and more, you can take care of your needs through bartering and you don't have to use the euro. This means a huge shift in logic, in your time, in the day-to-day, in work, in how you define work, in working for a salary, so maybe your work is less tied to a salary, working more for others in a way that involves bartering and that is free. It's all a debate that doesn't make much sense on a theoretical level. What makes sense is to live it. And feel it within yourself. (Text from two interviews on record.)

Similar goals inspire the growing practice of *ethical banking and alternative financial cooperatives*, which include close to 300,000 clients and members in Catalonia. Thus, according to one of the founders of financial Coop 57, their business "is quite simple: to collect money from its members in order to provide members with favourable conditions that are not provided by conventional banks." The director of a non-profit financial entity, Fiare, describes its activity as "a bank where social profitability is the most important thing, not economics but social values." However, "the project has to be profitable or it won't grow, or even survive." By focusing on ethical goals and bypassing intermediaries, they are both efficient and value oriented. The interesting matter is that, in the midst of a global financial crisis, some of these entities, such as FIARE and Coop 57, appear to be impervious to the crisis. Indeed, they are growing, and are in good enough financial shape to provide loans for projects that correspond to their ethical views.

Housing

The lack of affordable housing, particularly for the younger population, is felt deeply by those whom it affects. Alternative practices to deal with this crisis include housing cooperatives; agreements with landlords to repair and maintain vacant housing in exchange for low rents; agreements to cultivate the land in an abandoned farm to share the harvest and live on the premises; and self-construction of various housing structures adjacent to existing buildings, without legal permits—a growing practice below the radar of the authorities.

In addition there is a particularly significant practice of squatting in vacant apartments and buildings. Here we must differentiate between illegal occupation of empty apartments by individuals and families in need, and conscious, equally illegal occupations (the Okupas movement) that take over entire buildings as material support for an alternative way of life. The latter actions formed what is known as Occupied Social Centers, which organized cultural and social activities open to the neighborhood at large. These include services such as free repair of bicycles, legal and psychological support, exchange of services, and free lessons in a variety of skills, including music and programing. In 2010 there were sixty-two such centers in Catalonia (fifty-two in Barcelona and its metropolitan area) whose aim is to materialize the vision of a different city and a different culture. They are often the target of police-backed evictions, sometimes leading to violent confrontations.

Education

A number of collectives have attempted to create educational institutions to provide alternative education. There are three main types of alternative education: networks of knowledge sharing, free universities, and parental networks of alternative childcare. Knowledge-sharing networks are usually based in specific neighborhoods and operate on the basis of mutual agreements between persons to exchange lessons of their respective knowledge. Free universities are usually housed in occupied buildings and offer a wide range of courses given by voluntary teachers: some of them university professors, others persons with knowledge and skills who want to help educate the population at large. They offer formal courses, with a fixed duration and explicit rules and program for each course. There is an implicit philosophy of denouncing the emptiness and uselessness of formal higher education, and showing in practice how students can be fully engaged when the pedagogy is participatory and the course content is focused on personal development rather than on what they consider to be the bureaucratic degree-delivery logic of the universities. In 2011 in Barcelona, one of the free universities, La Rimaia, was enjoying considerable success in terms of attracting students. In 2010 there was a network of five free universities in Catalonia that shared programs and resources.

Parent-controlled childcare networks originated from parents' critique of the care received by their children in existing institutions. These networks are inspired by a free education philosophy with the goal of full development of the child's personality. Parents are usually intensely involved in the process, with the help of professional educators. These are largely private, self-managed experiments that sometimes include home schooling.

Communication and information technology

There are a number of free Wi-Fi networks, open and neutral, that operate via self-installed antennas on balconies around Catalonia. Users are connected by a free virtual network, guifi.net, which has over 9,000 nodes. Guifi.net was developed as a response to the lack of Internet access in some rural areas, and has been extended to cities as a free Catalan Wi-Fi. Thousands of prospective users are on the guifi.net waiting list.

Alternative communication networks include free radio stations (nearly thirty in 2011), publishing houses, dozens of magazines, and bulletins of all sorts. "Free," as they label themselves, should be understood to mean that in most cases they do not fulfill the legal requirements for their activity. Radio stations often use non-attributed frequencies, and are thus in direct violation of regulations. Contrabanda and RadioBronca are the most popular of these stations. Their programing breaks all habits of standard radio production. A popular program (Radio Nicosia) is conducted entirely by mentally ill persons. Around this nucleus of alternative communication there are bookstores, publishing houses, and websites that, while legally established, distribute the prints, images, and sounds of this alternative culture.

Free software and hacking of various kinds are also key components of the alternative culture, and are often central to establishing wireless Internet networks in sites of protest. There is a network of HackLabs that work as both training grounds for activists and centers of innovation for advanced free software programing. They also teach how to set up peer-to-peer networks for free downloading. These HackLabs are globally connected to the network of Hacktivists and other hacker networks, such as The Onion Router.

Alternative cultural activities

Although, strictly speaking, theater, filmmaking, music, plastic arts, and poetry are not considered economic practices, we want to include them in our observation because, in current thinking regarding economic development, "cultural industries" have a prominent role. Thus, it is important to emphasize the extraordinary blossoming of all of these cultural creations within the alternative cultures of Catalonia. Indeed, art and social protest have always been closely linked throughout history, everywhere. Music plays a central role in youth culture and lifestyle. But perhaps theater is the most openly critical medium in terms of its explicit message of resistance to the institutions of capitalism. There is a network of theater groups that call themselves the "theater of the oppressed": Plataforma Autonoma de Teatro del Oprimido (PATO). They are based on voluntary work and self-managed production, direction, and acting. They perform in streets, public places, and social centers in order to reach an audience outside of high culture sites.

Altogether, these economic practices embody an alternative culture in its multidimensional manifestation. But what is the meaning of these practices for those who practice them?

The meaning of alternative practices: the view from the actors

To investigate the meaning of these alternative economic practices for the actors themselves, we proceeded with an analysis of the internal debate within eight focus groups, designed according to our hypotheses, and studied according to the procedures presented in the methodological appendix to this chapter. The overall purpose of the exercise was to contrast the discourse and self-representation of those persons consciously and actively engaged in alternative practices, with people who are also involved in these practices but not deliberate in their behavior, and with people whose economic practices are mainstream and rarely overlap with the practices we intend to study. For the sake of clarity we will identify the first group as *culturally transformative*, the second as *alternative practitioners*, and the third as *culturally adapted*. The rationale for this terminology will be clearer as we proceed with the analysis. It is important to emphasize that the three categories are found in all of the groups in various proportions. However, our analysis will concentrate on the key themes emerging from the discussion in all groups. We will identify the positions of the different actors for each one of the themes that characterize the rise of a transformative economic culture in contrast with the other two categories in each one of the groups.

The economic crisis

It appears that alternative economic practices have been growing as the crisis of 2008 has taken full shape in the Spanish economy. Nevertheless, while everybody, regardless of his or her practice, is fully aware of the gravity of the economic crisis and affected by its consequences, people differ widely in their perception and evaluation of the crisis. For transformative persons, the crisis is a consequence of the logic of capitalism and should not come as a surprise. Indeed, it is an affirmation of their analysis of capitalism, which had previously led to their rejection of living according to capitalist rules. Thus, most of them had already begun to live differently before the crisis became visible in society, and now feel to some extent vindicated by their preventive move of setting up an alternative way of life before being forced to do so by the crisis. They do not identify themselves with those who change their practices because of their inability to maintain their pre-crisis consumption patterns and levels, to the point that they are sometimes reluctant to acknowledge the growth of new practices after the crisis. For them, capitalism is in perma-crisis, and it is a matter of being aware of it and escaping the trap of living to work and making money to consume instead of just *living*. They position themselves ideologically, and call for a political treatment of the crisis that will deal with its roots rather than adapt to its effects. For the alternative practitioners without a deliberate ideological position, the crisis has shaken their beliefs and their understanding of life. The crisis appears as a monster of uncertain profile that affects everything they used to do or think, so that adapting to the new environment is difficult and confusing. Thus, they change their practices: they consume less, they share, they become willing to try solidarity networks, and barter, and a number of other practices that are better suited to the economic unpredictability in which they currently find themselves, but without knowing why and how and toward which kind of future. While the transformatives had anticipated the crisis, the practitioners are reacting only now, and are learning by doing so in the new world they call, after the media, "the crisis." In contrast, the adapted, unable to accept these new conditions, are waiting, enduring the bad weather, and hoping for the best. As the crisis deepens, the shift from being adapted to being practitioners of the culture of austerity may be one of the most decisive trends in ongoing social change.

The culture of work

The "culture of work" has been central in the industrial society, the society where the majority of the mature and aged sectors of the Catalan population grew up (25 percent of the residents of Barcelona are older than 64). In the focus groups we conducted, retired persons were adamant in their defence of the culture of work, not only as a necessary economic practice but as a moral principle. Furthermore, the influence of the work ethic goes beyond the old age to influence the younger group engaged in conscious alternative economic practices. Their identifying characteristic is that they do not make a distinction between paid work and unpaid work. The key distinction for them is between rewarding work that has a creative or enjoyable component, and imposed, boring work that is done as a means of survival. Moreover, they value the kind of jobs that fit into their own schedule and complement their preferences. They see work as an expression of their choice and their autonomy, rather than meaningless toil (which was sometimes equated to slavery in the interviews). The majority of the transformatives seem to have the capacity to obtain skilled jobs or flexible working time. They are self-programmable workers. This self-programmable quality is actually amongst the same set of capabilities required to operate self-managed networks on which alternative cultures are based. Many of these people are educated enough to have a well-paid job. However, they have made a deliberate choice not to take such a job because it would limit their autonomy and free time.

They feel secure enough about themselves to prioritize quality of life, as they have defined it, over money. They are aware that not everyone has this kind of choice. People usually face constraints that make it difficult to reconcile work and personal life. They know that their cultural capital grants them the possibility of choice, and thereby wish others would also increase their cultural capital. Yet, they do not necessarily equate this handicap to social inequality; they also take into account the difference in personal attitudes and priorities. Some of them are aware that they could be blamed for elitism and accordingly feel uncomfortable. On the other hand, some redeem themselves by referring to the risks they take in order to follow an autonomous path, and thus conclude that they may deserve the freedom they obtain by sacrificing security.

The transformatives believe that one should begin by defining true economic needs, rather than falling into an endless spiral of consumption where new needs always appear as a result of enticement in the market. Thus, they cut unnecessary spending, and as a result do not need to earn as much and free themselves to find flexible jobs that allow time to live. Their discourse is constructed on the relationship between the consciousness of their needs and the satisfaction of the needs that are most worthy for them. Rather than starting from consumer preferences, as in the market logic, they start with personal life preferences and organize their needs accordingly. Needs determine how much money they must earn, and how much value they assign to free time. The result of this calculation is the choice of a certain job or activity that optimizes the combination of this set of self-defined needs. In some persons there is an acute awareness of an internal contradiction: if they are able to live more fully with less money, it is because of the subsidized services that capitalism provides. It soon becomes obvious that the system is not external to their practice, and they live within it as a contradiction. Moreover, they feel sometimes that they are members of an elite that has choices in a society where the majority do not. They console themselves by saying they are just middle class with a college education.

Amongst the practitioners, the discourse on the centrality of work in their lives is full of ambiguity. They value their own time and the enjoyment of life over work. They would certainly prefer to work less for lesser pay. For them, happiness is contingent on the ability of each person to choose work according to his or her preference of schedule and kind of activity. On the other hand, they are aware of the difficulty of finding a job under current economic conditions. They feel trapped by mortgage payments, their tight budgets, and their family responsibilities. Thus, they do engage in alternative economic practices as much as they can, and would envisage a new way of life in accordance with their quests for personal happiness. But such a project is perceived as an unattainable dream in contrast with the harsh reality of life.

For the adapted, work is of paramount importance because it anchors their lives. Yet, interestingly enough, they would also prefer to work less and be paid less. But what dominates their discourse and their perception is the need to pay the bills for everything they do in life. They refer again and again to having to pay for rent, the car, electricity, water, and a whole range of other family expenses; and, to be able to do so, they need a job that pays as well as possible. So, life could be different and better, but it is as it is, and there is no return to a situation freed of the constraints that have been derived from their constructed existence. They followed the socially established pattern in life, and any challenge to their routine would be disturbing and perceived as destructive.

The transition from a work culture to a personal fulfillment culture is better understood when we compare the discourse of the young adults (18–24) with that of the retirees in the focus groups. Most of the young persons consider alternative economic practices to be the most desirable lifestyle. But this lifestyle is somewhat abstract for them, because they often live with their parents and have not yet entered the professional world. Because most of them are studying, they try to make sense of their current efforts by projecting into the future, and picturing themselves as not only working, but working on what they would like to do, and in accordance with what they study. Thus, they do share the work culture, but in terms of chosen, meaningful work. On the other hand, facing the dire employment conditions during the crisis, they do not think that they can achieve their goals. Thus, they convey both the hope for a meaningful working life and the frustration of its perceived unlikelihood.

This is in sharp contrast with retired people. For them, work is of utmost importance, and is what has given meaning to their lives. They cannot understand why people would reject work, or be paid less in order to work less. There is an implicit disdain for the youth who resist working under any circumstances. The cultural divide between the industrial society and the current society is fully manifested in the sharp contrast in the mental representations of those who have already lived their lives and those who are now projecting their lives.

The risk society

To engage in alternative economic practices implies a certain risk in the current institutional environment. The risk increases with the depth and extent of each individual's involvement in these practices. Indeed, one striking finding in our analysis of focus groups is that the willingness to take risks appears to be the determining factor in jumping the fence and adopting a different way of life based on personal preferences rather than on the imperatives of the labor market. For instance, among the adapted or the practitioners, a recurrent fear of dropping the formal labor market is the loss of the rights to social security pensions when the time of retirement comes. However, in the discourse of the people who are most deeply committed to an alternative way of life, the fear of risk fades away under the effects of a powerful antidote: trust. They trust the people around them, they trust their networks of support, and, so, they do not feel the risk. Furthermore, they would not have it otherwise. This is the life they want. As for the concerns for the future, in terms of social security and other forms of public assistance, from the perspective of their relatively young age, they feel optimistic about the chances of seeing the problems solved once they have reached the point of needing assistance. When we asked how they could receive needed help, they projected a horizon of social change, and a belief that the exponential growth of networks of solidarity will be sufficient to care for each other when needs arise. Thus, rather than counting on a traditional welfare state, they hope for the self-management of networks of mutual support. This discourse in fact could be linked to the origins of the mutualist movement that preceded the modern welfare state.

Furthermore, when pressed on the question of the risks they face in their alternative lifestyle, the transformatives refer to what in their perception is the real risk: living under capitalism, as the current economic crisis shows. In their views, the risks are unemployment, low salaries, uncertainty of credit, cuts of basic social services—the insecurity of the whole institutional fabric on which the lives of people depend. In contrast, autonomous economic practices, accepting a much lower level of consumption, and with the meaning of life placed beyond the consumption realm, do not depend on business cycles, on financial speculation, or on failed public policies—processes that are all beyond people's control. In fact, some argue, to worry constantly about the future spoils the joy of the present. Since the future is out of our control, it seems wiser to construct a different future out of the dynamic of a succession of meaningful presents.

In contrast with this vital attitude, other persons are mired in the risk that these practices entail. They usually find the idea of having more free time or broadening the scope of their experience appealing. But, when considering the feasibility of these practices, social security and retirement weigh decisively in their choice of caution and resignation. They find security and stability in earning more money, even if there is unanimity that money does not mean happiness. Happiness is somewhere else, in a universe that could be closer to the blueprint of life present in alternative practices. But this is seen as a forbidden Eden.

The perceived risk diminishes with the size of the support networks that make alternative practices sustainable. The larger the network, and the more intense the expressions of solidarity that build trust, the greater the feeling of security. Large networks build trust. Small networks convey insecurity and, in addition, induce fatigue of living in a small world in constant tension with the dominant logic of society. The feeling of risk related to alternative practices dwindles when the support networks grow to the point of representing an alternative social organization. This effect of network size explains the exponential growth of some of these practices, particularly consumer cooperatives, exchange networks, and ethical banking. We know the value of a network grows exponentially with an increase in the number of its nodes. Trust and security grow exponentially with the growth of the number of participants in a given network of practices, while the feeling of risk, and associated fears, decreases accordingly. For a practice to become significant it has to reach a threshold of critical mass in terms of the number of people and organizations involved in the practice.

The adapted do not feel the risk, because they do not seriously consider engaging in alternative economic practices. They have a negative view of those who do. Retirees think this form of economic practice is simply wrong, and contradictory to what their own life is all about. Others, without being so critical, believe the transformatives do not in fact assume any risk, because of two opposite but often conjoined reasons: on the one hand, they are an elite that can afford to take risks because they are socially insured; on the other hand, some have no real chance of playing by the rules of the system, and, because they have nothing, they have nothing to lose. However, for those refusing to engage in alternative economic practices, the fear of risk is very real; it is in fact so overwhelming that they do not even consider taking it, and thus do not perceive it, and resent those who dare, dismissing them as elitists and freeloaders of the system they denounce.

The construction of alternative practices: identity, networks, and circles

Those who are deliberately engaged in alternative practices have a strong identity. They define themselves as people involved in a non-capitalist way of life, out of their conviction for seeking alternatives to a failed system. Their motivation is primarily ideological, and differentiates them from those who have engaged in similar practices out of economic need. They often use the term "we" and oppose it to "the people," it is "us" versus "them," "I versus the other." In their view, being transformative and deliberately engaged in alternative practices constructs a certain universe, a new society, in rupture with the mainstream, conventional world.

In the debates within the groups, two poles appear clearly: those who assume the alternative culture and those who reject it. However, the separation is not complete, because there is a group that says, "I do not do it, but I know people who do it," and the other, conscious group, who says, "I do it but I know people who do not do it." Thus, it would seem that there is a continuum of practices but a polarity in terms of deliberateness and identity. The construction of this identity largely depends on the social environment. Alternative identity arises from being in touch with persons equally critical of the social organization and ready to live differently and assume the necessary risk. For instance, in one focus group, one woman said she would like to practice an alternative economy but she had to yield to the pressures of her friends and family. Yet, another of the discussants said that, when confronted with lack of understanding in his environment, he simply changed his network of friends to find a cultural home more akin to his views. Both cases illustrated the decisive influence of the social environment in shaping practices one way or another.

One interesting debate on identity refers to the use of the term "alternative." Some of those engaged in these kinds of practices want to use it to mark their distance vis-à-vis conventional society. But others, more sensitive to strategies of broadening what they see as a movement, would rather not set up a terminological barrier to attracting people who agree with the content of alternative practices but refuse labels that would put them in a special, segregated category. Here again, the willingness to affirm an identity instead of just engage in practices depends on the existence of a favorable environment that provides emotional support and social capital conducive to breaking openly with the dominant norms of society. On the other hand, the practitioners usually agree with what the transformatives do on a small scale but would not like to see the whole society organized around alternative values. They refer to such an attempt as a "utopia": something impossible, thus not worth pursuing. Yet they see the possibility of living differently in their everyday life at a small scale; ready to change their lives, but not the world at large. They seek to set up a circle of practices, meaning a circle of directly known persons. There they see the possibility of social change. The reason for this, they argue, is that on this small scale personal trust can be established through direct knowledge and interaction, and so new social rules can grow organically. Trust becomes more difficult to establish within a much larger group, because there are unknown people, and it is difficult to trust people one does not know.

In sum, trust is essential to those engaging in alternative economic practices, and trust is built by social support and personal contact with networks of people with whom practice can be shared. Personal knowledge allows experimentation without fear: it is all right for people to make mistakes if they do it together. Yet networks cannot extend beyond a size that makes personalized contact difficult. To know that someone who knows someone is aware of similar alternative practices creates a connection that provides safety and learning experience. The intensity of the practice of sharing determines the likelihood of sharing practices.

Alternative practices as a process: information sharing and the dynamics of time

The discussion within the focus groups emphasizes the fact that most people in society are unaware of the extent and intensity of alternative economic practices. There is consensus on the fact that, the more people are aware of how many other people are engaged in this economic culture, the more alternative practices diffuse. The question, then, is how to diffuse the information. Two perspectives are confronted in the discourse. On the one hand, the process of building an alternative culture is seen as suffering from insufficient internal communication, thus diminishing the opportunity for synergy and cooperation. On the other hand, some of the transformatives believe that there are organic processes through which people will spontaneously discover what others do, connecting efforts without necessitating directed organization external to the process. The advantage, in this view, is that people integrate only what they find useful or desirable into their experience. There is a debate on the dynamics of organization in emergent economic practices: whether to have a deliberate agenda to build up an organizing effort, or else to let the networks grow and configure themselves in a much slower process that ultimately consolidates the connection between practices through the convergence of their values. The transformatives—particularly those who have been engaged consciously in alternative practices for some time—see these practices as a process. The development of these practices over time strengthens the social relations embedded in the practices. The process produces the practices. To live practicing an alternative culture generates new forms of culture embedded in new economic practices. It is an open-ended process of experimentation in which the sharing of the learning process induces new forms of living that were not originally intended, but ultimately discovered. People do not move toward a programed goal. They discover their goals, and themselves, in the process of learning by doing.

The invisible alternative economy: signs of non-capitalist economic practices among the population of Barcelona

The diffusion of non-capitalist economic practices and their connection to the economic crisis

Perhaps the most important finding from our survey is that virtually everyone we surveyed—97 percent of respondents—has engaged in some kind of non-capitalist economic practice since 2008, the year the current economic crisis was initiated.[1] Although one of these practices, ethical banking, does involve paying money for goods or services and sometimes looking for profits, most practices considered here are non-capitalist in the sense that their goal is not profit, but rather the pursuit of personal meaning. In fact, the vast majority of these practices do not involve financial payment or exchange at all. For this component of our research, we focus on the period 2008 to 2011, in order to focus on the practices and attitudes of people since the crisis hit.

Our survey shows that engagement in non-capitalist economic practices is not a marginal movement in which only a small number of people participate. Table 9.2 illustrates the percentage of survey respondents who participate in each activity, and shows clearly that the percentage of people participating is much higher than one might expect. Furthermore, we see that there is a wide range of economic activities taking place—from urban gardening to cooperative childcare—that do not involve the exchange of money. We show evidence of a surprising extent of entrenchment of these

---

[1] We will use the term "alternative" here as shorthand for non-capitalist economic practices.

practices, in terms of the breadth and depth of their use, and of the kind of people who engage in them.

Table 9.2 depicts the percentage of the total population that has done each of the practices at some point since 2008, the year in which the financial crisis began.[2] We grouped the 26 practices into three categories—self-sufficiency, altruistic, and exchange and cooperation. Self-sufficiency practices involve work people do for themselves rather than going to the market to pay for goods and services. For example, nearly 20 percent of respondents grow vegetables for their own consumption, a significant number for a dense urban area. More than half have performed their own home repairs, and more than a third have repaired their own household appliances; an equal number have made or repaired their own clothes. Less numerous but still important are those who have repaired their own car, motorcycle, or bicycle (21.5 percent) and those who have picked up useful objects or food on the street (16.1 percent). We know from the literature, and from our own qualitative observation, that people may do these things in order to save money—perhaps because they do not have the money to pay for them—or because they enjoy the practices themselves.

A second category of activity is what we call altruistic practices, the performance of acts of service for others that are worth something in the market, without receiving financial compensation. Twenty-one percent of survey respondents have repaired other peoples' homes without the mediation of money, and 11 percent have repaired the car, motorcycle, or bicycle of others without the mediation of money. Sixteen percent have cared for children, the elderly, or sick people who are not family members, and *more than a third have lent money without interest to people who are not family members.*

Cooperation and exchange is the term we use to describe the third group of activities. These involve exchanging goods or services—bartering or the like—without using money as the medium of exchange. Nearly 65 percent of respondents have lent or borrowed books, movies, or music to or from people who are not family members. Nearly 22 percent of respondents have exchanged clothing, home appliances, and other goods without the mediation of money. Twenty-four and 17 percent have engaged in teaching and service exchanges, respectively, without being paid monetarily.

---

[2] We specifically analyzed people who have engaged in non-capitalist economic practices since 2008, in order to focus on the period following the economic crisis. This group respects the representativeness of the survey, and constitutes 88 percent of the entire population surveyed.

Table 9.2 Data on a representative sample of the population of Barcelona, 2008–2011

Practice	Percentage of survey respondents who have participated in each activity	Absolute numbers
Self-sufficiency practices		
Have painted or performed their own home repairs	55.6	445
Have repaired or made their own clothing	39.0	312
Have repaired their household appliances themselves	34.6	277
Have repaired their own car, motorcycle, or bicycle	21.5	172
Have picked up food or useful objects found on streets or markets	16.1	129
Have planted tomatoes, vegetables, or other products for self-consumption	18.8	150
Have raised chickens, rabbits, or other animals for self-consumption	1.9	15
Altruistic practices		
Have lent or borrowed books, movies, or music from people who are not family members	64.5	516
Have shared the use of video cameras, tools, home appliances, and similar objects with people who are not family members	34.0	272
Have lent money without charging interest rates to people who are not family members	34.0	272
Have repaired the house of others without the mediation of money	21.3	170
	16.1	129

Have taken care of children, elderly people, or sick people without the mediation of money		
Have repaired the car, motorcycle, or bicycle of others without the mediation of money	11.1	89
Exchange and cooperation practices		
Have legally downloaded software from the Internet	39.8	318
Know an agro-ecological farmer	29.5	236
Use free software	24.6	197
Have engaged in teaching exchanges without the mediation of money	23.8	190
Have exchanged products, clothing, home appliances, and other goods without the mediation of money	21.9	175
Have shared the use of a car with people who are not family members	17.6	141
Have engaged in service exchanges without the mediation of money	16.9	135
Are or have been members of a food cooperative	9.0	72
Have participated in a community garden	6.9	55
Live with two or more adults who are not family members nor employees	6.0	48
Have taken care of other people's children in exchange for having others take care of their children	5.3	42
Have used social currency	2.3	18
Have participated in an ethical bank or credit cooperative	2.0	16

(continued)

Table 9.2 Continued

Practice	Percentage of survey respondents who have participated in each activity	Absolute numbers
Self sufficiency practices		
Have painted or performed their own home repairs	8.4	67
Have planted tomatoes, vegetables, or other products for self-consumption	4.5	36
Have raised chickens, rabbits, or other animals for self-consumption	2.6	21
Have picked up food or useful objects found on streets or markets	2.4	19
Have repaired their own car, motorcycle, or bicycle	2.3	18
Have repaired or made their own clothing	2.1	17
Have repaired household appliances themselves	0.5	4
Altruistic practices		
Have lent money without charging interest rates to people who are not family members	6.1	49
Have repaired the house of others without the mediation of money	3.0	24
Have taken care of children, elderly people, or sick people without the mediation of money	2.4	19
Have lent or has borrowed books, movies, or music from people who are not family members	1.5	12
Have repaired the car, motorcycle, or bicycle of others without the mediation of money	0.6	5

Have shared the use of video cameras, tools, home appliances, and similar objects with people who are not family members	0.3	2
Exchange and cooperation practices		
Know an agro-ecological farmer	29.5	236
Live with two or more adults who are not family members nor employees	6.0	48
Have or have been members of a food cooperative	3.1	25
Have engaged in teaching exchanges without the mediation of money	2.1	17
Have participated in a community garden	1.9	15
Have taken care of other people's children in exchange for having others take care of their children	1.1	9
Have shared the use of a car with people who are not family members	1.1	9
Have engaged in service exchanges without the mediation of money	1.0	8
Have legally downloaded software from the Internet	0.5	4
Have exchanged products, clothing, home appliances, and other goods without the mediation of money	0.4	3
Have used social currency	0.4	3
Use free software	0.1	1
Have participated in an ethical bank or credit cooperative.	0.0	0

More than 17 percent have shared a car with someone who is not a family member, and 34 percent have shared the use of video cameras, tools, or home appliances with people who are not family members.

A surprisingly high number of people—97 percent of respondents—have engaged in at least one activity. Eighty-three percent have engaged in three or more. The average survey respondent has engaged in six practices, a high number that implies that non-capitalist activities are a regular part of life in Barcelona. The relatively recent appearance of technological tools to abet this kind of activity points to growing demand among younger people, the primary users of such tools.

Only 22 of the 800 people surveyed have not engaged in any of these practices since 2008. Seventy-seven percent of this small group is over the age of 64; many reported that age-related health issues have kept them from doing more.

In addition to asking about concrete practices, we also asked people whether and how they have been affected by the economic crisis. *The majority of survey respondents—62 percent—indicated that they have been negatively affected by the economic crisis.* More than half reported that the crisis has adversely affected their spending and their income, and has caused them to worry about their future and the future of their families. Nearly one-third of respondents indicated that their employment has been negatively affected. The incidence of stress-related ailments, from depression and anxiety to substance abuse, has increased since the crisis began, and many attribute these increases to the financial crisis. As early as October 2008, the World Health Organization warned that mental health problems and suicides would probably increase as people were forced to cope with poverty and unemployment (Reuters, 2008). More than 29 percent of our survey respondents told us that their health had suffered as a result of the crisis.

We also gathered data on a range of attitudes toward capitalism and social change from survey respondents. The results of this component of our survey point to fairly broad disenchantment with the capitalist system. Over half of respondents answered "bad" or "very bad" to the question "What do you think about capitalism?" Only 2.5 percent answered "very good." Despite this negative attitude toward capitalism, the vast majority of respondents—77.4 percent—believe that society can change for the better, and 67.8 percent believe that they can contribute personally to this change.

Nearly 60 percent of respondents reported that they would like to work less and make less money if such an option were possible. This finding, coupled with the deep engagement of a majority of people in non-capitalist practices, implies dissatisfaction with the capitalist system, and a desire for other ways to organize their work lives, and for greater control over their time. Those who told us they would like to work less indicated that they would spend more time with their friends and family, and pursue other activities they enjoy with their newly available time.

Who does what? Social categories and the intensity of non-capitalist practices

When we look at particular socio-demographic groups, we see that there are several that engage in a relatively high or relatively small number of practices. Here, we dig more deeply into these groups in order to understand more specifically what they do and to consider why they might be more or less likely to engage in non-capitalist practices. Table 9.3 illustrates the average number of practices engaged by each group that we analyzed, and the difference between each group and the mean for the total population, which is 6.29 practices. There is clearly some overlap between particular groups, such as young people and students at the higher end of the spectrum, and between older people and the retired at the lower end.

Foreign-born people engage in a relatively high number of practices—seven on average. Significant portions of this group engage in nearly all of the self-sufficiency practices: 40.6 percent repair or make their own clothing and more than one fourth repair their own car, motorcycle, or bicycle, or glean food or useful objects from the street. Substantial numbers also appear to be engaged in networks of exchange, as evidenced by the above average percentages of people who: (1) have cared for the sick, the elderly, or children who are not family members without receiving monetary pay (32 percent versus 16 percent); (2) have lent money to people who are not family without charging interest (48 percent versus 34 percent); and (3) have taken care of other people's children in exchange for others taking care of their children (6 percent versus 5 percent). The focus on networks of exchange is not surprising, given that foreign-born people tend to live in close proximity and help each other. Interestingly, the foreign born who responded to our survey tend to be relatively well established. More than half have lived in Barcelona for more than ten years and another fourth

Table 9.3 Comparison of practice intensity by socio-demographic categories

Socio-demographic category	Number of practices performed (mean)	Above or below mean
Total population	**6.29**	
Gender*		
Male	7.08	0.79
Female	5.61	−0.68
Age*		
+ 64 years	4.08	−2.21
50–64 years	5.52	−0.77
35–49 years	7.13	0.84
25–34 years	7.9	1.61
18–24 years	8.28	1.99
Educational level***		
Master's degree and above	7.29	1.00
College degree	6.77	0.48
Upper secondary education	6.37	0.08
Lower secondary education	5.55	−0.74
No education/primary studies not completed	4.35	−1.94
Occupation*		
Liberal professional, entrepreneur, middle manager	7.69	1.40
Autonomous worker	7.24	0.95
Employed, manual laborer	6.86	0.57
Housewife	4.39	−1.90
Retired	4.36	−1.93
Unemployed	7.57	1.28
Student	8.21	1.92
Marital status*		
Single	7.66	1.37
Married	5.47	−0.82
Unmarried living in couple	9.48	3.19
Divorced/separated	7.31	1.02
Widow(er)	4.5	−1.79

Birthplace**

City of Barcelona	6.53	0.24
Rest of Catalonia	6.05	−0.24
Spain	5.17	−1.12
Foreign born	7.01	0.72

Time of residence in Barcelona***

Has always lived (was born in) Barcelona	6.3	0.01
More than twenty years	5.33	−0.96
Between ten and twenty years	7.88	1.59
Between five and ten years	7.4	1.11
Less than five years	8.88	2.59

Income***

Above €5,000	7.65	1.36
Between €4,001 and €5,000	7.11	0.82
Between €3,001 and €4,000	6.83	0.54
Between €2,001 and €3,000	6.99	0.70
Between €1,001 and €2,000	5.82	−0.47
Up to €1,000	6.82	0.53
Does not know	6.1	−0.19
Does not answer	5.23	−1.06

Note: *** statistically significant at the 0.00 level; ** statistically significant at the 0.01 level.

have lived in Barcelona between five and ten years.[3] Fully 68 percent are between the ages of 25 and 49, and 37 percent describe themselves as employees. The foreign born tend to be on the low to middle part of the income spectrum, with 35 percent earning between €1,000 and €2,000 per month, and another fifth earning between €2,000 and €3,000 per month. Another fifth earn less than €1,000 per month, a figure that is commensurate with the 19 percent unemployment rate reported by this group of respondents, and a figure that approaches the overall unemployment

---

[3] Note that we did not ask them when they had immigrated to Spain, so it is possible they have lived in this country for a longer time.

rate for Barcelona. If we relate this analysis on the practices of the foreign born to the results of our immigrant focus group, we may conclude that immigrants tend to be more willing to engage in non-capitalist practices than the native population at large. The paradox, of course, is that they emigrate from a more traditional to a more predominantly capitalist culture: this indicates that non-capitalist practices are insufficient for making a comfortable living in a capitalist environment, however desirable they may be in terms of human relationships.

Students are also a highly active group in alternative economic practices. Like the foreign born, their activities tend to be concentrated in the self-sufficiency and exchange-oriented categories. More than a third (34 percent compared to the average in our sample, 16 percent) have gleaned food or useful objects found on the streets, and 31 percent have repaired their own car, motorcycle, or bicycle. This group tends not to engage in more home-based self-sufficiency practices such as growing vegetables and repairing their homes because they are the most footloose of all of the age groups we studied. With respect to exchange-oriented activities, nearly 90 percent (versus 65 percent on average) have lent or borrowed books, movies, or music to or from people who are not family members, and 58 percent (versus 34 percent on average) have shared the use of video cameras, tools, and home appliances with people who are not family members. Students, by virtue of being students, have an easily accessible network of other students, along with ready systems with which to communicate with their peers, which helps to explain their heavy involvement in exchange-oriented activities.

With respect to employment status, those who are in middle management are quite active. The majority of people who constitute this group (64 percent) are men, and most (43 percent) are between the ages of 35 and 49. Forty-six percent are single, and an equal number are married. Most—71.4 percent—are highly educated, having obtained a college degree. Eighty-six percent have painted or repaired their own homes, 100 percent (versus 65 percent) have lent or borrowed books, music, and movies to or from non-family members, 64 percent (versus 34 percent) have lent money without interest to non-family members, and 64 percent (versus 40 percent) have legally downloaded software from the Internet. Forty-three percent (versus sixteen percent of the total population) have taken care of children, the sick, or the elderly without receiving money for their services.

Men tend to engage in more practices than do women—7.1 versus 5.6, although this is probably due to the high feminization rate among the oldest group of the population, who are less prone to engage in alternative practices. Perhaps not surprisingly, we see rather stark gender differences in terms of the kinds of activities that women and men engage in, indicating that the gender division of labor continues to exist both in the home and in the engagement of other activities. For example, 55 percent of women have repaired or made their own clothing, as opposed to 20 percent of men. Nearly half of male survey respondents have repaired their household appliances themselves, whereas only 22 percent of women have done so. Men are more likely to engage in activities related to technology—54 percent (versus 27 percent) have downloaded software from the Internet, and 34 percent (versus 16.5 percent) have used free software.

Unmarried couples are particularly active in alternative practices, which is probably a function of the cultural independence usually associated with this kind of household. Also especially active are the most recent residents of Barcelona (fewer than five years). This fits into the well-known pattern of entrepreneurialism and autonomy among those who come to live in a different environment.

Those who are unemployed tend to engage in a higher than average number of practices—7.6. Perhaps not surprisingly, their activity tends to be concentrated in the self-sufficiency category of practices. Thirty percent (versus 19 percent of the total sample) plant vegetables for their own consumption. Nearly half (versus 35 percent) repair their own household appliances, and nearly 70 percent (versus 56 percent) have done their own home repairs. These findings make sense, given that this group has more time and less money than they did before their unemployment.

The relationship between the economic crisis, attitudes toward capitalism, and alternative practices

Our analysis of the survey shows that people who have been negatively affected by the economic crisis are more likely to engage in a higher number of non-capitalist practices than those who say they have not been negatively affected (6.52 practices versus. 6.29).[4] Of the group that has been negatively affected, the

---

[4] We counted how many practices each respondent had participated in. We use this number, but very cautiously, as a kind of proxy for the extent of their engagement in non-capitalist practices. We did not ask respondents how much time they spent per day or per week actually doing these practices.

subgroup whose employment has suffered engage in the greatest number of practices—7.4, on average. *This provides some evidence in support of our hypothesis on the intensification and diffusion of alternative economic practices in the wake of the economic crisis.*

There also appears to be an interesting relationship between attitudes toward capitalism and intensity of engagement in non-capitalist practices (see Table 9.4). On the whole, those who are disenchanted with capitalism and would like to see change also tend to engage in a higher number of alternative practices. People who think capitalism is "very bad" engage in 7.6 practices, on average. Those who believe that capitalism is very bad for their personal lives engage in 8.9 practices, on average, and respondents who are interested in working less and receiving less pay engage in nearly 7 practices, on average. We also see that those who believe they can contribute to positive social change tend to engage in a greater number of practices, 7.1.

Interestingly, those who expressed an interest in working less for less money tend to be on the low to middle part of the socio-economic spectrum; more than one-third earn less than €2,000 per month. More women (56.3 percent) than men (46.4 percent) would prefer to work less and earn less, which makes sense, given the household and care-giving activities that typically fall to women. The group that holds this attitude is distributed relatively evenly across the age spectrum; the largest subgroup—at 27 percent—is 35–49-year-olds, who are most likely to have reached a plateau in terms of their income, and be responsible for small children and older parents. Half of this group is married, implying that it might be easier for them to earn less if they have a spouse who also contributes to the household income; however, nearly a third are single and not living with a partner.

We did not find that the youngest group we surveyed—18–24-year-olds—felt very negatively about capitalism, or thought they could contribute personally to making the world a better place. Those who felt they could positively impact on the world tended to be between 25 and 49 years of age, and relatively well educated. Our guess is that, since most 18–24-year-olds are still living with their parents, they do not feel the world is such a harsh place.

We wanted to understand the profiles of respondents who had positive and negative attitudes toward capitalism. For this part of the analysis, we collapsed the responses of "good" and "very good" and "bad" and "very bad" to the question "What do you think of capitalism?" We see little difference

Table 9.4 Attitudes towards capitalism and intensity of non-capitalist practices

Attitude	Average number of practices
Capitalism is very bad	7.6
Capitalism is very bad for my personal life	8.9
I would like to work less and earn less	7.0
I believe I can contribute to positive social change	7.1

between those with positive and negative perceptions when we look at gender, education, and age, but we do when we consider income levels. Not surprisingly, 45 percent of respondents with a negative perception of capitalism earn less than €2,000 per month. Most are older—26 percent are over the age of 64.

An analysis of our survey produces two critical findings. The first is the existence of a broad set of non-capitalist practices that people engage in to lower their cost of living, to connect to local and far-flung communities, to help others, and simply to fulfill themselves. The second is major dissatisfaction with capitalism and its trappings. Further, the correlation between disenchantment with capitalism and engagement in a greater than average number of practices implies that those who are not happy with the dominant economic arrangement are opting out, albeit quietly, by seeking out alternative ways to manage their lives and take control of their time. Despite their dissatisfaction, they are an optimistic bunch, believing that the world can change for the better, and that they can be a part of that change.

Conclusion: from economic culture to political movement

On May 15, 2011, street demonstrations were called for over the Internet in Madrid, Barcelona, and other Spanish cities, to claim "real democracy now" a few days before municipal elections were to be held. This was an initiative of a group of activists who wanted to protest against the incapacity and dishonesty of the political class in its mishandling of the economic crisis. Without any kind of organization or leadership, tens of thousands of people responded to the call. At the end of the demonstration in Madrid, about two dozen demonstrators camped for the night in Plaza del Sol, the main square of the town, to discuss how to reverse the destructiveness of a crisis out of control as a result of the irresponsibility of politicians. The next night, a group of people decided to do the same in Barcelona, at Plaça Catalunya, the main square of the town. They tweeted their friends to come and join them. Hundreds came, who tweeted their friends as well, so that, after three days, there were thousands camping in the square, and additional thousands in Madrid and other cities and towns of Spain and Catalonia. They called themselves "The Indignants," as their protest was born from the indignation they felt about mass unemployment, housing evictions, mediocre education, cuts in public services, and widespread injustice in the entire realm of their experience. They focused their indignation on bankers, politicians, political institutions, and governments. In their view, the crisis was not really a crisis, but the consequence of the failure of capitalism to provide a decent living and of the inability of pseudo-democratic institutions to represent the interest of the people. They camped for weeks and debated in assemblies and multiple commissions about what should be done and how to do it. They adamantly rejected any formal leadership, ideology, or permanent organization. Only the assemblies could make decisions after hours of respectful debate and open voting. After almost one month, the assemblies in each locality decided to leave the camps but called for organization of assemblies in neighborhoods and towns around the country, for demonstrations and protests focused on political institutions, for mobilizations against the austerity measures imposed by the European Union (EU) and the International Monetary Fund (IMF) to avoid the bankruptcy of entire countries and the fall of the euro. The majority of Spaniards were sympathetic to "The Indignants"—as many as 84 percent, according to a survey commissioned by the prestigious daily *El País*. The gap between politicians and citizens grew wider than ever, and the Spanish parliament began to debate some of the movement's proposals for political reform, in spite of the skepticism of "The Indignants" about the sincerity of any political opening.

What is significant from our analytical perspective is that many of those who are the object of our analysis in this chapter as participants in alternative economic practices were present in the "Indignants" movement. For them, there was a logical continuity between their distance from the norms and institutions of capitalism and the protest against the indignity of political leaders that, in their view, led most people in Catalonia, Spain, and Europe to the dead end of the crisis in the labor market and in social services, while banks recorded unprecedented high levels of profit. Moreover, the resonance we found between the alternative economic practices of a conscious minority and the wide diffusion of non-capitalist economic practices in a sizable segment of the population of Barcelona is mirrored in the support of the majority of public opinion (exemplified by the attendance of hundreds of thousands to protest demonstrations on June 19, 2011, and then on October 15, 2011), to the projects of alternative democracy put forward by those camping in the public squares. Furthermore, these protests were spontaneous, without formal leadership, and without any participation of the trade unions and political parties. While the protest originated as a reaction against the economic crisis and its social costs, the demands of the protesters were not limited to the usual catalogue of economic demands, but rather configured a project of a new economy based on many of the alternative practices that we have observed in this study. Yet, for this project to prosper, in the views of the movement, a new politics must arise, as the necessary lever to move from the margins of society to a new social organization of life. Thus, the alternative economic culture that preceded the economic crisis by virtue of its prescient critique of capitalism rose to the forefront of the public debate when it became clear for many that the return to the happy days of debt-driven capitalism was questionable. The stage was then set for the confrontation between a disciplinary model of hardened, shrunk, financial capitalism, and the deepening and diffusion of an alternative economy that a conscious minority had dared to start living in. This is a direct political conflict whose outcome will determine the world we will live in during the years after the crisis.

METHODOLOGICAL APPENDIX

Our research design comprised four different operations:

1. Identification and analysis of alternative economic practices by participation observation and interviews of some of the key actors involved in the practices.
2. Production of a documentary film on alternative economic practices based on the interviews of our study.
3. Organization of eight focus groups to discuss the values and issues involved in alternative economic practices. The film was used as a stimulus to trigger the debate.
4. Survey of a representative sample of the population of Barcelona (800 interviews), with a questionnaire elaborated on the basis of the findings of our qualitative studies.

We summarize here the features of each one of these research operations:

Conill, Castells, Cardenas, and Servon

Selection of organizations and networks of alternative practices and interviews of the participants in these practices

Between October 2009 and May 2010 we interviewed seventy persons engaged in alternative economic practices. The interviews were videotaped and transcribed. To select the interviewees, we first conducted in 2009 participant observation in a number of organizations and networks of alternative economic practices. We constructed a typology of practices in the following categories: production, consumption, exchange, social currency, ethical banking, housing, education, communication, information technology, and arts. For each category we selected specific networks and organizations and we interviewed individuals engaged in each one of these practices. We relied on the advice of the actors themselves to identify the most significant practices and the most significant interviewees. For the most extended practices (consumer cooperatives, exchange networks, urban orchards, and agro-ecological producers), we selected the cases to be analyzed using three criteria: practices that were older than three years in contrast with practices less than three years old; size of the network engaged in the practice; urban versus rural.

In most cases, the collective itself decided who should be interviewed, using two criteria: it should always be one man and one woman together; it should be someone with more than three years of experience and someone with less than three years of experience in the collective.

All of the interviews were conducted in the place where the practices took place. While interviewing, we observed and filmed the meeting place and, when possible, the practices themselves. The duration of interviews varied between 40 minutes and 2 hours. Fifty-seven percent of the interviews took place in Barcelona and 97 percent took place in the Metropolitan Area of Barcelona (including the city), of which 3 percent were in a rural environment. Three percent of interviews were in the rural areas of Tarragona.

Fifty-five percent of the interviewees were men; 45 percent were women. The age distribution was as follows:

9%   18–24 years old
48%   25–34
37%   35–49
2%   50–64
4%   64 +

Focus groups

We designed eight focus groups. The procedure was the same for each group. Prior to the meeting they watched the documentary film *Homage to Catalonia II* (one hour). In the meeting they engaged in a debate directed and moderated by the research team following a thematic guideline prepared in advance. The debates were recorded and transcribed. The design of the focus groups was based on criteria of the different intensity of engagement in alternative economic practices, as well as socio-demographic composition, as we set out to understand the cultural attitudes of specific groups, such as youth, retired workers, women with family responsibilities, and immigrants. These are the groups that we studied:

1. group of persons with a high level of participation in alternative economic practices;
2. group of persons with low levels of participation in alternative economic practices;
3. mixed group of persons with high levels of participation and low levels of participation in alternative economic practices;
4. group of mothers with high level of participation in alternative economic practices;
5. unemployed persons;
6. group of youth 18–24 years old;
7. group of retired persons of a working-class background;
8. group of immigrants.

Within each group (with the exception of specific age or gender groups) we included persons of different age, gender, and educational level.

The immigrant group included persons from Morocco, Romania, Uruguay, Cuba, and El Salvador.

The number of participants in each group oscillated between seven and twelve, with the exception of the group of persons with low levels of alternative practices, which was made up of five persons.

The focus groups met between November 2010 and May 2011, usually in a room at the university, except for the groups of unemployed persons, retired workers, and immigrants, which met on the premises of their respective associations.

The survey of alternative economic practices in the population of Barcelona at large

We administered a questionnaire of 43 questions to a statistically representative sample of the population of Barcelona. Eight hundred telephone interviews were conducted between February 9 and February 10, 2011. The questions focused on a list of 26 alternative economic practices, on attitudes toward capitalism and social change, and on the socio-demographic characteristics of the respondents. The questionnaire was elaborated by our research team. The design of the sample, the pretest of the interviews, and the interviews were realized by the technical team of Instituto Opina, one of the leading private survey research organizations in Spain

(<www.opina.es>). Technical details of the sampling and interviews as well as the questionnaire are available upon request (<accardenas@uoc.edu>).

References

Adaman, F., and Madra. Y. M. (2002). "Theorizing the Third Sphere: A Critique of the Persistence of the 'Economistic Fallacy'," *Journal of Economic Issues*, 36/4: 1045–78.

Gibson-Graham, J. K. (2002). "Beyond Global vs Local: Economic Politics outside the Binary Frame," in A. Herod and M. Wright (eds), *Geographies of Power: Placing Scale*. Oxford: Blackwell, 25–60.

——(2006). *The End of Capitalism (as we Knew it): A Feminist Critique of Political Economy*. Minneapolis: University of Minnesota Press.

Leyshon, Andrew, Lee, Roger, and Williams, Colin C. (2003). *Alternative Economic Spaces*. Newbury, CA: Sage Publications.

Miller, E. (2006). "Other Economies are Possible: Organizing toward an Economy of Cooperation and Solidarity," *Dollars and Sense*, 266 (July–Aug.).

North, Peter (2005). "Scaling Alternative Economic Practices? Some Lessons from Alternative Currencies," in *Transactions of the Institute of British Geographers*. Oxford: Blackwell, 221–33.

Reuters (2008). "Financial Crisis may Increase Mental Health Woes" <http://www.reuters.com/article/2008/10/09/us-financial-health-mental-idUSTRE49839M200810 09> (accessed June 24, 2011).

PART FIVE

The Non-Global Global Crisis

Is the 2008 crisis global in the sense that the whole world is experiencing similar effects, suffering comparable ordeals, and enduring the same unfolding processes that lead to diminishing hopes toward the future? Is the world system feeling the crisis through the institutions that structured its core, semi-periphery, and periphery during previous generations? Under the startling eyes of the peoples of the Western world on both sides of the Atlantic, the world system is evolving violently and oscillating chaotically, seemingly ready to bifurcate into a different self-organized architecture for the span of some generations. Because of the economic and cultural interdependence between the core and the peripheries, and taking into account the outcome of past chaotic transitions between old and new areas of capitalist accumulation, one could in principle expect disturbances of considerable amplitude in Asia, Latin America, and Africa. But the crisis in what have been called the emerging economies is social, not financial: no signs of major economic disturbances are observed, although there are symptoms of potential social disruptions linked to the dynamics of societies, not to the world economy. The full crisis is a crisis of the West and the rift between the two shores of the Atlantic is widening, suggesting the contours of a new configuration—whether more or less multipolar, we do not yet know—of the global economy.

This is why we thought it necessary to reflect on the non-global nature of this crisis in the global world, analyzing the dynamics of the development of global capitalism through the eyes of social science scholars from China and Latin America. These chapters provide us with a fresh and unique opportunity to look at present perceptions and thoughts of key economic and political actors who are also contributing to the shape of the new world that is piercing through the curtains that still veil the aftermath of the crisis.

Chapter 10

No Crisis in China? The Rise of China's Social Crisis

You-tien Hsing

A grain of salt in China's post-2008 economic expansion

The continued growth of the Chinese economy since the 1980s, which has set China apart from other transition economies, is a well-known story. What is more intriguing is China's continued economic expansion since the 2008 financial crisis. China seems to have emerged from the crisis unscathed, if we look at the following figures:

Despite the fact that consumer spending in the USA and in other major markets of Chinese exports was slashed after the 2008 financial crisis, China managed to keep its growth rate above 9 percent from 2008 to 2009. In 2010 China returned to a double-digit growth of 10.3 percent (see Table 10.1 for a comparison with other economies). Also in 2010, China's trade balance bounced back and made a 25 percent increase from 2009 (see Table 10.2 for a comparison with other economies), even though its currency was on a steady rise (*The Economist*, 2011a). In terms of the governmental debt, the official data showed a reasonable and stable rate of around 17–18 percent of the GDP from 2001 to 2010 (see Table 10.3), compared to the USA (91.5 percent), Japan (220.3 percent), and Germany (79.9 percent) in 2010.

These figures have encouraged some economists to suggest that China has been "de-linked" from the global economy in a positive way. David Dollar (2008), until 2009 Country Director for China and Mongolia in the East Asia and Pacific Region of the World Bank, for example, suggested that China's

Table 10.1 GDP annual growth, 2001–2010 (%)

Country	2001	2002	2003	2004	2005	2006	2007	2008	2009	2010
China	8.3	9.1	10.0	10.1	11.3	12.7	14.2	9.6	9.1	10.3
USA	1.1	1.8	2.5	3.6	3.1	2.7	1.9	0	−2.6	2.83
India	5.2	3.8	8.4	8.3	9.3	9.3	9.8	4.9	9.1	10.37
Brazil	1.3	2.7	1.1	5.7	3.2	4.0	6.1	5.2	−0.6	7.49
Germany	1.2	0.0	−0.2	1.2	0.8	3.4	2.7	1.0	−4.7	3.50
Japan	0.2	0.3	1.4	2.7	1.9	2.0	2.4	−1.2	−5.2	3.94
South Korea	4.0	7.2	2.8	4.6	4.0	5.2	5.1	2.3	0.2	(6.11)

Source: IMF (2011); World Bank (2012a).

Table 10.2 Trade balance, 2001–2010 (change over time in %)

Country	2001	2002	2003	2004	2005	2006	2007	2008	2009	2010
China		103.5	29.5	49.7	134.2	57.48	46.81	17.2	−31.8	25.27
USA		−15.3	−13.7	−21.1	−18.6	−7.36	10.53	6.85	43.42	−24.2
India		400.6	24.3	−91.1	−1,418	9.58	13.16	−283	13.98	−134.7
Brazil		67	154.6	181	19.14	−2.6	−88.6	−1917	13.79	−95.5
Germany		10,580	14.01	176.3	11.69	31.98	34.63	−3.16	−32.0	5.45
Japan		39.7	11.06	26.3	−3.7	2.86	23.78	−25.5	−9.75	37.39
South Korea		−10.5	106	107.3	−42.4	−24.3	54.58	−85.3	9.25	−13.9

Source: IMF (2011); World Bank (2012b).

Table 10.3 General government gross debt, 2001–2010 (% of GDP)

Country	2001	2002	2003	2004	2005	2006	2007	2008	2009	2010
China	17.7	18.9	19.2	18.5	17.6	16.2	19.6	16.9	17.7	17.7
USA	54.7	57.1	60.4	61.4	61.7	61.1	62.1	71.2	84.5	91.5
India	75.8	80.1	81.2	81.2	78.8	75.7	72.9	72.9	71.1	69.1
Brazil	70.2	79.8	74.6	70.6	69.1	66.6	65.1	70.6	67.8	(66.0)
Germany	58.5	60.4	63.9	65.7	67.8	67.6	64.9	66.3	73.5	79.9
Japan	151.7	160.9	167.2	178.1	191.6	191.3	187.7	195.0	216.3	220.3
South Korea	17.4	17.6	20.7	23.8	27.7	30.4	29.7	29.0	32.6	(30.9)

Source: IMF (2011).

domestic demand contributed 9 percent to the country's growth, while net export contributes only 2–3 percent. The International Monetary Fund (IMF) also projected that between 2011 and 2013 China will be the largest contributor ($1.6 trillion) to the expansion of global output, outweighing the USA (1.43 trillion), Japan, and Germany (*The Economist*, 2011b). The counter-argument includes the "Middle-Income Trap" thesis, which says that China's fast-paced economic expansion will not sustain itself long. Eichengreen, Park, and Shin (2011), for example, argued that, once a country's GDP per capita exceeds $17,000, the country will experience considerable economic slowdown. This is because (1) it will be more difficult to boost productivity by shifting workers from agriculture to industry, and (2) gains from importing foreign technology will diminish (see also *The Economist*, 2011c).

China's impressive post-2008 growth record is to be read with a grain of salt. At the end of 2008, the Chinese central government announced a stimulus package of RMB 4 trillion (about 13 percent of China's 2008 GDP) to combat the global financial crisis and offset the recession in China's export sector. Meanwhile, local governments in China took advantage of the liberal macroeconomic climate brought by the "stimulus package" and added another RMB 20 trillion in "supplementary" investment proposals. Together, the Chinese central and local government committed RMB 24 trillion, or $3.5 trillion (compared to Obama's $800 billion stimulus package in 2009) to keep the Chinese economy afloat. Now the question is: how did the Chinese government manage a reasonable budgetary deficit with such an extraordinary level of investment after 2008? The answer of political scientist Victor Shih (2010) was: it did not. Shih's research shows that the size of the Chinese governmental debt has been astronomical. It was incurred mostly by local governments, and has been off the official balance sheet. After much probing, Shih estimated the total governmental debt, as a share of China's 2008 nominal GDP, was about 77 percent instead of the official figure of 17 percent, and over 100 percent, if the debt leveraged by the state-owned enterprises was added. The Chinese local governments have been borrowing very heavily to finance the stimulus projects. As the local government budget had already been running in the red since the late 1990s, and the central government regulations forbid the local government to borrow excessively or issue bonds, local governments came up with the strategy of setting up another platform to deal with local financial issues. Since 2008, more than 8,000 urban development and investment companies (UDICs) were set up by China's local governments at the provincial, municipal, district, and county levels. The UDICs, separated from the governmental budgetary system, functioned as the investment platform to issue bonds and to borrow from state-owned banks. By 2012 they will have borrowed up to RMB 24 trillion (about $3.5 trillion), if we include both what the local governments had already borrowed by 2009 (RMB 11.4 trillion) and the credit lines that were promised to them (RMB 12.7 trillion) (Shih, 2010).

This amount of debt, more than eight times larger than the total of local government revenue, Shih argued, could never be paid back. While the local governments' investment projects in infrastructure, real estate, and other businesses were extremely ambitious, they were not always profitable. To service the debt and to continue funding new projects, local governments resorted to establishing more companies under the umbrella of UDICs, again off the balance sheet, in order to take out new loans. It is habitual for newly appointed local government leaders to start signature projects, and these new projects were funded by new loans. The financial game of "restructuring old debts with new debts" and triangular debts is not novel in China. Nor is the game of confidence manipulation. China's non-performing loans were estimated to be as high as 50 percent. This has just not been admitted by the People's Bank of China.

Understandably, Shih worried about the financial sustainability of China's post-2008 expansionism. And there have been heated debates both in and outside of China over the issue of how "delinked" the Chinese economy is. Before we can go further into the question of China's financial sustainability, we need to examine what kind of political foundation has helped sustain China's expansionist model this far, what could be the social consequences of this spectacular expansion, and the implication of such social processes on the overall political economy of China's development in the coming decade. I argue that China's expansionist model is built on a political system that integrates the interests of the political and economic elite at all levels for the purpose of sustaining the dominance of the Chinese Communist Party, aided by an effective restructuring of the party–state system. As the integration of political and economic elite and the expansionist model reinforce one another, the economic and political crises are shifted to the social front.

For a start, what comes with the excessive expansion is inflation. The official figure of inflation, as of April 2011, was 5 percent, one percentage point higher than projected. While this figure was sufficient enough to set off all sorts of policy debates over whether and how to control the inflation, most residents in China that I spoke to believed that the real inflation rate was much higher than 5 percent, especially if one takes into account the skyrocketing housing prices (again, not fully reflected in the official figures), which have gone way beyond the reach of the salaried class; not to mention rising food prices, which are felt most heavily by the poor: landless peasants, retirees, the unemployed, and migrant workers. The Central Bank of China has raised the interest rate four times since 2010, and it has also ordered banks to set aside more cash reserve. Both *Bloomberg* (2011) and the Barboza (2011) predict that the bank will raise the interest rate again soon.

Another direct and critical link to China's debt-financed expansionism is land. Most of local governments' debt was collateralized with land appropriated from peasants. Each time the local government needed to restructure its debt, it injected some land parcels into the UDICs. This additional asset helped the UDICs obtain new loans from the bank. This scheme has created a massive number of dislocated peasants and triggered an increasing amount of social unrest. Furthermore, in order to negotiate better borrowing conditions and larger-sized loans with the bank, the local government tried to boost the commercial value of the land in its jurisdiction. It would encourage bidding wars over land parcels, and repeatedly boast the birth of the new "king of land" (the parcel that fetched the highest unit price in local history). In China today, there are no private landownership rights. But landuse rights can be sold and bought through land auctions at the government-monopolized land lease market. The local government is the only legitimate supplier of land in the land lease market for commercial development. Under the state monopoly of land circulation, the government-sponsored bidding wars over land leases, as an indispensable part of the local finance scheme, inevitably led to housing price hikes. It was reported that, in the 2010 round of government-controlled land lease sales in Chengdu municipality (of Sichuan province in central China), the land price of its new town project went up ten times in 2007–10. The land-financed expansionism has created massive dispossession and housing price hikes, affecting not just the poor at the bottom, but also those in the middle strata.

But this is just the beginning. Before we go further into the question of the social impact of China's expansionism, an analysis of the political sustainability of such an expansionist model is in order.

Integration of political and economic elites and continued domination of the Chinese Communist Party

China's expansionist model is ultimately a political project. The economic expansion has a clear political goal of sustaining the dominance of the Chinese Communist Party (CCP) through economic expansion. The model was made possible by the integration of a political and economic elite under the statist economy. In other words, both the foundation and the goal of China's economic expansion and market reform is the party state-centered political system. So, as long as the economy continues to expand, it is politically viable, and vice versa.

Politically, China diverged from other transition economies in Eastern Europe and Russia in the continued and uninterrupted dominance of the Communist Party. The CCP managed to do so by making itself the most formidable capitalist player in the growing market and by streamlining the party–state organization to keep its elite young, motivated, and loyal.

Before we get into the new ruling class, let me briefly describe the Chinese economy in the post-Mao era.

China's market reforms since the late 1970s have been characterized not by a wholesale-style privatization of the economy, but by continued state intervention and direct participation in the market. China's market expansionism did not follow a lineal path of diminishing the state sector, nor did it lead to an increasingly strong private sector.

However, the continual and increasing state intervention in the process of market expansion has not been a straightforward story of state monopoly and a corresponding disappearance of market competition. This is because, when we talk about the Chinese state, or any state for that matter, we are hardly talking about a homogeneous entity with a coherent set of bureaucratic organizations, evenly allocated resources within the machine, and consistent policy mandates and implementation capacities. The state of China, in fact, as a legacy of a planned economy and, as it continues to be a socialist state, is a vast galaxy of state agencies, which include institutions like government or party organizations, public utility and service agencies, military units, universities, hospitals, research institutes, state-owned enterprises, and banks. In addition, the government is hierarchically organized, from the highest, central level, to the provincial, municipal, county, township, and village levels. And at every level there is a wide array of functional agencies. After the 1980s, many of these state agencies, and especially local governments at various levels, were granted fiscal autonomy to control a good portion of locally generated revenues. Along with the fiscal autonomy was the fiscal liability: local governments had to take much greater fiscal responsibility for overheads, social welfare spending, and infrastructure investment. As a result, local government leaders, who were appointed instead of elected, except for the village heads, became highly motivated to search for new sources of revenue, engaging directly in profit-making businesses such as land sales and real-estate development.

As a result of continued state intervention and participation in the market undertaken by a highly fragmented and diversified state sector, the post-Mao Chinese statist economy can be characterized as follows.

First, increasing significance of the local state in the process of market formation and expansion. But again, this "local state" is not a homogeneous entity. In the three decades since the 1980s we have observed a major shift in terms of the motor of growth. In the 1980s and early 1990s, the rural, lower-level government at the township and village levels took the lead in industrialization and market expansion. The heroes of the 1980s were the legendary township and village-owned collective enterprises (TVEs). Huang Yasheng (2009) argued that the rural-based liberalization and industrialization presented a historical opportunity to develop a private sector. But the opportunity was missed. The rural TVEs did not follow that "inevitable" and lineal path of private-sector growth in the process of market-making. Quite the contrary, the infamous TVEs started to decline by the mid-1990s, and were being blamed for their lack of scale economy. Meanwhile, the new development ethos endorsed the integration model of growth led by high-level and urban-based municipal governments. Large municipal governments would consolidate the urban centers and rural hinterland within their jurisdiction, which can be as large as a European country. These municipalities are leading cities of large metropolitan regions, including the usual suspects of Beijing, Shanghai, and Guangzhou along the coasts, and the latecomers in the coast and interior regions, such as Chongqing, Tianjin, Nanjing, and Wuhan, as well as Qingdao, Zhengzhou, Changsha, Jinan, and so on. China's new territorial order is structured by these powerful metropolitan regions.

Second, as a response to the overly decentralized economy of the 1980s, and to balance the emerging metropolitan regions led by powerful municipal governments, the central government strived to recentralize control over the economy after the late 1990s. The state council took a series of actions to restructure state-owned enterprises (SOEs), aiming at consolidating state assets. The campaign peaked in 2004 with the establishment of the State-owned Assets Supervision and Administration Commission (SASAC).

SASAC initiated a nationwide campaign of consolidating SOEs, with the principle of "keeping the big fish and letting go the small shrimps." The smaller SOEs were merged into hand-picked large and strategic SOEs, and oligopolistic or monopolistic central state-owned corporate groups were formed. The consolidation campaign covered a wide range of strategic sectors, including finance, hydropower, logistics, petroleum, petrochemical, steel, ship-building, telecommunication, media, precious metal, defense, aerospace, food, infrastructure construction and real estate, tobacco, and so on. Meanwhile, the less strategic and weaker state firms were privatized. A lion's share of the national stimulus package in 2009 was channeled into these strategic, top-tiered SOEs.

Third, under the principle of "keeping the big fish and letting go the small shrimps" in SOE restructuring, small SOEs were privatized through merger or manager buyout. The restructuring created a very complex ownership structure and elaborate business networks within and across different sectors and industries, making it impossible to draw a definite line between the "state" and the "private" sectors. As a result, small and medium-sized businesses continued to exist; competition among them is particularly fierce, and mortality and birth rates very high. They were also the ones that were deeply affected in the recent credit crunch.

The key link in China's statist economy is what I would call the bureaucratic entrepreneurs (BEs) and entrepreneurial bureaucrats (EBs). By EBs I refer to current government officials whose primary responsibility is to run

1.Top-tier EBs   2. Second-tier EBs   3. Third-tier BEs

State ←--→ Market

Entrepreneurial Bureaucrats   Bureaucratic Entrepreneurs

Fig. 10.1 Spectrum of bureaucratic entrepreneurs and entrepreneurial bureaucrats

businesses directly, such as the directors of special development zones or heads of government-owned investment firms. By BEs I refer to business owners, CEOs, and top level managers of profit-making corporations who have strong connections with, or backgrounds in state institutions, including government or party organizations, public utility and service agencies, military units, or state-owned enterprises.

What the BEs and EBs have in common is that, as the major actors in the market, they have strong affiliation with the state bureaucracy. Based on the nature of their affiliation with the state, we can build a three-tiered typology of the BEs and EBs. My basic presumption is that the level of their affiliation with the state has direct implication on their position in the market, such as their access to finance and key resources such as land and energy at highly subsidized prices. The position also affects whether they are in the strategic sector and with what level of monopoly. In this typology of the political–economic elite, those at the top tier are the closest to the core of the state: they are "entrepreneurial bureaucrats"; and those at the third tier are closer to the market, hence "bureaucratic entrepreneurs" (see Figure 10.1).

Type 1: the top-tier entrepreneurial bureaucrat class

As mentioned before, in 2004 the SASAC launched a massive-scale, nation-wide merger of smaller SOEs by hand-picked large SOEs, to form oligopolistic or monopolistic corporate groups. The CEOs of the winner SOEs make the top-level social elite. These CEOs are not just merely "dependent on," but are an "extension of," the state. The CEOs and top-level managers of the high-level SOEs are ranked in the same bureaucratic hierarchy as government and party officials. The top ones are ranked as high as a minister. The job of the CEO of an SOE is a bureaucratic position with the mandate of accumulation. These CEOs are GDP promoters with a political agenda of continued party–state dominance. Most of the CEOs of top-tier SOEs have long and extended experiences in the party, government, or military systems. Veteran CEOs of top-tier SOEs are often appointed as provincial governors or party secretaries, and vice versa. In the campaign for scientific management of SOEs, the SASAC started to recruit high-level managers of SOEs from outside the existing state bureaucracy in 2004. But, according to a survey, only 30 percent of the new recruits were still in their positions by 2009. And the majority of those who had stayed on had had a previous background in the state sector (Zhou and Liang, 2010).

The top-tiered CEOs also possess cultural capital. In China's long tradition of a statist society and culture, the central state is still entrusted with, and somewhat legitimized by, the mandate of heaven, and the top state leadership continues to command political and moral legitimacy and obligation. Such moral legitimacy of the top-level state leadership is transferred to high-level SOEs and their CEOs, who are seen as extensions and representatives of the state.

One example of such moral legitimacy is that central-level SOEs have carried the nationalistic mission of building a strong new China since the beginning of the socialist era. The new mission of the central-level SOEs in the 2000s is to put China on the world map and win a global leadership. One way of doing this is to export Chinese capital and technological know-how to the world. The former is represented by the Chinese investment in African and Central Asian resource and energy sectors, and in hydropower projects in Africa and south-east Asia. The central-level SOEs play an important role in this nationalistic mission of economic expansion and international influence and status. Another example is Lenove's acquisition of the manufacturing division of IBM in 2004. The level of economic success of the top-tier SOEs in this mission is open for debate. In any event, this nationalistic mission has helped to justify the macroeconomic policies of state-sector expansion since the late 1990s. The argument goes like this: scale economies are a must in achieving global competitiveness, and scale economies can be achieved, and have to be undertaken only by the state, as declared by the former Director of the SASAC, Mr Li Rongrong, who served as Director of the SASAC for seven years, one of the longest tenures of such a high-level position since the late 1970s, when China's market reform started.

Another example comes from the consumer sector. In the new economy, top-tier SOEs are seen as the guardian of consumer citizens. In a market survey in Shenyang, the capital city of Liaoning province in China's north-eastern "rust belt," for example, 60 percent of the surveyed homebuyers still considered projects that were developed by central-level state-owned development firms to be more reliable in terms of quality, credibility, and management (Yang, 2010). Homebuyers in Beijing were also said to prefer commodity housing projects developed by state-owned enterprises (Fleischer, 2010: 39). Top-level SOEs' brand-name effect could be shared by brand-name multinational corporations (MNCs)—hence the popularity of joint ventures of large SOEs and MNCs since the 1990s.

Top-tier SOEs bear the prestige, expectation, and obligation that few local state enterprises or private firms can match. Their CEOs and top-level managers together make the key link between political and economic powers, and form the highest-level social elite.

Type 2: mid-tier entrepreneurial bureaucrat and bureaucratic entrepreneur class

Below the top-tier SOEs there is a more diverse economy, which accounts for more than half of the national GDP and more than 80 percent of the employment, making the structural base of the second- and third-tiered elite class.

As mentioned earlier, there has been a shift from rural to urban-centered growth since the 1990s, and the rise of leading metropolitan centers, such as Beijing, Shanghai, Chongqing, Guangzhou, Chengdu, and Nanjing, as the predominant regional powers in China's new territorial order. These leading urban centers have become new sites of central–local contention as well. The high-level local state leaders had the advantage of both the administrative authority granted by the central state and the territorial power earned from the entrepreneurial maneuvering of urban development projects such as economic zones and new towns. Municipal leaders acted as landlords relying on land-related revenues. They used planning and zoning authority to create locational advantage for their development projects. They were also urban boosters whose performance was ultimately evaluated by increased property value. Their political agenda was framed by urban development, and their political aspiration was set in urban modernity.

The urban-centered municipal leaders and their development allies in urban development businesses in the metropolitan regions make the second-tiered bureaucratic entrepreneur and entrepreneurial bureaucrat class. They can be characterized by the following:

First, compared with the top-tier elites, the mid-tier elites have a larger membership, and they face a much more competitive, less monopolistic market. This group also bears greater political and social liability. This is because, since the 1990s, the local government has been accumulating an increasingly negative reputation for being too eager to grab land and too quick to retreat from the obligation of social protection in the face of market invasion. As a result, this group of elites commands less moral capital and more ambiguous political mandate than the top-tier group. Their identity as urban boosters and builders brought them as much positive performance evaluation as damage to their legitimacy in the eyes of peasants and inner-city residents. Under the new political discourse that prioritizes social harmony in the 2000s, such a dilemma could bring down local state leaders. I will elaborate on this point further in the next section on social crisis.

Second, this group is advantaged by urban development at the expense of the rural sector. The decline of TVEs and rural entrepreneurship in the mid-1990s and the reduction and abolition of agricultural taxes in the early 2000s stripped the financial base of the low-level rural government at the village and township level. Meanwhile, the urban government was granted greater control over a large area of rural hinterland within its administrative jurisdiction, many times larger than the city proper itself. As mentioned above, this has given the urban government more assets that could be used as collateral for bank loans, to finance more new urban mega-projects such as ports, airports, bridges, highways, convention centers, sports complexes, and new towns. The making of the entrepreneurial bureaucrats and their allied bureaucratic entrepreneurs of the second-tier elite class, therefore, is based on the political divide between urban and rural sectors, and supported by massive conversion of rural farmland for urban expansion. The debt-financed expansionism is built upon this territorial and political–economic structure.

Type 3: the third-tier of bureaucratic entrepreneurs

The making of the third-tier bureaucratic entrepreneurs has followed two opposite directions. One is a movement from the private sector to the semi-state sector, the other from the collective to the state sector. Because they are positioned at the lower level in the state-topped hierarchy, they are more akin to bureaucratic entrepreneurs than entrepreneurial bureaucrats.

The most representative case of the first group of this third tier can be found among the business people who originally started as private entrepreneurs rooted in rural villages, undertaking small industrial or commercial ventures supported by family savings, private loans, or/and collective funds (and land) in the form of joint venture. Their initial success earned them respect from fellow villagers, and they were elected as heads of villagers' committees. (The village election is the only open election in China today. But the party secretary of the village CCP branch is still appointed. For an analysis of China's village election, see O'Brien and Li (2000).) Once elected into the villagers' committee, this so-called neng-ren (competent person) in the village started to learn the ropes of government bureaucracy from the bottom up. They also accumulated political capital as they won awards as model entrepreneurs from township or county offices, and received financial support through their political connections. Some of the more ambitious neng-rens managed to move up on the bureaucratic ladder and got into more diverse segments of the local government at the township level, such as the party organization or local People's Congress and Political Consultation Committee, while they kept a strong footing in their businesses. (There has been research on the significance of the political connection in facilitating private entrepreneurship, focusing mainly on the effect of party membership for entrepreneurial success. Chen Zhongshi (2011) shows that the entrepreneur turned representative of the People's Congress and Political Consultation Committee proved to be an even more important type of political capital.) With the stagnation of small and medium-sized rural industries and the aggressive expansion of the urban and the state sectors, many of these small rural-based firms were bought out by urban, larger SOEs. This group of entrepreneurs became managers of the state firms, and so became more deeply entrenched in the state enterprise and bureaucratic network. Their economic capital got them political dividends, and vice versa.

For this first group of the third-tier bureaucratic entrepreneurs, their affiliation with the state was acquired after their initial success in private businesses. The second group of the third tier started from the opposite end: these were former officials "diving into the sea of business" (*xia-hai*) in the 1980s or 1990s, starting small businesses while keeping their close connection with the state sector. Such a connection served as an important asset in their operation as private firms. This type of entrepreneur is found in many single project-based firms in the real-estate industry, in start-ups in the high-tech sector, and in trading and other establishments in the service and commerce sectors.

Also belonging to the second group are the formerly collective-owned or small, uncompetitive local state-owned enterprises at the county or township level that were facing bankruptcy. After being bought by large SOEs, they managed to build a stronger affiliation with the state sector. As county and township governments tried to deal with the financial and social burden created by waves of bankruptcy of local firms, the best scenarios the townships could hope for was to have a top or second-tier SOE buy out the firms to keep them in the same location. If the local government simply sold the firms to private or foreign investors or arranged a management buyout, local government leaders could easily be accused of selling state assets at a loss, and be suspected of craftiness. The political risk could be too high for the official to undertake a straightforward "privatization" of failing collective firms. A buyout by an SOE would be safer politically. It would be more justifiable, even if the sales were a total financial loss to the local government. It saved local officials from corruption charges, since the transaction would be within the "state sector." In other cases, the local state-owned enterprises had less competitive edge, because of the central state's monopoly of key resources. This mechanism of merger also brought those at the edge closer to the state system.

The state's dominance of the economy is consolidated through the integration of the political and economic elite at these different levels, through bureaucratic entrepreneurs and entrepreneurial bureaucrats. It is centralized around the party state, but decentralized within the organization of the party state. This statist economy is the foundation of China's continued economic expansion, while sustaining the power of the CCP. An interesting question about this relatively decentralized model is the organizational and ideological capacity of the CCP to maintain an effective level of coherence in the era of globalizing market economy. As the party organization went through waves of reforms to keep the leadership circle young and motivated, especially in strategic areas, the state sector continued to attract talented and ambitious college graduates from top universities. At the time when unemployment rates started to rise, state-sector jobs became even more desirable. In July 2011, one Beijing official of a Street Committee, the lowest-level local government in urban China, told me that an opening for an entry-level position in her office attracted more than a thousand applicants, and all of them were college graduates.

In any case, there is a downside to this model: by keeping the economic and political crises at bay, the crisis could be shifted to the social front.

The regime of social stabilization

The other side of the concentration of power and money is growing social disparity. China's Gini coefficient rose from 0.25 in 1984 to an alarming 0.47 by 2006, one of the highest in the world. If we calculate the distribution of property assets instead of income (which is skewed because of continued welfare subsidies to selected groups and under-reported income), the figure rises up to 0.661. The rural–urban income gap was about 1:4 by 2006, if we take into account the welfare benefits available only to urban residency holders (Li et al., 2008).

But income gaps alone do not necessarily create a social crisis. China's social tension since late 2010, which could be seen as a crisis in the making, was made by a specific process that was meant to resolve the tension and prevent the crisis.

China's social crises started at the moment when the representatives of the state at the grass-roots level, including local officials and the police, clashed with the masses during unrests. The cause of the conflicts could be excessive fines for and punishment of family planning violators, or violence against street vendors, and so on. But land-related conflicts have been the most important cause. Jian-rong Yu, a Beijing-based sociologist, suggested that about 80 percent of the recorded cases of social unrest in China since the early 2000s were land related, caused by under-compensation of land appropriation, inadequate relocation arrangements, and forced demolition and relocation. My research showed that between 1990 and 2009, farmland conversion and inner-city redevelopment have displaced at least 75 million rural and urban residents. The number could reach 150–200 million, one seventh of the national total, if we include the destruction of migrant settlements and the subsequent dislocation of people who have been dis-located multiple times. The number of protests increased as destruction of homes and communities accelerated (for more detailed analysis, see Hsing, 2010). It was reported that, in 1993, there were about 8,000 reported cases of "public order disturbance," including protests, demonstrations, picketing, and group petitioning. The number rose to between 90,000 and 100,000 in 2007, with more than four million participants, according to Jian-rong Yu

(2009). The following are two officially reported incidents in the mid-2000s that involved land grabs and violence.

Incident 1: Anhui Province, 2004

In the late spring of 2004, in Ningda Village in north-west Anhui Province, tracts of village land were appropriated by the local county government to build a planned highway. Villagers were to receive compensation for appropriated land. Although households within the village held different amounts of contracted land, the land was owned by the collective. The county government therefore imposed the decision that the cash compensation would be divided evenly among all households that had lost their land without considering the difference in each household's contracted land. The village leader was to distribute the cash compensation and redistribute the village's remaining land among all village households as contract land.

But the Ningda party secretary did not disclose the total amount of appropriated land, nor the total cash compensation the village received from the highway construction agency. Villagers suspected the village party secretary of embezzling the funds. They requested that the village leadership open the books on the deal before reallocating the remaining land to villagers. But the party secretary ignored the request and began to reallocate the land. On May 25, without the consent of the villagers, the party secretary and other village and township cadres began to reallocate village land by placing new boundary marks between land lots. That evening, villagers erased the new marks. Two days later the party secretary and his two sons killed a villager, named Wang Yong, who had participated in erasing the boundary marks. Wang died in front of his 71-year-old father after being stabbed eleven times.

The murderers were arrested that evening as there had been several witnesses to the killing. But, even after the arrest, few villagers dared to talk to Wang Yong's father. Old Wang said he felt he had become a "counter-revolutionary" in the village after he had lost his son over the conflict with the powerful party secretary. Frightened villagers were reluctant to talk about the party secretary with an investigating journalist. The party secretary was known as a local bully with significant political clout. He had been effective in collecting fees and taxes for the township government, and was rewarded as an "advanced party cadre" by the township in 2001. The villagers feared that, if they talked, the party secretary would retaliate after his release from jail (Bao, 2004).

Incident 2: Hebei Province, 2005

Yousheng Village, Dingzhou City, Hebei Province, is about 100 miles south-west of Beijing. According to the official Xinhua news agency and the *New Beijing Daily* (*Xinjingbao*), Yousheng villagers had been camping out in their fields from July 2004 to June 2005 to resist a compulsory and under-compensated appropriation of 380 mu of fertile farmland for a power plant project. The resisters dug earthen fortifications under more than ten large tents on the field and dug deep trenches around their tents for defense. At 4 a.m. on June 11, 2005, the day of the Dragon Festival, more than 300 men in helmets and camouflage attacked the camps. The men came in five buses, one truck, and three cars. Some had shotguns. Others came with sharpened steel tubes with blades attached to the end. Villagers were armed with bricks and sickles. In the ensuing battle, six villagers were killed and another forty-eight were injured. The attack was captured on a three-minute video by a protester and was circulated widely on the Internet.

The attack was not the first on the village. About two months earlier, thirty men had attacked the camps at night. But that attack resulted in one of the assailants being taken prisoner by Yousheng villagers. Before that, more than fifty construction trucks, eighty police cars, and hundreds of public security officers and construction workers made more than ten attempts to force the start of construction work by first destroying the field to demoralize the peasants. But none of these attacks successfully "cleared the site," to use the official term for forced eviction. These unsuccessful attempts eventually led to the final all-out attack and the deaths.

Two days after the incident, the party secretary and the mayor of Dingzhou City was sacked. A month later, 31 people involved in the crime were arrested and another 131 hired hit men were detained. The provincial government ordered a halt to the appropriation of the village land. The incident was mostly presented as a criminal case in media coverage, with blame placed primarily on the construction contractors, who were said to have initiated the attack and hired the thugs (*San Lian Life Weekly*, 2005).

The number of unrests has gone up since 2008 (Li, 2010), and so have the number of participants and the level of violence (Xu, Chen, and Li, 2011). A critical change in the unrests since 2008 is that they have often taken place in an ad hoc fashion, without organization or an identifiable source of conflict. Most of the participants took action without a specific purpose, nor did they have clearly framed grievances or demands such as higher wages, job security, or fair compensation. Participants joined the riots upon hearing some rumors, receiving text messages, or seeing conflicts between the authority and people in the street. As the size of the riots grew, they also turned more violent. Burning, smashing, crushing, and looting were common in these incidents. Rioters in a number of cases, totaling between 10,000 and 30,000, physically confronted the police and paramilitary by throwing rocks and broken glass bottles, and burned down public buildings and police cars, and the incidents could last for several days. Jian-rong Yu suggested that these large yet spontaneous riots were signs of people's frustration with the system and resentment toward the authority at a more general level.

But we still need to ask what turns a clash into a social crisis, and whether these clashes represent a social crisis; and, if they do, what kind of crisis. If we define social crisis as events that lead to a drastic collapse of existing social orders and power relationships, we have yet to see that happening in China. But it is fair to say that these unprecedentedly violent incidents did have a significant effect on the way the government responds to social contestations. If there is a crisis brewing in these clashes, the mechanisms that the Chinese government have installed to deal with it do not seem to have helped reduce the tension.

The Chinese government took action to vent the heat as early as 1990, one year after the Tiananmen massacre, by establishing the Administrative Litigation Law, which allowed a citizen to sue the government. In addition, governments of all levels set up specifically designated agencies to deal with people who would write to local leaders or visit their offices in person, to voice grievances and lodge complaints. But peasants and inner-city residents' experience of seeking justice through the legal and administrative routes was largely disappointing, and often antagonizing (Lee, 2007). Indeed, many municipal and district courts, which were under local governments' jurisdiction, with judges who were on local governments' payroll, would not accept cases related to highly explosive issues such as one-child policy violation, land grabs, and forced donation imposed by the local government. People who chose to take the administrative route to voice grievances were also met with a bureaucracy that was more inclined to stop or retaliate against the protestors than to resolve the conflicts.

Disillusioned, some people turned cynical, whilst others became perpetual visitors to government offices at higher levels to lodge complaints.[1] Still others turned radical. A more extreme example of this was found as recently as May 26, 2011. On that day a farmer in Jiangxi province used explosives to bomb three municipal government buildings, causing three deaths, including his own, and six injuries. The tragedy originated in 2002, when the farmer's house was demolished by the district government for a highway project. The farmer decided the compensation was too low. So he took the government to court, and, like many others, lost the lawsuit. The farmer then started his long march of taking the complaints to various government officials without any results for nine years. The disillusion finally led to the tragedy.

Officials at the lower level were feared, resented, mocked, suspected, outwitted, even attacked during mass riots, but rarely trusted. As the central government became alarmed by the scale and scope of the contention, the masses became more skillful in dealing with the state after these first encounters.

By the late 2000s, to deal with the mounting social conflicts that were not resolved by the legal institutions and bureaucratic system, the Chinese government instituted a new regime of "social stabilization." Local officials' performance evaluation and promotion were strictly conditioned by whether there had been any reported cases of very broadly defined "disturbances of social order" in his or her jurisdiction. Just one such case would be sufficient to terminate their hope for promotion, and often their career. Consequently, social stabilization began to take the top priority in local governments' daily operation. Again designated offices of Social Stability Maintenance were set up at all levels of local government. Long and comprehensive checklists of conflicts that were considered threatening to social stability were sent to different departments and agencies of the government.

---

[1] My interviews show that, once people start to make trouble, or are seen as trouble-makers or as leaders of some outbreaks, they have taken a path of no return. Once people have taken part in a riot, they are blacklisted by local governments and seen as a stability threat. They are constantly harassed and watched by the government, and many can no longer lead a normal life or even keep their job. In this process, these people found more reasons to lodge complaints to the higher level of government, and continued their protests. As a result, they turned into long-term "trouble-makers" for the regime of stability maintenance.

The listed threats ranged from demolition conflicts, youth unemployment, counterfeits, media reporting, veterans' employment, natural disasters, ethnic and religious conflicts, ecological destruction, enterprise restructuring, food and drug safety, infrastructure and ecological construction projects that entail relocation, and so on. Various parts of society were mobilized to help maintain social stability, including middle schools and high schools. Students were encouraged to report signs of social instability, such as excessive fees, electricity safety, food safety, students' bringing knives to schools, unsafe building, traffic problems around the campus, and political thoughts of teachers (for example, see a report on a high school in Fujian province responding to the provincial Bureau of Education's campaign to prevent instability in school (Fuqing High School, November 17, 2011)). During the politically sensitive time of the Annual People's Congress meeting and the CCP national meeting, blacklisted troublemakers were put under surveillance 24/7 by security agents equipped with expensive electronic surveillance devices. The high-security regime has added a tremendous workload and financial burden on the local government. The government had to mobilize volunteers to patrol communities and commercial streets to help them maintain social stability. As a result of mass mobilization and the concentration of government resources on social stabilization, many other regular government functions of public affairs were reduced or halted, especially during the time of high-security alert.

Social stability is not just yet another bureaucratic routine, but a political campaign that demands results. To keep their jobs, which were still some of the best career options around, officials became more coercive. Most government officials were shrewd enough to avoid applying violence right from the beginning, as the political cost could be high. They would first send officials to persuade the non-compliant; if this failed, gangsters were brought in to take over the task of persuasion. In the case of forced demolition and relocation, to prevent conflict escalation and to facilitate the smooth operation of the project, local governments would begin by deploying hundreds of employees from various government agencies, including schoolteachers, to accompany demolition crews to the sites to demonstrate the government's authority. Hired private security guards, paramilitary, armed police officers in armored vehicles, and even helicopters were deployed as a show of force, and remained on standby in case of confrontation. For local cadres, carrying out hugely unpopular policies like family planning or demolition and forced relocation could be as tense as a mini-warfare. And wars were expensive financially. From time to time, gangsters and thugs (many were migrants from other provinces) were hired to attack stubborn relocation holdouts physically, as in the case of the second incident presented above. In some occasions, enraged villagers would attack demolition crews and clash with the security force. Physical injury and death could happen on either side, and confrontations threatened to interrupt the demolition process and slow construction, which caused negative publicity for local leaders. Under the regime of "social stabilization," such confrontation could cost their jobs.

So the carrot was offered along with the stick. To prevent the conflicts from escalating or spreading, and under the pressure from the central government to avoid physical confrontation, local officials used monetary compensation to quieten the stubborn yet shrewd troublemakers. After 2008, an increasing number of municipalities, districts, and counties set up a special Judicial Supplementary Fund to pay off those who threatened to create negative PR for the leaders. Under the centralized local authority, top leaders would mobilize all resources to combat a crisis. The size of the campaign was conditioned by the political priority. The goal was an immediate solution and restoration of social order as quickly as possible, with either violence or cash.

With either approach, conflicts were resolved only in extra-legal platforms. For most of the aggrieved people who were disillusioned with the judicial and bureaucratic system, the cash compensation was often the best possible result of their struggle for justice. Through time, people also learned that the size of the compensation is often conditioned by the scale and scope of the trouble they make. More troublemaking and media coverage, more cash, regardless of whether the government action or people's reaction was within the realm of legality or justice.

The threat of suicide was a common tactic to demand more compensation. In such cases, protestors would bring a can of gasoline to visit the officials in charge, threatening to self-immolate as a show of determination. Some death threats succeeded in winning protesters higher compensation, but some backfired. The threat could, for example, be dismissed as a hoax, thereby forcing the protestor to set him or herself alight to save face. The resulting injury or death might be recompensed with better compensation for surviving family members. Most people seemed to believe that it would take death to get the government's attention, as the amount of compensation seemed to be determined by the number of deaths. The cost of justice is life, and the measure of justice is cash. Meanwhile, to buttress its authority, the government has to show that it is not easily threatened by troublemakers. An authoritative news source in China published a "rumor" that the governor of a district of Xian municipality in north-western China, which has been going through massive redevelopment and demolition projects, had told the demolition crew that they were allocated a "quota" of four deaths in a demolition project of a particular neighborhood (Liu, 2010). In many of the cases, those who were severely injured or lost their lives in physical confrontation were not necessarily government officials. The confrontation often occurred face-to-face between holdouts, lowest-level cadres "in the frontline," and hired migrant workers of the demolition crew, at the very moment of demolition. The violence occurred not just between the state and society, but between different groups of the society as well.

A riot, or a "mass incident" in Chinese terms, that took place in Hubei province of central China in June 2009 is representative of what the Chinese would describe as "oppressive officials and recalcitrants coproduce one another."

On June 17, 2009, a 24-year-old chef of a hotel in Shishou City, Tu, was found dead by the gate of the hotel. Local police announced that Tu's death was suicide and claimed to have found his suicide note. The hotel was known as the hub of drug trafficking. The boss, who was known to be a relation of the mayor of Shishou city, offered $4,700 to Tu's family for compensation in exchange for immediate cremation of the dead body, and requested the family to sign a public statement that said Tu's death was suicide.

But Tu's family did not believe that it was suicide, and decided that the compensation was insufficient. Meanwhile, the police tried forcefully to remove the body from the hotel for cremation. To protect the body, which was critical evidence in a criminal case, Tu's family brought cans of gasoline to barricade the body, and started sending out text messages, contacting media, and mobilizing relatives and friends to block the traffic around the hotel. In front of the hotel, Tu's family and supporters used speakers and spoke the language of justice, and offered cigarettes and beers to passers-by, pleading them to join the effort of stopping the police from removing the dead body by force. The incident that began with about 200 people became a mass riot involving over 10,000 people and 10,000 police force and para-military. During the riot six police vans and fire trucks were smashed and the hotel was also burned down. It was reported that at one time between 60,000 and 70,000 people were on the street, throwing rocks and empty beer bottles at the police. More than 200 injuries from both sides were reported. Videos of the confrontation posted on YouTube showed thousands of paramilitary police marching with riot shields, then beating a hasty retreat as the crowd pelted them with stones and other objects.

The riot lasted for four days. Two top leaders of the city, including the party secretary, were sacked, and five participants were sentenced to jail for up to five years. Five others were convicted of inciting trouble but given suspended sentences. But the members of Tu's family were exempted, in exchange for their signing an agreement to cremate the corpse before they saw the forensic report, and after Tu's father had threatened to immolate himself in front of the city hall (Zhang, 2011). The government also promised the deceased's family a higher cash compensation of a total of RMB 80,000 ($11,764), including RMB 30,000 offered by the Hotel, RMB 35,000 by the Shishou municipal government and RMB 15,000 by the township government (Cai, 2009).

Following the incident, an editorial of the *People's Daily*, the official newspaper of the CCP, cited the "failure of the government to provide timely and detailed information about the circumstances surrounding the suspicious death, combined with the spread of rumors and unofficial information via the Internet" as the key factors that fomented the violent protests (Ren-hou, 2009).

Another consequence of the "social stabilization" campaign was the ballooning budget for public security. It was estimated that, in the city of Guangzhou in 2007, social stability maintenance cost the municipal government RMB 4.4 billion (close to $70 million), higher than its unemployment insurance expenditure of RMB 3.5 billion. Nationwide in 2010, the expenditure on public security was RMB 514 billion, an increase of 9 percent from 2009; this was compared to the national defense budget of RMB 532 billion, which was an increase of 7.5 percent from 2009. It is not a total coincidence that, by 2010, China's public security expenditure nationwide surpassed the national defense budget, two years after the stimulus program had started.

A more fundamental issue, it seems to me, is not just the setback of the rule of law or the swollen state budget of public security. What this new regime of social stabilization has brought is the commodification of citizens' perception of justice and rights. For the aggrieved and the unjustly treated, either in the case of farmers facing industrial pollution or land appropriation, or in the case of migrant workers facing unpaid salaries and work-induced injuries, many measure the success of their effort to seek justice by the size of cash compensation. Constrained by the limited political space in their struggle, cash has become their goal and the only measure of justice.

Meanwhile, the combination of local officials' retreat to governance by violence and cash, and the dominance of the political and social elite at all levels, means the legitimacy of state is weakened, and the state has lost the trust of its citizens.

According to a 2006 national survey conducted by the Chinese Academy of Social Sciences, more than 70 percent of the 7,000 plus surveyed, who included peasants, workers, and migrant workers as well as urban professionals and government employees, believed that government officials have been the group that has benefited the most from China's economic growth since the late 1990s. Following the government officials with some distance were pop stars (54 percent), private entrepreneurs (52 percent), and managers of state-owned enterprises (48 percent) (Li et al., 2008: 64–5).

When asked to choose among the following sets of relationships the respondents perceived as the most explosive—that is, between the officials and the masses, between the rich and the poor, between management and laborers, or between employers and employees—more than 73 percent of the respondents chose the relationship between officials and the masses as the most important source of conflicts in China today, followed by the relationship between the poor and the rich. More than 73 percent of the respondents also said they had either experienced or heard about corruption of government officials (Li et al., 2008: 79).

The distrust of the state and its legal system has made citizens more susceptible to cash compensation. Cash seems to have supplemented the justice that the legal system cannot deliver and the sense of security that the state has failed to provide. (Paralleled with this mechanism of governance, the 2006 social survey showed that more than 88 percent of the respondents chose "making more money" as the most important goal in life.) The realms of justice, morality, and legality have turned into matches of willpower and muscle as well as contests of trickeries and tactics, and are often settled by violence.

The regime of social stabilization has produced a paradoxical result: the more government resources have been devoted to stabilizing the society, the more frequent, violent, and larger the riots have become. The regime of social stabilization that was designed to maintain China's expansion model and party-centered political system has created a monster of increasingly agitated society. A crisis emerges as the social question of distribution, rights, and justice brings up a cultural question about the meaning of these ideals, and what the state and society perceive as the best way of achieving them. In short, what are being threatened are not only human rights, but also the value of humanity and the vision of development.

References

Bao, Xiaodong (2004). "Investigation into a Murder Committed by a Village Party Secretary in Funan County, Fuyang Municipality, Anhui Province" (*Anhui Fuyang Funanxian cunzhishu sharen shijian diaocha*), *Southern Metropolitan Daily*, July 5; for a partial report online, see <http://news.163.com/40705/9/0QH3133D0001126G.html> (accessed Feb. 10, 2009).

Barboza, David (2011). "Inflation in China Poses Big Threat to Global Trade," *New York Times*, Apr. 17 <http://www.nytimes.com/2011/04/18/business/global/18yuan.html> (accessed May 17, 2011).

Bloomberg (2011). "China Inflation over 5 percent Signals Officials May Boost Yuan Interest Rates," May 11 <http://www.bloomberg.com/news/2011-05-11/china-inflation-over-5-signals-officials-may-boost-yuan-interest-rates.html> (accessed June 1, 2011).

Cai, Ke (2009). "Cook Killed Self: Autopsy," *China Daily*, June 26 <http://www.china-daily.com.cn/china/2009-06/26/content_8324868.htm> (accessed May 2, 2011).

Dollar, David (2008). "Is China Delinking from the US Economy?" <http://blogs.worldbank.org/eastasiapacific/node/2804> (accessed June 1, 2011).

The Economist (2011a). "Appreciation for China," Apr. 22 <http://www.economist.com/blogs/freeexchange/2011/04/chinas_economy_1> (accessed May 3, 2011).

The Economist (2011b). "In Search of Growth," May 25 <http://www.economist.com/blogs/dailychart/2011/05/world_gdp> (accessed July 2 2011).

The Economist (2011c). "China's Economy: The Middle-Income Trap," Apr. 5 <http://www.economist.com/blogs/freeexchange/2011/04/chinas_economy> (accessed Aug. 3, 2011).

Eichengreen, Barry, Park, Donghyun, and Shin, Kwanho (2011). "When Fast Growing Economies Slow Down: International Evidence and Implication for China," NBER Working Paper No. 16919 (Mar.).

Fleischer, Friederike (2010). *Suburban Beijing: Housing and Consumption in Contemporary China*. Minneapolis: University of Minnesota Press.

Fuqing Experimental High School Plans of Stability Maintenance (2011) (*fuqing shiyan zhongxne 2011 nian weiwen gongzuo jitma*) <http://www.8qsygz.cn/E_ReadNews.asp?NewsID=404> (accessed Dec. 18, 2011).

Hsing, You-tien (2010). *The Great Urban Transformation: Politics of Land and Property in China*. Oxford: Oxford University Press.

Huang, Yasheng (2009). *Capitalism with Chinese Characteristics: Entrepreneurship and the State*. New York: Cambridge University Press.

IMF (2011). "World Economic Outlook Database, April 2011" <http://www.imf.org/external/pubs/ft/weo/2011/01/weodata/weoselgr.aspx> (accessed June 5, 2011).

Lee, Ching Kwan (2007). *Against the Law: Labor Protests in China's Rustbelt and Sunbelt.* Berkeley and Los Angeles: University of California Press.

Li, Lin (2010) (ed.). *The 2010 Report on Rule of Law.* Beijing: Chinese Academy of Social Sciences.

Li, Pei-lin, Chen, Guangjin, Zhang, Yi, and Li, Wei (2008). *Social Harmony and Stability in China Today* (zhongguo shehui hexie wending baogao). Beijing: Social Science Press.

Liu, Jinsong (2010). "Lianhu District Government of Xian Municipality Denied Setting Death Quota in Demolition Projects" (*xianshi lianhuqu foren chaiqianzhong fenpei siwang minge*), May 31 <http://www.eeo.com.cn/2011/0531/202511> (accessed June 5, 2011).

O'Brien, Kevin, and Li, Lianjiang (2000). "Accommodating 'Democracy' in a One-Party State: Introducing Village Elections in China," *China Quarterly*, 162: 465–89.

Ren-hou, Shi (2009). "Beijing Aims to Stem Mass Incidents," *Asian Times*, July 2 <http://www.webcitation.org/5wUpA8gNk> (accessed Mar. 2011).

San Lian Life Weekly (2005). "The Attack on Villagers in Dingzhou, Hebei: The Village under the Shadow of Horror" (Hebei Dingzhou xiji cunmin shijian shimo: bei kongju longzhao de cunzhuang), *San Lian shenghuo zhoukan*, July 1 <http://news.qq.com/a/20050701/001470.htm> (accessed Feb. 12, 2009).

Shih, Victor (2010). "Big Rock-Candy Mountain," *China Economic Quarterly*, June: 26–32.

World Bank (2012a). "GDP Growth" <http://data.worldbank.org/indicator/NY.GDP.MKTP.KD.ZG> (accessed June 5, 2011).

World Bank (2012b). "Current Account Balance" <http://data.worldbank.org/indicator/BN.CAB.XOKA.CD> (accessed June 5, 2011).

Xu, kai, Chen, Xiaoshu, and Li, Weiao (2011). "A Bill of Public Security" (*gonggong anquan zhangdan*), *Canjin Magazine*, May 8.

Yang, Mengyu (2010). "Property Projects Developed by State-Owned Enterprises Were Popular: Brand Name Projects Guarantee High Quality" (*yangqibeijing loupan shouqinglai; dapinpai defangzi zhiliang youbaozheng*) <http://news.sy.soufun.com/2010-05-21/3364689.htm> (accessed Mar. 6, 2011).

Yu, Jianrong (2009). "Defending the Last Frontier of Social Stability" (*shouzhu shehui wending de dixian*), public lecture in the auditorium of the Ministry of Finance, Beijing, Jan. 6 <http://www.zjyizhan.com/newsdetail.php?case=2&classid=22&id=90> (accessed July 2, 2011).

Zhang, Jinghong (2011). "Participants' Logic of Action in Value-Oriented Mass Incidents" (*jiazhi zhudaoxing qunti shijianzhong canyu zhutide xingdong loji*), *Chinese Journal of Sociology*, 31/2: 73–96.

Zhongshi, Chen (2011). "Empowering State Capitalism in China: The Revival, Legitimization and Development of Private Enterprises," doctoral dissertation, Department of Sociology, University of California, Berkeley.

Zhou, Limin, and Liang, Xiao (2010). "Central Level SOE Management Recruitment Started Again, less than 30% of the Previous Recruitment Stayed" (*yangqi quanqiu haixuan zaiqihang wangjie kongjiang liucun buzu 30%*) <http://finance.sina.com/bg/chinamkt/sinacn/20100702/181789396.html> (accessed Mar. 2, 2011).

Chapter 11

A Non-Global Crisis? Challenging the Crisis in Latin America

Ernesto Ottone

Introduction

Latin America's relation to the 2008 global financial crisis reveals a unique situation that allows us to question, both in relation to the specific region, but also with reference to emerging countries in general, whether we really are faced by a global crisis or, paradoxically, whether we are witnessing a global crisis that has global effects but is not properly global.

Even if we are cautious in analyzing a phenomenon that is in full swing, and is still causing problems as much in its place of origin, the USA, as it is in Europe, we can at least point out that we are experiencing a decoupling amongst developed and emerging countries that, without being absolutely due to the interdependency levels of the global economy, has generated very different realities amongst them, which are reflected in very different levels of growth.

Emerging economies have maintained high levels of growth since the crisis, but the economy in developed countries has grown very little and runs the risk of growing even less (see Figure 11.1).

Such a decoupling with global tendencies has no precedent in the economic history of Latin America. But previous crises have affected the region itself. The Great Depression of 1929 had devastating effects for the region. The worst affected country in the world, according to a report from the Society of Nations, was a Latin American country, Chile (Pinto, 1962). Then the turbulence in the global economy during the 1970s contributed in a determinant way to the debt crisis that exploded in 1982, hurting Latin American economies and giving way to the period that the Economic

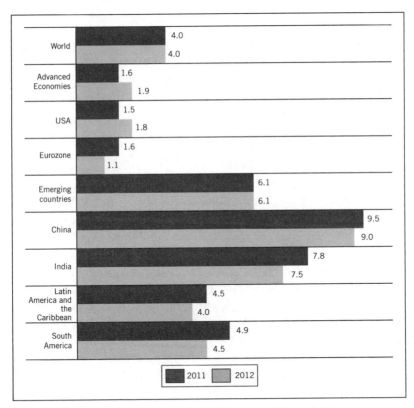

Fig. 11.1 Expansion of GDP, 2011–2012 (annual % variation)
Note: The figures for 2012 are projected.
Source: IMF (2011).

Commission for Latin America and the Caribbean (ECLAC (Comisión Económica para América Latina y el Caribe (CEPAL))) characterized as "the lost decade." The 1990s were marked by several crises of endogenous and exogenous origin. The so-called Tequila Crisis in Mexico in 1995 had some repercussions in the region, but the subsequent Asian, Russian, and Turkish crises had serious effects in several Latin American countries and tainted the regional economy at the end of the twentieth century and the beginning of the twenty-first century.

This new situation has been so surprising that the Latin Americans themselves do not seem fully aware of their ability to resist the global crisis, an ability they have accumulated over years of hard-learned experience during previous crises, which had compelled them to introduce into their economies contra-cyclical elements, more financial regulations, and increased public intervention. To this must be added the importance of their exports to the great emerging markets in Asia, which have resisted the crisis since 2008.

Thanks to all of these factors, the 2008 crisis has had less of an impact than previous crises. Even if growth did slow down, this lasted for scarcely a year, and its social impact was not dramatic. The decline was concentrated in 2009, but was followed by a strong recovery in 2010 and a strengthening in 2011, though at a more moderate level (see Figure 11.2 and Table 11.1).

As for future years, this recovery seems to be holding in the projections of the IMF, even though it will depend upon the size of the problems experienced by countries that up to now have been considered to be central to the world economy, and upon the ability of China and India to resist the effects of the crisis. Such projections indicate that Latin America will continue to grow until 2016 at an average of 4 percent, and that a group of countries in the region will grow even more. Some of them will even reach levels of per capita GNP that will take them to the "threshold of development" (see Tables 11.2 and 11.3). Only a huge global depression could create a kind of catastrophically new convergence.

To understand the magnitude of this change it is necessary to investigate more thoroughly the relationship among globalization processes and the process of development in Latin America.

At the time when globalization was becoming a dominant trend in the world, Latin America was going through the final stages of an unfinished modernization period, consisting of a state-led process of industrialization

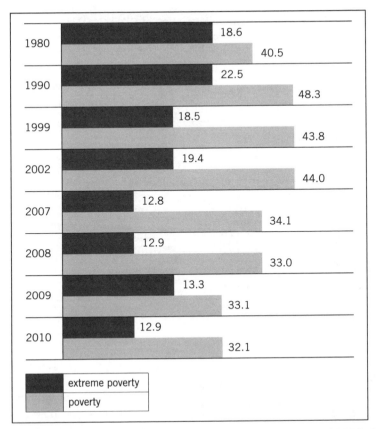

Fig. 11.2 Latin America: evolution of poverty and extreme poverty, 1980–2010 (in percentages)
Source: ECLAC (2011).

oriented mainly toward the domestic market, which started around the 1930s and came to a close in the 1980s.

This model of modernization had been preceded, first, by an oligarchic form of modernization based on export-led development, which began in the mid-nineteenth century, and second by an interregnum between 1914 and 1930.

I will not discuss the oligarchic modernization model except to note that it drew the map of Latin American states, created nations, and integrated

Table 11.1 Latin America, annual variation of GDP, 2001–2010 (%)

GDP	2001	2002	2003	2004	2005	2006	2007	2008	2009	2010
GDP	0.3	−0.4	2.2	6.1	4.9	5.8	5.8	4.2	−1.9	6.0
GDP per capita	−1.1	−1.7	0.8	4.7	3.6	4.6	4.6	3.0	−2.8	4.8

Source: ECLAC (2011).

Table 11.2 Higher GDP In thousands of US$PPP

Country	2011	Country	2016
Argentina	17.376	Argentina	21.452
Chile	16.172	Chile	20.187
Uruguay	15.470	Uruguay	19.514
Mexico	15.121	Mexico	18.033

Note: The figures for 2016 are projected.
Source: IMF (2011).

Table 11.3 Higher annual growth of GDP

Country	2011	Country	2012
Argentina	7.99	Peru	6.01
Chile	6.55	Bolivia	4.50
Paraguay	6.40	Chile	4.47
Peru	6.25	Argentina	4.04
Uruguay	6.00	Paraguay	4.00

Note: The figures for 2012 are projected.
Source: IMF (2011).

the region into the world economy of the time. Accordingly, this model gave rise to several features that persist to this day in Latin America, such as the region's gap with respect to the developed countries and the great social inequity and intraregional heterogeneity that are its hallmarks today. For better or for worse, the region's birth certificate was written in that period.

The unfinished modernization

The unfinished modernization model may be summarized in three main points:

1. The creation of a more inclusive state and of a popular national identity: in most of the countries, emerging social sectors were absorbed in the absence of a representative democratic system (that is, without elections, respect for minorities, or institutions responsible for checks and balances). Most states were forged by authoritarian processes, popular revolts, and military interventions of different political persuasions (such as the Mexican revolution and the movements of Getulio Vargas, Perón, Rojas Pinilla, Pérez Jiménez, and Villarroel, among others). Chile, Uruguay, and Costa Rica, in particular, were partial exceptions in this regard.
2. The end of the oligarchic state did not spell the end of oligarchy as a dominant class. Albeit transformed and weakened in some cases, this class continued to exist, representing the landowning component in a new political compromise with the emerging commercial, financial, and industrial sectors in the block of post-oligarchic power, which also included organized labour and the political representation of workers.
3. The process of state-led, domestic-market-oriented industrialization was not a doctrinarian decision; neither was it a free choice or—to dispel a myth—an invention of the Economic Commission for Latin America and the Caribbean (ECLAC). On the contrary, it was a reality created by the crisis of 1929. Let us recall that the exports of six major Latin American economies plummeted by 33 percent between 1929 and 1932, while the USA and Europe adopted protectionist stances.

This is the global economic landscape into which the state-led, domestic-market-oriented industrialization model was born.

The economic and socio-political developments that took place in the framework of this state model combined important advances with large inequalities.

On the one hand, great economic expansion was achieved between 1950 and 1980. During this period per capita GDP more than doubled, despite a twofold increase in the population (ECLAC, 1991). Hand in hand with this expansion went significant urbanization and the modernization of the lifestyles and consumption patterns of certain social groups. Notable social achievements were made, particularly in health and education and in infrastructure. However, economic expansion was achieved at the cost of external indebtedness and financial imbalance, and coexisted with large technological shortcomings and insufficient saving-investment processes (Fanjzylber, 1992).

The fruits of economic expansion were distributed in a notoriously unequal manner, with large sectors of the population continuing to live in poverty and even extreme poverty.

Despite its undeniable achievements, the Latin American development model, with its clientelistic State occupying a central role, was unable to overcome the concentration of wealth in a few hands or to shed its own heterogeneous nature.

The clientelistic model was unable to build a democratic system or a welfare state, notwithstanding the fact that some important social advances were taken as far as possible. During the 1970s poverty reached 35 percent of the population. All of these processes were framed politically by the Cold War and its landmarks, such as the Cuban revolution.

Towards the late 1960s and early 1970s, the region's pattern of growth with little equity—and, mostly, practically no democracy—generated what Lechner (1987) termed "ideological inflation" driven by "the threat of dissolution and atomization of the social order" in the framework of the Cold War.

Such ideological inflation led to a clash of "global ideological approaches and polarizations" that diminished the possibilities of compromise that the clientelistic state could arbitrate. Then, in the 1970s, a conservative alliance sprang up as authoritarian or military regimes were established in many Latin American countries.

According to the United Nations Development Programme (UNDP), only three democracies still survived in Latin America in 1976.

Under the military–authoritarian regime, the state loses its vocation for compromise and for economic intervention. It plays a fundamental repressive role, in this case to ensure the application of neo-liberal doctrines that arose in response to the crisis. In particular, it is a matter of attempting to impose hegemony through the disarticulation of civil society.

But the neo-liberal doctrines were hegemonic even in those countries where the democratic system survived. During this period, de-regulation and privatization were promoted and production was steered toward exports.

Between the 1970s and 1980s—in other words, the period in which the globalization process began to gather momentum and the world economy shifted dramatically toward internationalization—the unfinished moderni-zation model lost all effectiveness and became stagnant even in the demo-cratic countries.

The region had built up serious shortcomings in savings, investment, and addition of value. It was shouldering unwieldy external debt and lacked competitiveness, and was suffering depredation of natural resources and inflationary processes, while its industry and technology were becoming obsolete. The external debt, the raising of interest rates in the United States, and the fall in commodity prices paved the way for the crisis of 1982.

But this was not only an economic and social collapse; it was also a political and cultural one. The clientelistic state was the main source of shared identity in Latin America: the end of this model also created a vacuum in the sense of belonging, because the new neo-liberal minimal states and dictatorships were simply articulating the process of integration into the global economy, without any filter or attempt to build a national identity (Castells, 2003).

It must be stated, however, that it was during this period and in the framework of the cold war crisis that the conditions for democratization of political systems and advances in democratic pluralism were created.

Thanks to internal developments and the end of the cold war crisis, democracy was restored in the region by 1990, but the poverty rate had reached 4 percent.

The 1990s

The 1990s are commonly described as a period of neo-liberal domination reflecting the nature of the globalization process underway in the world at the time.

But, at the theoretical level, at least one important alternative school of thought existed in Latin America: the school of productive transformation with equity, inspired by and developed within ECLAC by Fernando Fajn-zylber (ECLAC, 1990).

On the basis of the empty box theory, which proved empirically that none of the Latin American countries had been able to achieve an acceptable level of per capita GDP growth at the same time as a reasonable degree of equity, ECLAC presented a theory to the Latin American governments in 1990 in which it proposed changing production patterns with social equity.

This theory may be summarized in five points:

1. The central idea around which all the other points revolve is that the changing of production patterns must be based on the systematic and deliberate incorporation of technical progress, which must encompass the entire system within which enterprises operate.
2. Coherent and stable macroeconomic management is necessary, although not sufficient in itself.
3. A symbiotic relationship between growth and equity is possible and feasible, and economic progress is sustainable only with social progress and inclusion.
4. Open regionalism is necessary.
5. There is a recognized need for a democratic, pluralistic, and participatory setting with a minimal level of consensus around fundamental development goals.

All these ideas were endorsed, but applied only partially. Chile has been the sole successful exception. Brazil, under the administration of F. H. Cardoso, also followed a number of these guidelines with good results.

By the mid-1990s, the balance of economic transformation showed both advances and shortcomings. Most of the countries in the region achieved moderate economic recoveries, with average growth of 3.2 percent between 1991 and 1996, significant advances in macroeconomic stability, rising export growth and diversity, improved access to external financing, and a significant increase in economic interdependence within the region, spurred by a new generation of formal integration agreements.

However, growth levels still fell far short of those necessary to overcome technological and social shortcomings, and the economies still showed large degrees of vulnerability.

Domestic savings levels were too low. Expansion of total investment was insufficient, and the structural heterogeneity typical of the region's productive systems sharpened.

There were profound disparities in national poverty levels. During the first half of the 1990s the poverty rate decreased from 48 percent to 39 percent—an important advance but not enough to counteract the previous decade's rise from 35 percent to 48 percent. Nor was it enough to reduce the overall numbers living in poverty.

The advances achieved in the region toward the mid-1990s became more fragile. The Tequila Crisis and, later, the Russian and Asian crises were decisive points for the Latin American economies.

The "dark" phase of globalization brought with it episodes of turmoil that proved devastating for the region. The early years of the twenty-first century were marked by profound economic, political, and social crisis. The region's GDP took a negative turn. Despite a brief recovery in growth in 2000 (3.7 percent), the figure in 2001 was only 0.4 percent in 2002, and, in 2003, 1.5 percent.

This situation, whose main cause lay in the world economy—in particular in financial market volatility—produced setbacks in poverty reduction and widened the gap in income distribution.

In relation to poverty, ECLAC figures again showed the loss of the advances achieved during the 1990s. In 2003, poverty reached 43.9 percent of the population, or 225 million poor in absolute terms. This reflected previously unheard-of figures in many countries, such as Argentina, where the poverty rate reached 40 percent, of which 20 percent were indigent. The only country to remain an exception to this was Chile, which managed to maintain and even slightly lower the figures of the 1990s, reducing poverty from 40 percent to 18.8 percent and indigence from 14 percent to 4.7 percent. Chile's situation largely reflected its ability to apply counter-cyclical policies.[1]

Facing the global crisis

Fortunately, the negative situation in the region began to turn around thanks to the new global economic cycle that started to gain momentum from 2004 on. As a result, the economy of Latin America and the Caribbean grew by 6 percent in 2004 and by over 4.5 percent from 2005 until 2008. This enabled strong recoveries in the economies that had suffered most in the previous cycle.

This new cycle afforded breathing space in the short term. It was strongly driven by a favorable external scenario, the lowering of interest rates, and the temporary rise in raw material prices caused by numerous factors, including burgeoning demand from huge economies—principally China and India.

---

[1] All the figures are quoted from the yearly ECLAC reports on economics and social development in Latin America and the Caribbean.

These factors combined to create a highly positive set of conditions in Latin America between 2003 and 2008, the like of which had not been seen for at least forty years. Growth stood at around 4.5 percent per year, all social indicators improved, and poverty levels decreased in nearly every country in the region, coming down to 33 percent overall in 2008. Income distribution improved, albeit moderately, and the overall quality of development rose: more saving and investment, first steps toward implementing counter-cyclical policies, reduction of unemployment, and higher and better-quality social expenditure.

Although the advances were greater in South America and smaller in Mexico and Central America—whose economies compete with China in exporting low-tech manufactured goods to the US market—the situation overall improved, seemingly opening up new opportunities for the region as a whole. Already in 2007, however, ECLAC had drawn attention to certain problems in the global economy, particularly in the USA. Even so, the expectation was for another "soft landing" in the world economy, whose impact on Latin America would slow up improvements but would not be dramatic.

The global crisis erupted in the third quarter of 2008 and shook the Latin American economy: as is well known, this crisis was of American and European origin, and Latin America had no responsibility in creating it.

So true is this that the Latin American financial system, much more regulated than those of the USA and Europe, did not suffer financial contagion.

The effects of the crisis began to hit Latin America at the end of 2008 and continued until the third quarter of 2009, when some signs of recovery emerged. GDP growth fell to –1.9 percent in 2009.

The reasons for the drop in GDP growth are all linked to the combination of reduced exports in the global economy, a collapse in investment, a decrease in tourism, the rise in unemployment, and the fall in migrant remittances—though not for long.

The counter-cyclical policies implemented in the region account for the only slight increase in poverty and extreme poverty and for the fact that, when the world economy—particularly the large emerging economies—recovered, Latin America also embarked upon a rapid recovery in the aspects mentioned above. GDP growth in 2010 was 6 percent and the projection for 2011 was 4.2 percent.

The primary problem of the Latin American economies relates to the uncertainties of the developed countries' economic recovery.

It may be asserted, therefore, that we are in a historically new situation, inasmuch as a global crisis did not dramatically hurt the region, which was then able to recover more quickly than the global economy.

Of course, prudence must be exercised. Latin America faces enormous challenges in consolidating sustainable development and achieving a positive and sustainable form of integration with the globalization process. But there is something new: for the first time the region's performance in the face of global crisis was relatively autonomous and successful. It could be said that we are moving, even if only a little, from dependency to interdependency. There is reason to think that Latin America could develop into a new protagonist in world affairs.

A strategic look

If we look at things objectively, Latin America is a region with a composite cultural identity, an intermediate economic situation, and political systems that are historically marked by fragility.

Latin America is not a low-income region like sub-Saharan Africa, but nor is it a developed region. It is in the middle, like many parts of Asia and some of Eurasia. It is middle income. It is midway between the African continent and the group of more advanced economies: Latin American per capita income represents a fifth of the per capita income of the countries of the Organization for Economic Cooperation and Development (OECD) and more than twice that of sub-Saharan Africa.

The region is vastly heterogeneous, both geographically and economically speaking: its economies range from Haiti, with per capita income close to $400, to Chile, Argentina, and Mexico, whose per capita income nears $15,000 in purchasing power parity (PPP) terms.

The region also has countries of continental dimensions, such as Brazil, as well as small island states in the Caribbean (Ottone and Vergara, 2007).

Nevertheless, the region overall faces similar problems throughout, including high rates of poverty and indigence, persistently unequal income distribution, and uneven opportunities, unsatisfactory economic growth and the permanent "black box of technical progress," and a lack of solid political systems.

In order to comprehend the relationship between today's Latin America and the globalization process, it is necessary to analyze some of the most salient aspects of its current situation.

Still fragile democracies

As noted earlier, the advances achieved by the region in terms of democracy have few precedents in its own history. With the exception of Cuba, all the countries have governments formed from elections that conform to international standards of acceptability, and have resolved serious conflicts in this way.

Latin American countries with fragile democratic systems today face difficulties similar to those experienced by all democracies in the present ("doxocratic") world: the distance between its citizens and institutional crises of political parties and parliament; the problems that public opinion, supported by the new information technologies, present for the democratic representative; and the omnipresence of image and interactive communications. All of this is, moreover, aggravated by the deficit of Latin American states in terms of responding to the challenges of highly unequal societies with mediocre levels of social cohesion.

Just when it is beginning to firm up its still-weak representative democracies, Latin America must deal with the challenges to democracy presented by the globalization process.

Latin American governments show a variety of political orientations today: center-right, center-left, neo-Jacobean. Democratic systems are suffering particularly in the neo-Jacobean governments (Ottone, 2010).

The regimes that I have termed "neo-Jacobean" in orientation show differences in representation that may arise from initial popular or citizen support in response to a broad perception of lack of governance and corruption, as is the case of Venezuela and Ecuador, or the exclusion of an entire universe, as was the case with the indigenous majority in Bolivia.

But beyond the rhetorical or practical differences and the varying economic and social outcomes of these regimes, in their refounding they share a clear vocation for power accumulation that stresses and polarizes the democratic logic, and erodes the separation of powers and, sometimes, freedom of speech as well. Their situation is paradoxical, inasmuch as their electoral democratic origin and regional and global surroundings compel them, sometimes at the limit, to give more or less respect to a democratic system that they do not truly value and for which they appear to have no love: this is certainly the case of Venezuela—that is, they are compelled in some degree to a democratic practice that, by its nature, empowers the negotiation of disagreements and is dysfunctional vis-à-vis great foundational ideological projects.

Although the fragility of democracy may be more acute in regimes of neo-Jacobean persuasion, it is not limited to these. Institutional weaknesses, the tendency to achieve power through demonization of the adversary, the mixing of politics and money, the absence of legal certainty and respect for rules, are shared partially by different political tendencies (such as that of Uribe and Kitchner), and the penetration of the state by criminal elements and corruption are all very common in the region and encompass countries with governments of diverse political orientation.

In Latin America the impacts of global crime, and especially of drug trafficking and its related ills, have long ceased to be the sole preserve of the sensationalist press. Crime has grown into a major political problem in a number of countries: Latin America is now the region with the world's highest crime rates, and this is weakening its political systems and taking a toll on the whole of civil society. The emergence of barbaric groups, their hold on particular territories, and the perpetration of acts of unthinkable cruelty and inhumanity in countries as large as Mexico throw up unprecedented challenges for still-fragile democratic systems and jeopardize the state's very ability to function. How these new developments are to be tackled is far from clear. What is clear, however, is that the approaches taken thus far have failed.

Persistent inequalities

As we have observed, social inequality in Latin America, particularly inequality in income distribution, is characterized by its persistence. Globalization did not cause inequality in Latin America, but it has reinforced and modernized it, extending its reach to education and communications.

The latest developments with regard to the high degree of inequality in Latin America, one of whose traits is excessive income concentration in the richest decile of the population, are not, however, all so negative. The 2010 edition of the *Social Panorama* of Latin America published by ECLAC shows a fall of poverty to 32.1 percent and of indigence to 12.9 percent in 2010 (ECLAC, 2010a). It also signals that income distribution improved through-out Latin America with few exceptions between 2002 and 2009. In some countries, such as Venezuela, Argentina, and Brazil, the drop has been very significant; in others it has been more moderate, but it reveals a tendency that could be prolonged.

I remark upon the fall in poverty and the improvement in income distri-bution at the same time, because, if they constituted different processes, then a rise in inequality starting from a certain average per capita income level would also lead to greater poverty.

Nevertheless, income inequality is still very high in the region. Some Latin Americans like to say, with a kind of perverse pride, that it is the world's highest. But this seems not to be the case. If the Gini coefficient for Latin America were compared with that of sub-Saharan Africa, the latter would be the winner, but Latin America would take a comfortable second place before the OECD countries, Central Asia, Western Asia, and the Pacific. The difference with Europe is enormous: 0.52 compared with 0.34. The Latin American country with the most equal income distribution still has a higher Gini coefficient than the European country with the worst distribution.

Where poverty levels are concerned, the comparison with other develop-ing regions has a different outcome: here Latin America is better placed, though this is not true of social mobility, consumption patterns, or access to property or basic services.

Consequently, it is necessary to consider the unequal income distribution theme in all its seriousness but also in all its complexity. Inequality in income distribution should not be equated with inequality in general, and it is necessary to address other aspects that capture the complexity of the subject.

As already noted, the globalization process has widened gaps in market incomes with the rest of the world. The gap with Europe in this regard has also increased; accordingly, what largely explains the enormous difference between Gini coefficients in Latin America and Europe is the action of the welfare state in Europe—that is to say, the income differences after payment of direct taxes, social assistance, unemployment insurance, and, ultimately, the whole array of transfers that act upon income. In Latin America the difference produced by state intervention is scarcely two percentage points; in Europe it is about ten, signalling distributive efforts of very different dimensions (Perry and López, 2008).

What made it possible to reduce inequality, starting with the boom period described, was the combination of higher labor income and transfers to poorer households. This is why the distribution improvement was able to navigate the 2008 crisis while remaining on a positive path.

To accentuate this trend, end the persistent inequality, and break its dynamics of production and reproduction throughout the lifecycle of the Latin American people are crucial steps toward building societies with greater well-being in the future. This depends, in the first place, on the generation of better and more stable employment for youth, particularly those in the poorer deciles. Simply keeping those groups in the labor market would by itself bring about an enormous jump in equality.

All this implies giving continuity to the increase in social spending and making it counter-cyclical. If it is accepted that social expenditure must be used efficiently, it is impossible to disregard the need for a new fiscal covenant in the region, one that provides more resources for social policy and can collect more revenue in a more progressive manner.

It must be recalled that, compared with other world regions, Latin America has a regressive tax structure and a larger proportion of indirect taxes. There is room to raise the tax income of the state without undercutting growth and to collect more revenues more efficiently, because most of the countries have a low tax burden, a high evasion rate, and too many exemptions. As a counterpart, this new fiscal covenant requires greater levels of social trust and a strong legitimization of state action.

In the long term, the fundamental factor that shapes a more egalitarian society is education, although here different factors work to prevent the rupture of inequalities of origin, such as territoriality, which causes acute social fragmentation in the very arteries of the region's countries. As in education, the advances obtained in territorial matters have a bearing on equality, productivity, and the building of a modern citizenry.

A spotlight must also be turned upon the new forms of inequality brought by the information society. Latin America has taken great strides in digital development since 2000 and is considered an emerging market in terms of ICT access and use. Yet new gaps are opening up with respect to the developed countries and even other emerging regions, as well as within countries, owing to segmented access to new information technologies.

Latin America accounts for 8 percent of the world's Internet-users, far short of the 39 percent for the Asia–Pacific region. Mobile telephony development, however, has been huge, with subscribers actually outnumbering inhabitants in some countries. Chile, for example, has twenty million

subscribers for a population of around eighteen million. This has not translated into productivity gains, however, or into greater internal equality, and
it has produced only partial convergence with the more advanced countries.
More strenuous efforts are needed, therefore, to design new strategies for
the information era (*comScore*, 2010; ECLAC, 2010b).

Open identities

Even though the subjects of identity in the region have undergone changes,
starting with the fall of the clientelistic national state and, within this
framework, as a result of globalization, Latin America does not show the
identity conflict seen in other world regions. Moreover, the existence of
700 ethnic groups does not appear to imply that such potential exists.

The problem is not irrelevant, however. It is a fact that Afro-descendants
and indigenous people, the most numerous minorities in this order, suffer
discrimination, racism, and accumulation of economic, social, and political
disadvantage.

Yet the identity concept is strongly present in the political discourse in
some Latin American countries today, particularly in those that have a
numerically large indigenous population with strong identity links with
their communities, as is the case of Bolivia in particular. In that country
thirty-six different identities have been acknowledged, which explains the
complex relationship between identities in local, territorial, ethnic, and
national plans (Ottone and Sojo, 2007).

In Bolivia, there are discussions that compare the notion of an indigenous
state with the idea of either a liberal or a Marxist nation state along Western
lines, coming down in favour of the first in the light of Aymara precepts of a
multicentric state of diverse territories (Mamani, 2006).

The issue of ethnicity and identity is not confined to Bolivia, however, but
is common in one way or another to all the countries of the region and is
particularly ingrained in Guatemala, Peru, Ecuador, Mexico, and Colombia,
and in other countries, like Chile, whose indigenous population is smaller
but enshrines a powerful symbolic heritage. What is more, it should not be
overlooked that the strong Afro-descendant presence in the region in fact
outnumbers the indigenous population.

The political treatment of indigenous issues differs substantially within Latin
America. Mexico's population has a considerable indigenous contingent, yet

political discourse in the country does not revolve particularly noticeably around its interests. Then there are paradoxical cases such as Guatemala, where the indigenous presidential candidate Rigoberta Menchú failed to garner sufficient support among the indigenous peoples canvassed in opinion polls. Several countries show a broad range of positions with respect to indigenous identities, running the gamut from those that point to the failure of the biological and cultural blending of *mestizaje* in Guatemala to those that elevate *mestizaje* to a national virtue. This latter concept of *mestizaje* weighs heavily in the history of Mexico and at times in that of Brazil, where it has been a research subject for decades. The discourse and reality of *mestizaje* are, therefore, an important subject for analysis in the different countries as an element of union and of tensions born of real inequalities.

Fortunately, while in other latitudes religious conflicts tend to cross over ethnic or cultural identities, with impacts moving increasingly from local to global in recent years, in Latin America freedom of creed and the secular nature of most states has averted the outbreak of significant religious conflicts. This has been aided by the fact that secularism, understood as a regulative principle, is a social link that determines people's participation in public life as citizens, adding to the value of this principle as a driver of social cohesion. As a result, conflict arises mainly over restrictions on the effective enjoyment of citizenship that impose profound exclusions and social inequalities.

The modernity of the region lies, precisely, in its openness to the world from the moment it was named. From then on, its modernity was defined by syncretism, which supposes a continuous resignifying of its cultural identity.

From the cultural point of view, the challenge of globalization for Latin America revolves around two questions. The first is how to capitalize on the region's historical experience in intercultural crossover and turn it into a competitive advantage in the new landscape of an interconnected and globalized world. The second is how to make use of the region's long conflicting and syncretic history to tackle in greater depth the challenge—which industrialized societies also face—of rethinking the content of citizenship, starting from the progressive coexistence of several cultural–ethnic identities.

For the region to come to terms with its own intercultural fabric is, perhaps, the most authentic way of recognizing itself today within the context of a modernity marked by a growing complexity of "identity."

Ernesto Ottone

The unresolved productive transformation

Despite the advances made in terms of social well-being, greater equality in Latin America is still a pending issue. Likewise, despite the economic progress achieved in the past few years, from a strategic perspective the region's productive transformation also remains pending.

Unless this transformation is achieved, the current growth will not be sustainable over time. What is needed, then, is not only to build solid macroeconomic policies and fiscal responsibility, but also to raise the productivity of all the factors, adding value to the whole of production activity.

How will Latin Americans position themselves within the global economy? Clearly, the region will lose yet another opportunity if it stands still and does not add value to its current form of integration in the world economy. The boom may last for several more years, but without a new type of economic integration, there can be no certainty of a positive future. On the contrary, a future fraught with weaknesses is almost certain.

Although the Latin American people have advanced, little has been done with any strategic intent. The region is still marginal to the traditional concentration of trade, research, and development in the United States and Europe. Unlike Latin America, Asia has advanced remarkably in this aspect.

The region's empty box, that of growth and equity, is still unfortunately unfilled. Investment is still insufficient, exports do not produce dynamic effects across the production structure, and market share has been lost in services trade. Latin American regional integration is not moving forward, scant resources are allocated to research and development and knowledge-intensive industries account for a very low proportion of industry overall. Lastly, the region is not creating the basis for sustained growth and a good position in the world economy in the long term.

Despite the crisis, the possibilities of bringing about this transformation lie open for Latin America. Today consumption has expanded to encompass a substantially larger part of the world population, which has increased demand for all types of raw materials and services, and opened spaces for very specialized manufacturing.

It seems very probable that raw materials prices will remain high, which would enable the region to gain time. In addition, new technologies are cheaper and thus the region can advance faster in its adaptation and access to them. Latin America must therefore act more rapidly to position itself in the world production structure and take its place in value chains.

This will require a jump in innovation, in export quality and in all kinds of diversification, from manufacturing, mining, agricultural feeding complexes and services to tourism and finance.

All of this calls for a strategic vision in each country and a region-wide effort to project itself ten or twenty years hence. None of the countries outside of the region that have developed recently have done so without a strategic vision and an alliance between a vigorous State and a dynamic private sector, and without building consensus and inclusive understandings which enable the generation of strategies that outlast political-electoral cycles. The absence of strategy could mean several decades' delay.

The nucleus of an efficient development strategy is to diversify and develop arenas in which technological learning and competition are linked. Even if much of technological change lies in manufacturing, innovation and technical progress must be extended across the entire fabric of production.

The twenty-first century must not be allowed to be marked by the "natural resources curse" of past centuries, when the bondholder and lazy spirit of the ruling classes led them to lose their opportunity, as they did by the end of the nineteenth century (oligarchic modernization).

Today, the new technologies, biotechnology, and the rapid transformation of information technologies, make it possible to add value very broadly. There are no impenetrable walls between the outputs of production; what matters is how they are produced.

It is clear that this productive transformation process will not arise spontaneously; momentum must be provided by a State that drives technological steps to a higher level.

To live better, in a better world?

Strengthening democracy, ending inequality and ethnic discrimination, and achieving productive transformation—together with other strategic tasks such as environmental stewardship and the fight against crime—form the universe of challenges that Latin American countries must overcome in order to live better and to assume a greater and more positive leading role in a world that is beginning to redesign itself.

The supranational character of some of these problems and the need for all countries to cooperate to solve other national issues make it an urgent task to leave behind integrationist rhetoric full of bombastic phrases and historical quotations but little real content, and embark upon a serious and exhaustive process of regional integration. Two things are fundamental for this. The first is to change the missionary slant of certain convictions. Governments of neo-Jacobean orientation make their anti-North American phobia the axis of their foreign policy, at least in declaratory terms, in a form that is almost non-temporal and non-historical, without distinguishing between the neo-conservatism of George W. Bush's imperial vision and Barack Obama's new vision: they appear to envision Latin American unity as an outpost of a hazy twenty-first-century socialism. All this does is to paralyze less ideological and more pragmatic visions aimed at building a basis of shared infrastructure, interaction, and cooperation, all of which advance too slowly.

The creation of new subregional and regional organizations does little to drive the real contents of this process. Worst of all would be if radical ideological initiatives such as the Bolivarian Alliance for the Peoples of Our America (ALBA) were opposed by other, more conservative ones, such as the Pacific Rim. If organizations with no ideological persuasion, such as the Union of South American Nations (UNASUR), the Common Southern Market (MERCOSUR), and the Rio Group (whose functioning has not so far excelled) are added to the mix, we find too many acronyms engaged in pursuing the same effort, which continues without yielding the integration fruits so badly needed.

The second element is to change the treatment of foreign policy as an adjustment variable for national policies, such that, whenever a particular country experiences internal problems, it rekindles a border or trade conflict with a neighboring country for the sole purpose of politically propping up the president in office, and inflaming the most primary nationalist feelings.

What is needed, conversely, is for the Latin American countries to understand that they have a common destiny, which they can seize only with initiatives that allow all to grow according to their possibilities, while favoring the weakest economies.

The countries all have responsibilities, but they are not the same. For the first time in its history, Latin America enjoys the potential of having one of its countries, Brazil, recognized by the international community as a global actor: not only it is one of the BRICs (Brazil, Russia, India, and China); it is also one of the Eagles, the countries beginning to acquire weight in the world economy.

Brazil has overcome many international and economic problems, even if it still has a long road ahead of it to reach economic, political, and social development. Together with Mexico, Brazil is the country whose role will be fundamental in increasing Latin America's weight in the world.

It is true that Latin America has developed a greater capacity to solve, within the region and with a democratic orientation, certain specific conflicts, such as the Colombia–Venezuela dispute and the Bolivian internal situation. It had less success in the Honduras crisis, but was able to generate an immediate alert regarding the situation in Ecuador. All of this is still too little, because a stronger political density is required, which demands an effort of an entirely greater magnitude.

If it were assumed that passing the development threshold meant simply breaking through the threshold of $22,000 per capita income in purchasing power terms, and that threshold were reached with an income distribution structure similar to the current one in the region, the resulting state of affairs would be one in which the richest quintile would enjoy a standard of living on a par with that of the world's richest countries, but the poorest quintile would continue to live very badly.

Reaching the development threshold does not consist simply of attaining a determined level of growth. It must result from the combination of many factors, which include a considerable increase in yearly per capita income, but also an increase in the share of the lowest quintile in income and in that group's capacity to pursue life plans according to their aspirations and capacities and not to be constrained by their origins. This requires a society in which social ascriptions are reduced to a minimum and disadvantages do not accumulate within the same groups or pass from generation to generation.

I am absolutely convinced that growth is not development, just as income is not equal to quality of life, although the French singer Mistinguette was right to some extent when she said "Money doesn't bring happiness but it calms the nerves."

Discussions in academic and political circles today touch on the expansion of social indicators beyond the economic vision to measure other values that encompass a wider conception of quality of life, including happiness itself.

I am more skeptical on the matter of happiness because I have a certain conviction that it depends on a delicate and precarious individual equilibrium that, of course, eludes social action.

This leads me to lean more on the concept of well-being, particularly on the idea of "being well," as the greatest outcome of public action, in the line of Claude Lévi-Strauss (1955): "Pessimism teaches me that it is necessary in all cases to promote, instead of an exaggerated humanism, a modest humanism."

Ernesto Ottone

When we talk of Latin America's advance toward a development that affords a better life to all its inhabitants, we are aware that each country has its own pace and manner, because the region is still very heterogeneous. The road to overcoming its asymmetries and obtaining greater homogeneity is, then, a long one.

A few of the region's countries are advancing with a reasonably firm tread, have crossed halfway over the ford, and can see the other side fairly clearly; others are making the crossing with a more uncertain step and over more rocky terrain; some have only just left the river bank, and others have yet to reach the start of the crossing.

Crossing that river would allow the region to adopt a more leading role in the world, but that possibility is not set in stone, because the world is changing rapidly.

The 2008 crisis had and is still having multiple effects. It threw into question geopolitical equilibriums and revealed a world economy functioning on the basis of de-regulation and unrestrained greed, which took it to the edge of the precipice. Moreover, the crisis weakened the most advanced forms of social well-being, unmasked enormous disequilibrium, and ultimately showed the weaknesses of an economic culture of globalization that had seemed able to last indefinitely.

Questions that yesterday seemed to be the sole domain of alternative organizations are gaining new legitimacy today. They refer, for instance, to planetary sustainability, decision-making at the global level, the international financial architecture, consumption patterns, and political transformations. It has become legitimate and necessary to think about new forms of globalization and development and about the economic culture prevailing in developed countries, many of whose citizens, as Manuel Castells has remarked ironically, have nothing to lose except their canceled credit cards.

This is a far cry from the old anti-capitalist nostalgia whose dreams ended in dictatorial nightmares. We must conceive a wide field of reforms sustained by the new technological possibilities and widen democracy to give way to a new phase of globalization in which market and profit have their place but where the public too has weight and where space is opened up to a society guided by citizenship values.

This Latin America, which is in the middle of the ford, which has endured all kinds of avatars and has begun to secure democratic values, whose cultural mix makes tolerance only sensible, and whose religious dimension is non-belligerent, may acquire a more potent voice and a greater presence in the world in the near future. Perhaps it will position itself in the world, not in a desperate and all-accepting manner, as if it were entering "ne la città dolente" under the inscription "lasciate qui ogni speranza voi che entrate,"[2] but as a region that has acquired a reforming capacity that, amongst other things, carried it intact through the previous global crisis and that has learned the hard way to appreciate the intrinsic value of democracy and the need to advance gradually. This region has arrived at the conviction that the diversity of political and social actors is not an obstacle to "living together." Latin America can, therefore, make a meaningful contribution to the creation of that new diversified cosmopolitanism that requires the globalized world to be—let it be said once more—not the best of all worlds but a better world.

References

Castells, Manuel (2003). "Panorama de la era de la información en América Latina ¿Es sostenible la globalización?," in Fernando Calderón (ed.), *¿Es sostenible la globalización en América Latina*. Santiago: Fondo de Cultura Económica.

comScore (2010). "State of the Internet with a Focus on Latin America," June <http://www.comscore.com>.

ECLAC (1990). Economic Commission for Latin America and the Caribbean, *Transformación Productiva con Equidad: La Tarea prioritaria del desarrollo de América Latina y el Caribe en los años noventa*. Santiago: ECLAC.

—— (1991). Economic Commission for Latin America and the Caribbean, "Nota sobre el desarrollo social," *Primera Cumbre Iberoamericana, Guadalajara, México*. Santiago: ECLAC, July 18–19.

—— (2008). Economic Commission for Latin America and the Caribbean, *La Transformación Productiva veinte años después: Viejos problemas, nuevas oportunidades*. Santiago: ECLAC.

—— (2010a). Economic Commission for Latin America and the Caribbean, *Panorama Social*. Santiago: ECLAC.

—— (2010b). Economic Commission for Latin America and the Caribbean, *Las Tic para el crecimiento y la igualdad: Renovando las estrategias de la sociedad de la información*. Santiago: ECLAC.

—— (2011). Economic Commission for Latin America and the Caribbean, *Balance Preliminar de las Economias de América Latina y el Caribe*. Santiago: ECLAC.

Fajnzylber, Fernando (1992). "Industrialización en América Latina: De la 'Caja Negra' al 'Casillero Vacio'," Santiago: ECLAC.

[2] Dante Alighieri, *La Divina Commedia*, "Inferno," canto II.

IMF (2011). World Economic Outlook 2011. International Monetary Fund.

Lechner, Norbert (1987). "Problemas de la democratización en el contexto de una cultura post-moderna," quoted by J. J. Brunner, in Gonzalo Martner (ed.), *Diseños para el cambio*. Caracas: Nueva Sociedad.

Lévi Strauss, Claudes (1955). *Triste Tropiques*. Paris: Librairie Plon.

Mamani, Pablo (2006). "Hacia un estado multicéntrico construidos con tecnología indígena comunal," interview by Juan Ibarrondo and Luis Carlos Garcia, *La Paz* (Sept.).

Ottone, Ernesto (2010). "Izquierdas, Centro Izquierdas y progresismos en América Latina Hoy," *Algunas distinciones Estudios Públicos*, 118 (Autumn).

—— and Sojo, Ana (2007). "La sociabilidad de la Cohesión Social en América Latina y el Caribe," *Pensamiento Iberoamericano*, Segunda Epoca, 1: 5–30.

—— and Vergara, Carlos (2007). "La desigualdad social en América Latina y el caso chileno," *Revista de Estudios Públicos*, 108 (Spring).

Perry, Guillermo, and López, J. Humberto (2008). "Determinantes y consecuencias de la desigualdad en América Latina," in Jose Luis Achinea and Oscar Altimir (eds), *Hacia la Revisión de los paradigmas del Desarrollo de América Latina*. Santiago: ECLAC.

Pinto, Aníbal (1962). *Chile: Un caso de desarrollo frustrado*. Santiago: Universitaria.

Aftermath?

By the time you read these words, the economic crisis that unfolded in 2008–12 may have metamorphosed again. But you, and the world at large, will still be living in its aftermath, regardless of the timing and evolution of the business cycle. The aftermath we are referring to is the social, economic, and institutional landscape that is emerging from the wreckage of the near collapse and patchy rescue of the global informational, financial capitalism that had transformed economies and societies since the early 1990s. What the future holds, nobody knows, because, among other things, one of the features of the mighty financial system at the heart of the crisis was the privatization of the future, replaced by a futures market to be traded according to short-term gains. The result, as you may know if you have read this volume, has been systemic unpredictability and the breakdown of intergenerational solidarity.

But if we do not know the contours of the future, we do know something very important: we cannot return to our recent past. The virtualization of capital, the securitization of everything in a largely unregulated environment, the decoupling of the production of goods and services from the process of their valuation, the disconnection between currencies and fiscal policies, the fiction of full integration of European economies with vastly different levels of productivity and divergent public deficits, and the financing of the debt of the economies at the center of the global network by lending from capital accumulated in what used to be the periphery; all this has reached the limits of its sustainability. What is being debated is not the need to restructure the system, but what is to be done and how to do it. In particular, who pays for what, and how much, who gets the benefits and who endures the suffering of the transition to a new set of institutions and rules. This will be ultimately decided according to power relationships that underlie the values, interests, strategies, and policies being debated in the global networked economy, in the nation states, and within each specific network society.

Indeed, social systems do not collapse as a result of their internal contradictions. The crisis, its conflicts, and its treatment are always a social process. And this social process is enacted and shaped by the interests, values, beliefs, and strategies of social actors. This is to say that, when a system does not reproduce its logic automatically, there are attempts to restore it as it was, as well as projects to reorganize a new system on the basis of a new set of interests and values. The ultimate outcome is often the result of conflicts and negotiations between the actors who are the standard-bearers of these different logics. The financial global capitalist system that induced the crisis was the expression of a certain set of interests, as well as the manifestation of a specific economic culture. These interests and this culture, which we have analyzed in this volume from different theoretical perspectives, are still dominant in the economy and society. Thus, the first effort to restructure the system is characterized by the attempt to restore the same rules of the game within a tighter institutional framework, lesser redistribution of wealth, and greater vigilance in enforcing the logic of the system over the excesses of some of its unruly managers.

In terms of economic policies, after the financial failures of September 2008 a number of strategies were considered, and some implemented, by governments, corporations, and international institutions. In the new policymaking environment, the state, both as nation state and as a network of different states, recovered its steering role to manage capitalism through the following mechanisms:

- *Refloating major financial institutions, and major corporations whose demise would bring havoc to the economy and society.* This entailed in some cases (for example, AIG, Citi Group, General Motors in the USA, Lloyds in the UK, Hypo Real Estate in Germany) de facto temporary nationalization of corporations to be transformed under the aegis of the government, and then returned to the private sector with viable business plans. According to the International Monetary Fund (IMF), in the immediate aftermath of the financial crisis, by mid-2009, governments around the world had invested $432 billion to recapitalize their banks, and had guaranteed bank debts for a total of $4.65 trillion. State-owned banks in China, India, Brazil, and Russia increased their decisive share in overall investment and lending in the economy. In the USA, two-thirds of government capital injected in the banks went to the five largest banks, which were those with the lowest capital ratios, and those that had suffered the biggest loan losses during the crisis. As soon as financial institutions had been stabilized, they were returned to the private sector. In some cases, they returned to the government the loans they had received, but refused to play an active role in stimulating the economy, concentrating instead in increasing their profitability. The European Union (EU) created a financial stability fund destined to bail out financial institutions and governments. The European Central Bank (ECB) intervened repeatedly to avoid public defaults by buying treasury bonds from Greece, Portugal, Italy, Spain, and Ireland, and EU governments arranged bailout packages for Greece, Portugal, and Ireland. The ECB also became very active in the market of inter-bank lending, becoming the intermediary for most of these transactions, as banks did not trust each other and needed guarantees of liquidity provided by the ECB. This strategy required major public funding, and therefore a massive transfer of money from taxpayers to corporations, and a significant indebtedness of governments vis-à-vis global financial markets and major private and sovereign funds lenders.

- *Enforcement of national supervision of financial institutions and lending practices.* The G20 countries agreed on a number of regulatory measures and recommended that all financial institutions should increase their assets to reach a level of 5 percent of the value of all securities sold, up from 1.5 percent in 2007, although the recommendation was not followed. In 2011, the EU forced a number of European banks to recapitalize, and established an increase of the capital ratio for all financial institutions, although the rule was contested and often circumvented by most of the banks. Surveillance measures on offshore financial centers, and vague limitations on bonuses for financial executives, were also considered, but few were implemented. The idea of a global financial regulator was never retained. Instead, an attempt was made to strengthen international economic institutions, such as the IMF, the World Bank, and the Bank of International Settlements, with a new power-sharing agreement in favor of those with capital in hand (China, India, Brazil, Russia, the oil producing countries). The G20 has already replaced the G-8 as the steering club of the global economy.

Aftermath?

- *At the national level, fiscal stimulus to restart the economy*. However, the stimulus strategy included two contradictory sets of policies. On the one hand, increasing public investment in some sectors, particularly industries that are particularly relevant for infrastructure and employment (for example, energy, public works). On the other hand, tax cuts. Obviously, the former requires increasing public revenue, while the latter shifts public revenue into the hands of consumers, particularly those at the highest levels of income. The debate between these two approaches, rooted in opposing class interests, undermined the stimulus effort by making it politicized and chaotic.
- Coverage of social needs in times of crisis (extending unemployment insurance, providing housing allowances, expanding health coverage, subsidizing education, overhauling public services, and so on). However, this effort lapsed when the crisis extended beyond the period of time that public spending could be sustained.

Underlying these measures to deal with the crisis was a growing policy debate between those who advocated restoring the financial health of the system and then letting the market play its way, and others who doubted the capacity of the market to restart itself, given the sharp fall of demand and of available credit. Accordingly, they proposed a new form of temporary neo-Keynesianism, emphasizing public spending to induce massive job creation in the short term. Only a few (for example, Obama, at the onset of his administration) saw the crisis as an opportunity to induce corporations to innovate and to produce differently, and also as an opportunity to provoke people to consume differently, particularly in environmental terms. It was perceived also as an opportunity to gather public support for an expansion of a reformed welfare state, particularly in health and education, on the basis of public funding in innovation and new technologies.

Yet, in the period 2008–12 none of these strategies really worked anywhere, except for the bailout of major corporations, financial institutions, and indebted governments. For the restoration approach, the problem was that the same mechanisms that provoked the crisis continued to lead to the same consequences: financial instability, market volatility, decline of investment, rising of unemployment, and shrinking of demand. The new financial system that emerged slowly after the crisis was a much leaner system, with less capital and less ability to create virtual capital or avoid regulation. Furthermore, some financial institutions collapsed, and most of the financial institutions had to undergo major internal restructuring; the system as a whole does not appear to be able to provide the capital supply for bringing back the economy, beyond a few, selected profitable segments of the market. The neo-Keynesian attempt, implying substantial increase in public spending, was short lived in the countries that tried to do it. There were fiscal limits, as the rapid increase of public debt increased the price of the strategy, and financial markets reacted, devaluing the bonds of over-indebted countries, and even downgrading the ratings of entire economies. There were also political limits, as conservative forces opposed both tax increases and public spending, effectively disabling any project of neo-Keynesianism, and making the dream of an informational welfare state a utopian ideal. Moreover, in country after country, political elites engaged in pitched battles to play the blame game, trying to take advantage of the pains of the crisis to destroy their political adversaries. The result was the absence of all coherent crisis management, both at national and at international levels, and the full de-legitimation of governments in the minds of their reactive and distrustful citizenry. Thus, the immediate aftermath of the 2008 crisis was characterized by the inability of governments to manage the crisis, inducing an aggravation of the economic crisis in 2010 and of the financial crisis in 2011. While financial corporations regained their profitability, the real-estate market collapsed; mortgage foreclosures skyrocketed almost everywhere; the lifeline of credit for small and medium business was sharply curtailed, prompting massive bankruptcies; unemployment soared; demand was depressed further; and citizens retrenched in their countries, expressing in every possible way their lack of solidarity with other people and other nations, even when their governments argued the absolute necessity of sharing the pain. Indeed, the vision of the business elites indulging in their high standards of living and of the political elites maintaining their arrogance vis-à-vis the uninformed populace deepened the distance between people and the powers that be and paved the way for uncontrollable rage, populist reactions, and alternative social movements.

So this is the aftermath of the crisis: the dysfunctional remnants of an economic model based on a financial system incapable of reforming itself; the shift of capital accumulation from the old centers that virtualized themselves to death to the new peripheries that own and produce the real economy without having yet the power to manage it; a political system in ruins in most of the countries embattled by internal self-destruction and external assaults from the disenfranchised masses that no longer believe in their leaders; a civil society in disarray, as old social organizations have become empty shells and the new actors of social change are still at a

Aftermath?

nascent state; and the most important feature of this new landscape: the old economic cultures that provided certainty, such as the belief in the market and the trust in the banks, have lost their communicative power, while the new cultures based on translating the meaning of life into economic meaning are still in the process of being created.

Index

Index

Index

Index